The *Focus on the Family*® Guide to

Growing A
Healthy
Home

The *Focus on the Family* Guide to

Growing A Healthy Home

MIKE YORKEY, General Editor

Wolgemuth & Hyatt, Publishers, Inc.
Brentwood, Tennessee

The mission of Wolgemuth & Hyatt, Publishers, Inc. is to publish and distribute books that lead individuals toward:

- A personal faith in the one true God: Father, Son, and Holy Spirit;

- A lifestyle of practical discipleship; and

- A worldview that is consistent with the historic, Christian faith.

Moreover, the company endeavors to accomplish this mission at a reasonable profit and in a manner which glorifies God and serves His Kingdom.

© 1990 Focus on the Family. All rights reserved.
Illustrations © 1990 by Wolgemuth & Hyatt Publishers, Inc.
Published August, 1990. First Edition
Printed in the United States of America
96 95 94 93 92 91 90 8 7 6 5 4 3 2 1

Library of Congress Cataloging-in-Publication Data

Focus on the family's guide to growing a healthy home / Mike Yorkey,
    general editor.
        p.   cm.
    Includes bibliographical references.
    ISBN 1-56121-020-X (hard cover)
    1. Family—United States. 2. Marriage—United States. 3. Family-
-United States—Religious life. 4. Marriage—Religious aspects-
-Christianity. I. Yorkey, Mike. II. Focus on the family (Pomona,
Calif. : 1982) III. Title: Growing a healthy home.
HQ536.F63   1990
306.8'0973—dc20   90-36195
                                                                          CIP

Wolgemuth & Hyatt, Publishers, Inc.
1749 Mallory Lane, Suite 110, Brentwood, Tennessee 37027.

CONTENTS

PART SEVEN: FOCUS ON EDUCATION

PART EIGHT: FOCUS ON DIFFICULT FAMILY PROBLEMS

FOREWORD

O ne of the best parts of my job as editor of *Focus on the Family* magazine is spending time with reader mail. Recently, this letter crossed my desk:

> I was deeply touched to read the story of how the father and mother helped their children make a commitment to God to remain sexually pure until marriage in your April 1990 issue.
>
> Being a great file maker, I recently started one for my little boy. I use it not only to store medical records and his Social Security number, but I also add articles that I think will help him (and me) in years to come.
>
> I've removed the article on keeping your teens sexually pure and safely filed it away. No doubt, I will reread it several times before my boy is ready for his own "key talk."

We know this mom is not the only parent saving favorite articles from *Focus on the Family* magazine—our mail tells us that. That's why Wolgemuth & Hyatt, with Focus on the Family's blessing, is publishing *Growing a Healthy Home*, a compilation of our "greatest hits." You'll find 54 articles—in eight handy categories—reprinted from the pages of *Focus on the Family* magazine.

In case you're not familiar with the ministry of Focus on the Family, we're here to serve parents and their children. Successful family living has always required time, attention and effort. And with all the social upheavals of the last three decades, the task hasn't gotten any easier.

Dr. James Dobson, a noted family psychologist and author of 11 best-selling books, founded Focus on the Family in 1977. Since its beginning, the non-profit organization has been committed to supporting families with the practical informational and encouragement they need.

There's a lot of practical information and solid encouragement in the pages of this book. We hope *Growing a Healthy Home* is a resource you'll want to pick up again and again.

—Mike Yorkey
General Editor

PART ONE

FOCUS ON MARRIAGE

1

PRESCRIPTION FOR A SUCCESSFUL MARRIAGE

Dr. James C. Dobson

In an effort to draw on the experiences of those who have lived together successfully as husbands and wives, we asked married couples to participate in an informal study. More than 600 people agreed to speak candidly to the younger generation about the concepts and methods that have worked in their homes. They each wrote comments and recommendations which were carefully analyzed and compared.

The advice they offered is not new, but it certainly represents a great place to begin. In attempting to learn any task, one should start with the *fundamentals*—those initial steps from which everything else will later develop. In this spirit, our panel of 600 offered three tried-and-tested, back-to-basic recommendations with which no committed Christian would likely disagree.

Christ-Centered Home

The panel first suggested that newlyweds should establish and maintain a *Christ-centered home*. Everything rests on that foundation. If a young husband and wife are deeply committed to Jesus Christ, they enjoy enormous advantages over the family with no spiritual dimension.

A meaningful prayer life is essential in maintaining a Christ-centered home. Of course, some people use prayer the way they follow their horoscopes, attempting to manipulate an unidentified "higher power" around them. One of my friends teasingly admits that he utters a prayer each morning on the way to work when he passes the donut shop. He knows it is unhealthy to eat the greasy pastries, but he loves them dearly. Therefore, he asks the Lord for permission to indulge himself each day.

He'll say, "If it is Your will that I have a donut this morning, let there be a parking space available somewhere as I circle the block." If no spot can be found for his car, he circles the block and prays again.

Shirley and I have taken our prayer life a bit more seriously. In fact, this communication between man and God has been *the* stabilizing factor throughout our 27 years of married life. In good times, in hard times, in moments of anxiety and in periods of praise, we have shared this wonderful privilege of talking directly to our Heavenly Father. What a concept. No appointment is needed to enter into His presence. We don't have to go through His subordinates or bribe His secretaries. He is simply there, whenever we bow before Him. Some of the highlights of my life have occurred in these quiet sessions with the Lord.

I'll never forget the time a few years ago when our daughter had just learned to drive. Danae had been enrolled in Kamakazi Driving School, and the moment finally arrived for her to take her first solo flight in the family car. Believe me, my anxiety level was climbing off the chart that day.

Someday you will know how terrifying it is to hand the car keys to a 16-year-old kid who doesn't know what she doesn't know about driving. Shirley and I stood quaking in the front yard as Danae drove out of sight. We then turned to go back into the house, and I said, "Well, Babe, the Lord giveth and the Lord taketh away."

Fortunately, Danae made it home safely in a few minutes and

brought the car to a careful and controlled stop. That is the sweetest sound in the world to an anxious parent!

It was during this era that Shirley and I covenanted between us to pray for our son and daughter at the close of every day. Not only were we concerned about the risk of an automobile accident, but we were also aware of so many other dangers that lurk out there in a city like Los Angeles.

Our part of the world is known for weirdos, kooks, nuts, ding-a-lings and fruitcakes. That's one reason we found ourselves on our knees each evening, asking for divine protection for the teenagers whom we love so much.

One night we were particularly tired and collapsed into bed without our benedictory prayer. We were almost asleep before Shirley's voice pierced the night. "Jim," she said. "We haven't prayed for our kids yet today. Don't you think we should talk to the Lord?"

I admit it was difficult for me to pull my 6' 2" frame out of the warm bed that night. Nevertheless, we got on our knees and offered a prayer for our children's safety, placing them in the hands of the Father once more.

Later we learned that Danae and a girl friend had gone to a fast-food establishment and bought hamburgers and Cokes. They drove up the road a few miles and were sitting in the car eating the meal when a city policeman drove by, shining his spotlight in all directions. He was obviously looking for someone, but gradually went past.

In a few minutes, Danae and her friend heard a "clunk" from under the car. They looked at one another nervously and felt another sharp bump. Before they could leave, a man crawled out from under the car and emerged on the passenger side. He was very hairy and looked like he had been on the street for weeks. He also wore strange-looking "John Lennon" glasses down on his nose. The man immediately came over to the door and attempted to open it. Thank God, it was locked. Danae quickly started the car and drove off . . . no doubt at record speed.

Later, when we checked the timing of this incident, we realized that Shirley and I had been on our knees at the precise moment of danger. Our prayers were answered. Our daughter and her friend were safe!

It is impossible for me to overstate the need for prayer in the fabric of family life. Not simply as a shield against danger, of course. A personal relationship with Jesus Christ is the cornerstone of marriage, giving meaning and purpose to every dimension of living. Being able to bow in prayer as the day begins or ends gives expression to the frustrations and concerns that might not otherwise be ventilated.

On the other end of that prayer line is a loving Heavenly Father who has promised to hear and answer our petitions. In this day of disintegrating families on every side, we dare not try to make it on our own.

Commitment

I attended the 50th wedding anniversary for two friends a few years ago, and the man made an incredible statement to his guests. He said he and his wife had never had a serious fight or argument in the 50 years since they were married. That was either a lot of baloney or he and his wife had a very boring relationship. Maybe both were true.

To newly married couples I must say: Don't count on having that kind of placid relationship. There will be times of conflict and disagreement. There will be periods of emotional blandness when you can generate nothing but a yawn for one another. That's life, as they say.

What will you do, then, when unexpected tornadoes blow through your home, or when the doldrums leave your sails sagging and silent? Will you pack it in and go home to Mama? Will you pout and cry and seek ways to strike back? Or will your commitment hold you steady?

These questions must be addressed *now*, before Satan has an opportunity to put his noose of discouragement around your neck. Set your jaw and clench your fists. Nothing short of death must ever be permitted to come between the two of you. *Nothing!*

This determined attitude is missing from so many marital relationships today. I read of a wedding ceremony in New York a few years ago where the bride and groom each pledged "to stay with you for as long as I shall love you." I doubt if their marriage lasted even to this time.

The feeling of love is simply too ephemeral to hold a relationship together for very long. It comes and goes. That's why our panel of

600 was adamant at this point. They have lived long enough to know that a weak marital commitment will inevitably end in divorce.

Communication

Another recommendation by our panel represents a basic ingredient for a good marriage—good communication between husbands and wives. This topic has been beaten to death by writers of books on the subject of marriage, so I will hit it lightly. I would like to offer a few less overworked thoughts on marital communication, however, that might be useful to young married couples.

First, it must be understood that males and females differ yet another way not mentioned earlier. Research makes it clear that little girls are blessed with greater linguistic ability than little boys, and it remains a lifelong talent. Simply stated, she talks more than he.

As an adult, she typically expresses her feelings and thoughts far better than her husband and is often irritated by his reticence. God may have given her 50,000 words per day and her husband only 25,000. He comes home from work with 24,975 used up and merely grunts his way through the evening. He may descend into Monday Night Football while his wife is dying to expend her remaining 25,000 words.

Erma Bombeck complained about this tendency of men to get lost in televised sports while their wives hunger for companionship. She even proposed that a new ordinance be passed which would be called "Bombeck's Law." According to it, a man who had watched 168,000 football games in a single season could be declared legally dead. All in favor say "Aye."

The complexity of the human personality guarantees exceptions to every generalization. Yet women do tend to talk more than men. Every knowledgeable marriage counselor knows that the inability or unwillingness of husbands to reveal their feelings to their wives is one of the common complaints of women.

It can almost be stated as an absolute: Show me a quiet, reserved husband, and I'll show you a frustrated wife. She wants to know what he's thinking and what happened at his office and how he sees the children, and especially, how he feels about her. The husband, by contrast, finds some things better left unsaid. It is a classic struggle.

The paradox is that a highly emotional, verbal woman is sometimes drawn to the strong, silent type. He seemed so secure and "in control" before they were married. She admired his unflappable nature and his coolness in a crisis.

Then they were married, and the flip side of his great strength became obvious. He wouldn't talk! She then gnashed her teeth for the next 40 years because her husband couldn't give what she needed from him. It just wasn't in him.

Lyricist and singer Paul Simon wrote a song entitled, "I Am a Rock," which expressed the sentiment of a silent introvert. The person about whom the song is written has been wounded and has pulled within himself for protection. As you read these lyrics, imagine the special communication problems such a man and his poor wife would experience in marriage.

> A winter's day
>
> In a deep and dark December:
> I am alone,
> Gazing from my window
> To the streets below
> On a freshly fallen silent shroud of snow.
>
> I am a rock.
> I am an island.
>
> I've built walls,
> A fortress deep and mighty,
> That none may penetrate.
> I have no need of friendship
> Friendship causes pain.
> Its laughter and its loving I disdain.
>
> I am a rock.
> I am an island.
>
> Don't talk of love;
> Well I've heard the word before;
> It's sleeping in my memory.
> I won't disturb the slumber of feelings that have died.
> If I never loved I never would have cried.

I am a rock.
I am an island.

I have my books
And my poetry to protect me;
I am shielded in my armour,
Hiding in my room,
Safe within my womb.
I touch no one and no one touches me.

I am a rock.
I am an island.

And a rock feels no pain;
And an island never cries.

Unfortunately, the wives and children of rocks and islands do feel pain, and they *do* cry! But what is the solution to such communicative problems at home? As always, it involves compromise. A man has a clear responsibility to "cheer up his wife which he has taken" (Deuteronomy 24:5). He must not claim himself "a rock" who will never allow himself to be vulnerable again. He must press himself to open his heart and share his deeper feelings with his wife.

Time must be reserved for meaningful conversations. Taking walks and going out to breakfast and riding bicycles on Saturday mornings are conversation inducers that keep love alive. Communication can occur even in families where the husband leans inward and the wife leans outward. In these instances, I believe, the primary responsibility for compromise lies with the husband.

On the other hand, women must understand and accept the fact that some men cannot be what they want them to be. I have previously addressed this need for wives to accept reality as it is presented to them in *What Wives Wish Their Husbands Knew About Women*.

Can you accept the fact that your husband will never be able to meet all of your needs and aspirations? Seldom does one human being satisfy every longing and hope in the breast of another.

Obviously, this coin has two sides: You can't be his perfect woman, either. He is no more equipped to resolve your entire package of emotional needs than you are to become his sexual dream machine every 24 hours. Both partners have to settle for human foibles and faults and irritability and fatigue and occasional nighttime "headaches."

A good marriage is not one where perfection reigns: It is a relationship where a healthy perspective overlooks a multitude of "unresolvables." Thank goodness my wife, Shirley, has adopted this attitude toward me!

I am especially concerned about the mother of small children who chooses to stay at home as a full-time homemaker. If she looks to her husband as a provider of all adult conversation and the satisfier of every emotional need, their marriage can quickly run aground. He will return home from work somewhat depleted and in need of "tranquility," as we discussed earlier.

Instead, he finds a woman who is continually starved for attention and support. When she sees in his eyes that he has nothing left to give, that is the beginning of sorrows. She either becomes depressed or angry (or both), and he has no idea how he can help her. I understand this feminine need and have attempted to articulate it to men.

Nevertheless, a woman's total dependence on a man places too great a pressure on the marital relationship. It sometimes cracks under the strain.

What can be done, then? A woman with a normal range of emotional needs cannot simply ignore them. They scream for fulfillment. Consequently, I have long recommended that women in this situation seek to supplement what their husbands can give by cultivating meaningful female relationships.

Having girl friends with whom they can talk heart-to-heart, study the Scriptures and share child-care techniques can be vital to mental health. Without this additional support, loneliness and low self-esteem can accumulate and begin to choke the marriage to death.

This solution of feminine company seems so obvious that one might ask why it is even worthwhile to suggest it. Unfortunately, it is not so easy to implement. A woman must often search for companionship today. We've witnessed a breakdown in relationships between women in recent years.

A hundred years ago, wives and mothers did not have to seek female friendship. It was programmed into the culture. Women canned food together, washed clothes at the creek together, and co-operated in church charity work together.

When babies were born, the new mother was visited by aunts, sisters, neighbors, and church women who came to help her diaper, feed and care for the child. There was an automatic support system that surrounded women and made life easier. Its absence translates quickly into marital conflict and can lead to divorce.

To the young wives who are reading these words, I urge you *not to let this scenario happen to you.* Invest some time in your female friends—even though you are busy. Resist the temptation to pull into the walls of your home. and wait for your husband to be all things to you. Stay involved as a family in a church that meets your needs and preaches the Word.

Remember that you are surrounded by many other women with similar feelings. Find them. Care for them. Give to them. And in the process, your own self-esteem will rise. Then when you are content, your marriage will flourish.

It sounds simplistic, but that's the way we are made. We are designed to love God and to love one another. Deprivation of either function can be devastating.

Excerpted from *Love for a Lifetime,* © 1987 by James C. Dobson. Published by Multnomah Press. Used by permission.

2

"WHY CAN'T MY SPOUSE UNDERSTAND WHAT I SAY?"

*Gary Smalley
and John Trent, Ph.D.*

A number of years ago, I (Gary) sat down to talk with an attractive woman who was in obvious pain. With tears streaming down her face, she sobbed, "I've tried to express what's wrong in our marriage, but I just can't seem to explain it. What's the use in bringing it all up again?"

After only five years of marriage, this woman had nearly given up hope of experiencing a loving, healthy, and lasting relationship with her husband. Opposed to divorce, she had resigned herself to a life that offered few of the wishes and dreams she longed for.

I had heard this kind of story before. For years, I had regularly counseled with husbands and wives, spending countless hours talking to them about improving their relationships. Only now, I wasn't sitting in my counseling office. I was seated at my kitchen table. And the woman sitting across from me wasn't a counselee—she was my own wife, Norma!

That day, I made a decision to understand what was happening, or not happening, in my marriage. And I also decided to find the answers to several important questions. Why was Norma feeling so frustrated in her attempts to communicate with me? Why did I have such a difficult time sharing my feelings with her? And why was it such a struggle to understand each other—particularly when we discussed important issues?

While I didn't realize it at the time, the answer to these questions was, in large part, all in our minds. It wasn't until we understood why males and females think and speak so differently that we began maximizing our communication. The bridge that spanned these differences proved to be "emotional word pictures."

Unlike anything we have seen, word pictures can supercharge communication and change lives, whether in marriages, families, friendships or businesses. Indeed, word pictures have the capacity to capture a person's attention by engaging both their thoughts and their feelings.

Have you ever tried to express an important thought or feeling with members of the opposite sex, only to have them act as if you're speaking a foreign language? Have you ever asked, "Why can't he (or she) *feel* what I'm saying?" Join the club.

Throughout history, many women have found it difficult (some say impossible!) to communicate with men. And an equal number of men have given up trying to converse with women. I ran into this problem myself on a shopping trip when my wife and I were using the same words, but speaking a different language.

"Shooooppping"

After that tearful session with my wife, I decided to commit myself wholeheartedly to understanding and relating to her. But I didn't know where to start.

Suddenly, I had an idea I knew would get me nominated for Husband of the Year. I could do something adventurous with Norma—like going shopping!

I'm not sure what emotional and physiological changes ignite inside my wife upon hearing the words "the mall," but when I told her my idea, it was obvious something dramatic was happening. Her eyes lit up like a Christmas tree, and she trembled with excitement—the same reaction I'd had when someone gave me two tickets to an NFL play-off game.

That next Saturday afternoon, as we drove up to the mall, Norma told me she needed to look for a new blouse. So after we parked the car and walked into the nearest clothing store, she held up a blouse and asked, "What do you think?"

"Great," I said. "Let's get it." But really, I was thinking, *Great! If she hurries up and gets this blouse, we'll be back home in plenty of time to watch the college game on TV.*

Then she picked up another blouse and said, "What do you think about this one?"

"It's great, too!" I said. "Get either one. No, get both!"

But after looking at a number of blouses on the rack, we walked out of the store empty-handed. Then we went into another store, and she did the same thing. And then into another store. And another. And another!

As we went in and out of all the shops, I became increasingly anxious. The thought even struck me, *Not only will I miss the halftime highlights, but at the rate we're going, I will miss the entire season!* And that's when it happened.

Instead of picking up a blouse at the next store we entered, she held up a dress that was our daughter's size. "What do you think about this for Kari?" she asked.

Taxed beyond any mortal's limits, my willpower cracked, and I blurted out, "What do you mean, 'What do I think about a dress for Kari?' We're here shopping for blouses for you, not dresses for Kari!"

That night, I began to understand a common difference between men and women. I wasn't shopping for blouses . . . I was *hunting* for blouses! I wanted to conquer the blouse, bag it and then get back home where important things waited—like my Saturday afternoon football game!

My wife, however, looked at shopping from the opposite extreme. For her, it meant more than simply buying a blouse. It was a way to spend time talking together as we enjoyed several hours away from the children—and Saturday afternoon football.

Like most men, I thought a trip to the mall meant going shopping. But to my wife, it meant shooooooppping!

Over the next several days, I thought back to our mall experience and my commitment to become a better communicator. As I reflected on our afternoon, I realized I had overlooked something important—the innate differences between men and women.

Gaining the Edge in Communication

Researchers have found that from the earliest years, little girls talk more than little boys. One study showed that even in the hospital nursery, girls have more lip movement than boys! That propensity keeps right on increasing through the years, giving them an edge at meaningful communication!

In our home, Norma noticed the same thing discovered by Harvard's Preschool Program in its research of communication differences between the sexes. After wiring a playground for sound, researchers found that 100 percent of the sounds coming from the girls' mouths were audible, recognizable words.

As for the little boys, only 68 percent of their sounds were understandable words! The remaining 32 percent were either one-syllable sounds like "uh" and "mmm," or sound effects like "Varooom!" "Yaaaaah!" and "Zooooom!"

Norma was comforted to discover that the propensity males had in our family to yell and grunt was caused by heredity, not environment. And after twenty-plus years of asking me questions and receiving monosyllabic answers like "uh" and "mmm," she claims this inability to communicate in understandable sentences remains constant throughout the male lifespan!

Are Men Really Brain Damaged?

From the Garden of Eden, when Eve needed more fig leaves than Adam, it's been clear that men and women differ physically. However, only recently has research shown that they have uniquely different thought patterns.

Specifically, medical studies have shown that between the 18th and 26th week of pregnancy, something happens that forever separates the sexes. Using heat-sensitive color monitors, researchers have actually observed a chemical bath of testosterone and other sex-related hormones wash over a baby boy's brain. This causes changes that never happen to the brain of a baby girl. Here's a layman's explanation of what happens when those chemicals hit a boy's system.

The human brain is divided into two halves, or hemispheres, connected by fibrous tissue called the *corpus callosum.* The sex-related hormones and chemicals that flood a baby boy's brain cause the right side to recede slightly, destroying some of the connecting fibers. One result is that, in most cases, a boy starts life more *left-brain* oriented.

Because little girls don't experience this chemical bath, they leave the starting blocks much more two-sided in their thinking. And while electrical impulses and messages do travel back and forth between both sides of a baby boy's brain, those same messages can proceed faster and be less hindered in the brain of a little girl.

Now wait a minute, you may be thinking. *Does this mean that men are basically brain damaged?*

Well, not exactly. What occurs in the womb merely sets the stage for men and women to "specialize" in two different ways of thinking. And this is one major reason men and women need each other so much.

The left brain houses more of the logical, analytical, factual, and aggressive centers of thought. It's the side of the brain most men reserve for the majority of their waking hours. It enjoys conquering 500 miles a day on family vacation trips; favors mathematical formulas over romance novels; stores the dictionary definition of love; and generally favors clinical, black-and-white thinking.

On the other hand, most women spend the majority of their days and nights camped out on the right side of the brain. It's the side that harbors the center for feelings, as well as the primary relational language and communication skills; enables them to do fine-detail work; sparks imagination; and makes an afternoon devoted to art and fine music actually enjoyable. Perhaps you now can begin to understand why communication is difficult in marriage.

However, there is a way for a man to boost his communication skills instantly and for a woman to multiply hers. By using the power of emotional word pictures to open his right brain, a man can move beyond "facts" and begin to achieve total communication with a woman. This same skill not only will help a woman get a man to *feel* her words as well as *hear* them, but it also will maximize her innate relational abilities.

Years ago, Norma proved this point to me. She illustrated a concern in such a way that her words immediately moved from my head to my heart.

Add Feelings to Facts

When I was working on my parenting book, *The Key to Your Child's Heart*, I asked Norma if she would write one of the chapters. It was a section that highlighted one of her strengths, and I thought the project would be an easy and pleasurable experience for her. I thought wrong.

As the days passed and time drew near for the chapter to be completed, Norma hadn't even started. Several times she tried to discuss how much of a burden the project was, but I always steered the conversation back to the "facts."

I decided it was time to motivate her. I told her that writing a book was absolutely no big deal. She wrote excellent letters, I pointed out. She ought to think of the chapter as just one long letter to thousands of people she'd never met. What's more, I assured her that as a seasoned publishing veteran, I would personally critique each and every page and catch her slightest error. I thought to myself, *Is that motivation, or what?*

Her emotional, right-brain appeals to duck the assignment made little impact on me, because I was armed with the facts. But my left-brain reasoning didn't impress *her* much, either. We traded words as if we were swapping Monopoly money. Frankly, we should have saved our breath. We were at loggerheads until my wife, in desperation, gave me the following word picture.

"Do you see those hills in the distance?" she asked, pointing out the window. "Every day I feel like I must climb them, wearing a twenty-pound backpack. Between getting the kids fed, dressed, to school, and to their athletic practices—and still managing our business office—I barely have enough energy to take another step.

"Now, don't get me wrong," she continued. "I work out to stay in shape, and I love walking those hills daily. But you're doing something that's like asking me to climb Squaw Peak every day—in addition to climbing those hills."

"I am?" I said, pondering her words. Several months earlier I had climbed Squaw Peak, a beautiful mountain near our home, and I knew firsthand how demanding its incline was. My mind shifted into the hyper-search mode to determine where Norma was headed with the story. "OK, I'm stumped," I finally said. "What in the world am I doing to force Squaw Peak on you?"

"You added Squaw Peak to my day when you asked me to write that chapter for the book. For you, carrying around a twenty-pound pack is nothing. But to me, the weight of my current responsibilities takes all my energy. Honey, I just can't add another pound, climb the hills, and take on Squaw Peak as well."

Suddenly, everything she had been saying before was clear. To me, writing a chapter wouldn't have added an extra ounce to my pack or caused the slightest additional incline to the hills I climb daily. But for the first time, I could feel the strain I'd unknowingly put her under.

"If that's what writing this chapter is like, then I wouldn't want you to do it," I said without a moment's hesitation. "I appreciate what you're already doing and don't want to weigh you down any more. You're far too valuable for that."

After the conversation, it was as if a cloud lifted from our relationship. But I didn't know what to make of things the next morning when I came down the hall for breakfast. Norma was sitting at her kitchen desk, furiously writing away.

"What are you doing?" I asked, dumbfounded.

"Writing my chapter."

"You're doing *what*? I thought you said it was like climbing Squaw Peak!"

"It was," she said. "When I knew I had to write it, I felt tremendous pressure. But now that I don't *have* to, the pressure is gone!"

Bridging the Communication Gap

No one says word pictures will help you understand *all* the differences between men and women. But they do help us bridge the natural communication gap—and better understand what another person is saying.

As mentioned earlier, there are two primary ways we process and remember information. The first is via the left side of the brain. It is the channel through which the literal words and factual data of conversation are stored. Since men are primarily left-brain oriented, they generally focus on the actual words being said and often miss the underlying emotions.

That's exactly what happened when Norma first discussed not

writing the chapter. Her words only registered through my left brain. Consequently, they had little effect. But when she used a word picture, it was as if she began talking in color instead of black and white. I immediately saw the colors and shades of her feelings, and as a result, both my attitudes and actions changed.

If a woman truly expects to have meaningful communication with her husband, she *must* activate the right side of his brain. And if a man truly wants to communicate with his wife, he *must* enter her world of emotions. In both these regards, word pictures can serve as a tremendous aid.

Indeed, a world of colorful communication waits for those who learn the skill of bridging both sides of the brain. Word pictures won't eliminate all the differences between men and women, but they can enable us to unlock the gateway to intimacy.

Excerpted from *The Language of Love,* © 1988 by Gary Smalley and John Trent, Ph.D. Published by Focus on the Family.

3

WORKING THROUGH MARITAL CONFLICT

Richard and Mary Strauss

I t wasn't a happy evening. From the moment I walked through the door, I knew that Mary was in an irritable mood.

I didn't know whether the kids had gotten to her, or some church member said something unkind, or if she just wasn't feeling well. But I suspected sooner or later she might turn her wrath on me. Besides, I hadn't had a particularly pleasant day myself and wasn't about to look for trouble by probing for the problem.

When we had finished eating and cleaning up the kitchen, I sat down to read the newspaper. That's when it started.

"You're not going to read that paper, are you?"

"Well, yes. Why shouldn't I?"

"If you have time to read the paper, then you have time to bathe the kids and put them to bed."

"Mary, I've had a tough day, and I have to leave for a board meeting in 45 minutes. Let me relax for a while."

Though I had suspected this would happen, I still wasn't ready for it. I could feel myself getting defensive, and my response was less than understanding. We argued until I left for the meeting. When I returned home, the atmosphere was sullen and silent.

Now we were lying in bed, six inches apart, yet hundreds of miles from each other emotionally, both bodies as stiff as Egyptian mummies. Neither one dared to move an arm or leg lest it accidentally touch the other and be interpreted as a desire to talk it out, or— horror of horrors—*apologize!* We were in for another long night of conflict.

Bumpy Roads to Resolution

Of course, there are as many ways to react to conflict as there are personality types.

Some people simply withdraw. They think the best way to solve a problem is to run from it. But that doesn't solve anything. It just builds a wall between them, as I can sadly testify.

Other people fight to win. They won't quit until they've proven that they're right and their opponent is wrong. But that just drives their mates farther away from them, as Mary can unhappily attest.

A third response is to yield. The person who always yields may think he is right, but it's not worth the hassle to prove it, so he just gives in and tries to forget the whole thing. But that builds resentment, which is sure to come out in one way or another.

A fourth method is to compromise—each one must give a little and try to meet in the middle. Sometimes that is the only way, but it does carry with it the danger that neither mate will feel they have been completely understood or that their needs have been met.

A Better Way: Love Fights

Must there be conflict in marriage? Can't two reasonably intelligent and mature adults live together in peace?

Yes, they can. There will always be differences of opinion; no two normal people will always agree on everything. But they can work through those inevitable disagreements and resolve their conflicts..

How?

The best way to resolve conflict is to seek a solution that will satisfy the needs of both. Here are several things Mary and I try to do as we work toward that desirable goal. We strive to turn our conflicts into *love fights*—exchanges that not only resolve the conflict, but actually *increase* our love for one another.

The following are six principles to follow in the process of a love fight:

Adopt a learner's posture. Both spouses will win if they can learn and grow through the experience. Couples need to establish this goal from the very beginning.

Once Mary and I realize there is tension between us, the most important thing is not to make the other person understand our point of view—not to win the argument. Instead, the important thing is to learn something valuable that will help us become the person God wants us to be.

If I really want to resolve a conflict, I need to reach out and begin to work toward strengthening our relationship—even if that means being vulnerable and making some changes in *my* life.

Since neither one of us has the natural inclination to do that, it will also help to pray: "Lord, help me to have a teachable spirit. Relieve me of my defensiveness, self-righteousness and anger, and help me learn something that will cause me to grow." If we can maintain that attitude, we're well on the way to resolving conflict.

Listen with our hearts. My normal response is to show Mary how unreasonable she is acting, correct her inaccuracies, refute her logic, pick at details, and explain why I spoke and acted as I did. But an inspired proverb says, "He whose ear listens to the life-giving reproof will dwell among the wise" (Proverbs 15:31).

We reach the root of the problem more readily if I invite her to tell me what she is feeling and what *her* needs are. I also ask her how she would have liked me to respond and what I can do to help resolve the problem in a way that is best for her.

My hope is that she can share her thoughts with me without hurting me. But whatever she says, my goal should be to listen—without arguing, without answering back, without justifying my actions, without trying to get her to acknowledge my needs. My only comments at this point should be to agree, or to seek further clarification.

If something sounds untrue or unfair, I should simply say,

"What I hear you saying is . . ." and then share my impression of what she said and ask her if I'm understanding her correctly. After that I must devote myself to listening.

Mary explains it from her vantage point:

"There are two things I would like from Richard—one is unconditional love, and the second is understanding. I want him to understand not only the meaning of the words I am saying, but what I really mean—the hidden meaning. I want him to try to feel with me—I want to feel his support even when he does not agree with me. I want to be considered valuable to him.

"But if I want him to understand me, I have to make myself understandable. I must be willing to answer questions, to share my mind honestly, to avoid becoming defensive, to make myself vulnerable, and to listen and think before I speak. And I must be willing to look at things from his viewpoint."

Keep our emotions under control. When we are falsely accused or misjudged, most of us get angry on the inside and reflect that anger in some way. Of course, our spouses can feel our displeasure.

Anger will never help us to resolve a conflict or help us grow: ". . . for the anger of man does not achieve the righteousness of God" (James 1:20). Ephesians 4:31 says that God wants us to put our anger away from us.

How do we overcome anger? *Not* by bottling it up. If we do that, it inevitably surfaces in one form or another. Neither should we direct the anger toward ourselves—that is one of the major causes of depression.

The healthiest way to dispel anger is to admit it audibly ("I'm feeling angry right now"); identify the reason for the anger ("I feel angry when you speak sharply to me like that"); forgive the other person for failing to meet our expectations; and finally, kindly express our needs and desires to our mate. If we can do this, a resolution is just around the corner.

Think before we speak. Some of us have our mouths in motion before our minds are in gear. And if we are trying to resolve a difference, that is like pouring gasoline on a brush fire. Thinking before we speak will help us tell our mates what we are feeling and what we want—without hurting them.

Focus on our own part of the blame. Blaming others usually stems from a low self-image; we feel that we must win in order to establish our worth. Sometimes we blame others simply to avoid admitting that we have contributed to the problem.

If we are serious about strengthening a relationship, we must ask ourselves what *we* have done to agitate the conflict. If our partner feels hurt, unappreciated, criticized or rejected, then we must examine our own attitudes, words and actions. What have we done to contribute to those feelings? Even if our actions were unintentional, the tone of our voice or the expression on our face may have fueled the feelings, and we must be willing to acknowledge that.

Only recently have I begun to realize the ways in which I contribute to the arguments in my marriage, if by nothing more than a disapproving glance, or a probing question that subtly belittles Mary. Her hostile attacks used to send me scurrying to my study, where I would sulk and pity myself for long periods of time.

Once in a great while she still comes at me rather aggressively, and my first reaction is still to run to the safety of my study. But I no sooner close the door than the Lord begins to deal with me. I don't hear any voices, but the thoughts are surely there: "What are you doing in here?"

"I just came in here to get away from the verbal barrage, Lord."

"You need to go out there and admit your part of the blame."

"But, Lord, You heard what she said to me. That was totally unreasonable and untrue. It hurt. I need time to heal."

"Go out and admit your part of the blame."

Keep short accounts. It doesn't take several days for Mary and me to confront the problem anymore—usually just several minutes. And by that time, Mary has started to think about her part of the blame as well. These days, we are more readily able to acknowledge our wrong, seek the other's forgiveness, embrace, and proceed joyfully.

As the years have progressed, my work in ministry has required more traveling—good-byes are an increasing part of our relationship. There have been times when we parted without resolving a conflict, and my thought has been, "What if this were our last good-bye?"

Suppose something happened to one of us before we were reunited. Could the other live with himself/herself? It would be extremely difficult. It is our desire to keep short accounts with each other and to resolve our conflicts quickly and completely in a manner that keeps our love for one another growing stronger.

"What Are You Thinking?"

If we were to choose the one area that has caused us more problems than any other—and continues to be our weakest link—it would be the area of communication. And in that we are not alone. Many other couples echo the same frustration over their desire to communicate more effectively.

My problem was simply that I *didn't!* I've always been a rather quiet person, not prone to revealing my thoughts. Mary would ask, "What are you thinking?"

I would answer, "Oh, nothing important."

In some instances, I was ashamed to admit what I was thinking. It may have been a doubt or a fear that I didn't want to admit because I thought it would make me look weak. It may have been a wild aspiration that I didn't want to disclose because I thought she would criticize the idea, or it may have been a lustful thought that I didn't want to acknowledge for fear of being seen as spiritually lacking.

It was safer to play the role of the silent martyr. And besides, I thought that would make her suffer some for hurting me.

Mary's problem was just the opposite:

"I blurted out almost everything that came into my mind, regardless of how it might have affected Richard. If I was angry about something, I seldom kept it a secret. Richard never had to guess what I was feeling. I told him in no uncertain terms, sometimes in loud, angry, insulting and belittling tones."

Neither of us was thinking about the other; we were each concerned about ourselves. Mary's attack would send me deeper into my shell for protection. But the more I retreated, the more forceful she became, desperately seeking to have her needs met and to be understood. We knew that if our marriage was ever to improve, we had to work on our communication skills.

For openers, I knew I had to open up, admit what I was thinking, share what I was feeling, and allow her into my world.

Now when I come home in the evening, I try to sit down for 20 minutes and rehash with her some of the events of the day—not only to recount the events themselves, but to relate my feelings about them. For instance, if I have had the opportunity to introduce someone to Christ, I share the details and describe my joy. If I have done something poorly, I explain it honestly and admit my anguish.

Honest communication does not mean that we must blurt out everything that comes into our minds. Some things are unmistakably hurtful and are better left unsaid. But it *does* mean that we begin to develop a greater transparency about our thoughts and feelings.

How Much Should We Tell?

One good rule is to share whatever affects our attitudes or actions toward our mates. If they are feeling the effects of our temper or mood, they have a right to know what is on our mind. If I am irritated with Mary because she has snapped at me, then she has a right to know. And I have an obligation to tell her about it in a kind, calm manner—without laying the blame on her.

Honestly admitting what is on my mind has helped make me more accountable to Mary, and this has helped me grow emotionally and spiritually. As I have grown, the pages of my mind have opened wider, contributing to a greater intimacy between us.

As Mary and I continue to open ourselves more to one another, share our souls, and then eagerly listen to each other, we are drawn closer together in an exciting and mutually satisfying bond of intimacy.

Excerpted from *When Two Walk Together,* © 1988 by Richard and Mary Strauss. Published by Here's Life Publishers, Inc. Used by permission.

4

HOW TO KNOW
IF YOU HAVE
FALLEN IN LOVE

David and Carole Hocking

The young lady standing in front of me after one of my sermons seemed deeply concerned. She was lovely, talented and intensely interested in spiritual matters. Her problem? She wanted to know how a person falls in love. Specifically, she wanted information on whether her feelings for a certain man were the kind that led toward marriage.

I told her that in a few weeks I would be speaking on that subject. She said, "I can't wait that long." When I inquired as to why, she said, "He just asked me to marry him." So much for patience!

People seem to be falling out of love as surely as falling in love these days. One 35-year-old man told me that he did not love his wife anymore: "I have fallen out of love with her."

"That's not a big problem," I replied. He seemed surprised at my answer.

"Why do you say that?"

"Because you can learn to love her again. Just as you have fallen out of love with her, so you can fall in love with her again."

But he didn't want to hear this because, as time proved, he had already "fallen in love" with another woman. I get tired of this story—it seems like a broken record that keeps repeating the same line.

The Symptoms of Falling in Love

There are many married couples who have never "fallen in love" with each other. They need to, but in so many cases they remain apathetic to the necessity of such romance. Their marriage is based on duty and responsibility, which, of course, is essential. But if all a couple has going for them is the fact of a past ceremony, a couple of kids and a few years under their belt, they are living together in a relationship that is less than what God intended. Romantic love is needed in every marriage. The Bible's Song of Solomon makes that fact abundantly clear.

Marriage is based on commitment, not romance. If no romance ever exists in a marriage, it is still a marriage in the sight of God if the man and woman have spoken vows to each other before two or three witnesses. In other words, marriages should be held together even if no romance exists. But, as we read the Song of Solomon we get a clear understanding that God's intention for marriage is that it be characterized by romance.

But, how does a married couple retain the romance of their courtship? Let's examine the Biblical writings of Solomon for some advice.

The Song of Songs

"The Song of songs, which is Solomon."

What an opening line to the most powerful romantic song ever written!

It tells us several things. It speaks of music; it is a song—not just an ordinary song, but the *Song of Songs*. Romantic love done in God's way is filled with music—the music of love.

Musical songs are poetic, and the Song of Solomon is saturated with romantic poetry and beautiful vocabulary. It tells us how couples who are in love communicate with each other. There is nothing here of crass, blunt, sarcastic or critical talk. It is sweet and refreshing to the heart.

This is one song with 117 verses. It should be read as a whole and captured in our heart as though every line were essential to its impact and importance.

The words we use today may be different than those used 3,000 years ago, but they should be the very best and beautiful of all that we know and have.

Help from Solomon

The Song of Solomon is romance *par excellence*. And, it is good advice for the unmarried. Singles desperately need help on this matter because of the intense pressure that a single lifestyle places upon an individual.

In fact, everybody seems to be searching for romantic love these days. People want to fall in love and to experience romance that is often found only in novels or movies. They picture in their minds the ideal situation in which boy meets girl and both go bananas over each other.

But Solomon gives God's viewpoint, and that's vitally important. The secular world speaks much of romantic love but offers very few guidelines for true love. Morals and ethics are usually left out. Solomon tells you how "falling in love" should happen when God's love is controlling and when His principles determine your feelings.

Where Are the Lovers?

The Song of Solomon portrays the man as the lover. He is the romantic one: tender in his approach, lavish in his praise, sensitive to his spouse's needs. Abishag refers to Solomon as her love; it is her favorite word. She, like women today, has a need for the romance of her husband, and she expresses throughout the book how much it means to her.

Solomon is an example to all husbands today. We need to be romantic toward our wives. Constant encouragement and praise must flow from our lips as we relate to our wives and describe their attractiveness to our hearts. It is not a mere feminine quality to be romantic. "Macho" men can learn to be romantic.

Carole and I met when she was in her final year of college and I was in my first year of seminary. We were in the same car with two other people traveling home to California from Indiana to spend the Christmas holidays with our families.

On the return trip (we were driving straight through) at about

3 a.m., I happened to look in the rearview mirror to the backseat. Carole was wide awake, and our eyes met through that mirror. I'll never forget the feeling: We fell in love.

Though no words were exchanged between us and it was days before we met again (and weeks before I was ever able to hold her hand), we both felt it that night—romantic love. What a feeling it was and is!

Several weeks later I had the joy of holding her in my arms and kissing her. I asked her to marry me that same night. What a thrill! Just touching her was sheer ecstasy to me.

And ever since that day, we have strived to enjoy the romance that Solomon so richly described thousands of years ago.

❦ INSIGHT ❦

Are You in Love?

Take this test:

1. I want to be touched, caressed and loved by my spouse more than any other human activity or event.

☐ Yes   ☐ No

2. I find my spouse's inward spirit, attitudes and character more attractive than his or her outward appearance, including clothes, cosmetics and physical body.

☐ Yes   ☐ No

3. I would rather be alone with my spouse than enjoy the company of anyone else on earth.

☐ Yes   ☐ No

If you don't score too well (less than three "yes" answers), don't give up—there's hope for you in the message of the Song of Solomon!

Excerpted from *Romantic Lovers*, © 1986 by David and Carole Hocking. Published by Harvest House Publishers. Used by permission.

5

LONELY HUSBANDS, LONELY WIVES

Dennis Rainey

M y daughter, Ashley, slipped into my study and asked me what I was writing about. "Isolation," I replied. "Do you know what that means?"

"Oh," said my blue-eyed, blonde-haired, freckle-faced 10-year-old, "that's when somebody excludes you."

I may be a bit prejudiced, but I like Ashley's answer better than the dictionary's definition, which says isolation is "the condition of being alone, separated, solitary, set apart."

Ashley's answer is a profound observation on human relationships. Husbands excluding wives and wives excluding husbands is exactly what happens when loneliness and isolation infect a marriage.

When you're excluded, you have a feeling of distance. You experience a lack of closeness and little real intimacy. You can share a bed, eat at the same dinner table, watch the same TV, share the same checking account, and parent the same children—but you can still be alone.

You may have sex, but you don't have love; you may talk, but you don't communicate. You may live together, but you don't share life with one another.

Because an alarming number of good marriages are unaware of this problem, I will venture a bold premise: *Your marriage naturally moves toward a state of isolation.* Unless you lovingly and energetically nurture your marriage, you will begin to drift away from your mate.

In 1976 we began the Family Ministry, which is part of Campus Crusade for Christ. We've now held hundreds of Family Life Conferences all over the world. From the comments we've received, it's obvious to us that isolation is the number-one problem in marriage relationships today.

Periods of Pruning

One of our foundational Homebuilders Principles is: *If you do not tackle your problems together with God's help, you will fall apart.*

Lloyd Shadrach is a good friend and a leader in our ministry to families. He is sensitive to the lessons God has for him. Recently, Lloyd took a walk after a fierce thunderstorm rumbled through Little Rock, Arkansas. As he walked down a road lined with massive, towering oak trees, he had to step over dead limbs that had been blown down. Decaying branches—once lodged amidst the greenery above—now littered the landscape below.

"It was as though God was giving me a personal object lesson of what 'storms' can do in our lives," said Lloyd. "In the middle of the storm when the wind is gusting, the lightning is popping and the storm clouds are getting darker, it's difficult to believe our troubles are purposeful. But God may allow a storm in our lives to clear out the dead wood so new growth can occur. Isn't it interesting how fresh the air feels after a storm is over? Sort of unused."

As Lloyd and I talked, I couldn't help but think about the dead wood—several cords of it—that has been blown out of my life. One of the most important things my wife, Barbara, and I have learned from these storms is that God is interested in our growth. He wants us to trust Him in the midst of the storms. He wants us to grow together as a couple and not fall apart.

However, I've seen marriages die from these periods of pruning:

- A child drowns in a swimming pool. The mother blames herself, then abruptly turns on her husband.

- A husband loses a job. The subsequent financial troubles cause a wife to stop believing in him. Their disappointment in each other causes them to retreat from meeting one another's needs.
- An unplanned pregnancy and increased pressures at work provoke a husband to question his commitment to the marriage.

What most couples don't realize is that trials represent an opportunity for them to sink their roots deeper and to gain stability in their relationship.

Once, scientist Lord Kelvin was lecturing his students on an experiment that failed to come off as planned. "Gentlemen, when you are face to face with a difficulty, you are up against a discovery," he said. As inevitable storms rumble through our lives, it's imperative that we turn *to* one another and not *against* one another.

How Couples Fail to Handle Trials

Families fail to respond properly to adversity in two major ways. First, and most typically, *they fail to anticipate the trials and problems that will come.* Somehow they think none of that will happen to them, but they are mistaken.

A well-known saying reminds us that nothing is sure in life except for death and taxes. To those two old foes, you can add troubles. As I read recently, "The man whose problems are all behind him is probably a school bus driver."

Second, when troubles do hit, *many couples simply don't know how to respond.* The trauma brought by the problem is not the real issue. The real issue is the response the couple makes to that trauma.

According to studies conducted by Dr. Mavis Heatherington, 70 percent of marriages in which a child dies or is born deformed end in divorce within five years.

Why does this happen? Couples simply have no strategy for living that goes beyond romance. They don't know how to hold their relationship together and even make it stronger during that desperate period of suffering and pain.

Part of the strategy for facing troubles is to realize that God allows difficulties in our lives for many reasons. I'm not saying He causes difficulties, but I do believe He allows them. Malcolm Muggeridge once wrote:

Contrary to what might be expected, I look back on experiences that at the time seemed especially desolating and painful with particular satisfaction. Indeed, I can say with complete truthfulness that everything that I have learned in my 75 years in this world, everything that has truly enhanced and enlightened my experience, has been through affliction and not through happiness.

I was just ending a Family Life Conference in Dallas when a trim, well-muscled man greeted me. He told me he was a Green Beret.

Apparently, the seminar had touched a nerve with him. "Dennis, in the Green Berets we train over and over and then over and over again," he began. "We repeat some exercises until we are sick of them, but our instructors know what they are doing. They want us so prepared and finely trained that when trials and difficulties come on the battlefield, we will be able to fall back upon that which is second nature to us. We literally learn to do things by reflex action."

I realized I'd just heard a great illustration of how Christians should face marriage together. We should be so well trained in God's plan that our reaction to crises and difficulties will be an automatic reflex, not a panicky fumbling around. If we wait until a crisis hits and then turn to the Scriptures, we won't be prepared—and we'll be more susceptible to the enemy.

The Best Way to Handle Trouble

If there's a simple principle for handling problems, it's contained in these five words: "Give thanks in all circumstances" (1 Thessalonians 5:18).

This isn't a simplistic excuse to put your head in the sand and ignore reality. On the contrary, I believe it's the key to dealing with the storms life can bring your way—and that includes the little things as well as the big upheavals and challenges.

If we want to practice giving thanks in everything, we have to ask ourselves: Is God really involved in the details of my life? Could God possibly want to teach me something through a flat tire, a kid's runny nose, or a toy-strewn floor? Does He really want to be part of every moment of my day, or is He willing to settle for the 9:30 slot on Sunday mornings?

Giving thanks in all things expresses faith. Those five little words express our belief that *God knows what He is doing*. And that He can be trusted. As Martin Lloyd-Jones put it: "Faith is the refusal to panic."

Don't Lose Your Perspective

One summer, we lived out of suitcases for seven weeks on the road. It definitely was not easy to give God thanks in everything. On the way to Colorado for a conference, we lost our billfold and purse and had to spend the night in a leaky tent in the middle of a thunderstorm.

When we finally arrived in Fort Collins for the training conference, we questioned whether the Lord really wanted us to start a ministry to families.

Then, a couple of days later, a flash flood swept through Big Thompson Canyon, just a few miles from our training site. It was the worst flash flood in Colorado's history. More than 100 people lost their lives, including seven fellow Campus Crusade for Christ staff women. Twenty-eight other Campus Crusade women narrowly escaped a 20-foot wall of water by going up the side of a canyon in total darkness.

As news of the disaster sank in, Barbara and I realized we really didn't have any problems at all. We had our lives and the privilege of serving the King of Kings and Lord of Lords. We understood that God has all kinds of ways of teaching His children valuable lessons. No matter what the circumstances might be, there is always something to be thankful for.

Adapted from *Lonely Husbands, Lonely Wives,* ©1989 by Dennis Rainey. Published by Word Books. Used by permission.

6

BECOMING ONE

Dr. James C. Dobson

Not long ago, I was spinning the channel selector on our television set and paused momentarily to watch the "All New Newlywed Game." It was a bad decision.

Bob Eubanks, the show's host, posed a series of dumb questions to a lineup of flaky brides whose husbands were "sequestered backstage in a soundproof room." He challenged the women to predict their husbands' responses to inquiries that went something like this:

"Where was the exact spot your husband saw you stark naked for the first time?"

"If you and your husband ever separated, which of his friends would be the first to make a pass at you?"

"How would you describe the first time you and your husband made 'whoopee' using these TV terms: First Run, Rerun, or Cancelled?"

"Where is the last place you would have, if you could have, made love?"

Without the least hesitation, the women blurted out frank answers to these and other intimate questions. At times I felt I shouldn't be watching, and indeed, past generations would have blushed and gasped at the candor. But Eubanks was undaunted.

He then asked the women to respond to this question: "What kind of insect does your husband remind you of when he's feeling romantic?" If you think the question was ridiculous, consider the answer given by one female contestant. She replied, "A bear." When her husband realized his wife couldn't tell an insect from a mammal, he pounded her frantically with his answer card. She said, "*Wellll* . . . I didn't know!"

Ingredients of Instability

It has been said that television programming reflects the values held widely within the society it serves. Heaven help us if that is true in this instance. The impulsive responses of the newlyweds revealed their embarrassing immaturity, selfishness, hostility, vulnerability, and sense of inadequacy.

These are the prime ingredients of marital instability, and too commonly, divorce itself. An army of disillusioned ex-husbands and ex-wives can attest to that fact all too well.

For every 10 marriages occurring in America today, five will end in bitter conflict and divorce. That is tragic . . . but have you ever wondered what happens to the other five? Do they sail blissfully into the sunset? Hardly! According to clinical psychologist Neil Warren, who appeared on my "Focus on the Family" radio program, all five will stay together for a lifetime, but in varying degrees of disharmony.

He quoted the research of Dr. John Cuber, whose findings were published in a book entitled *The Significant Americans*. Cuber learned that some couples will remain married for the benefit of the children, while others will pass the years in relative apathy. Incredibly, only one or two out of 10 will achieve what might be called "intimacy" in the relationship.

By intimacy, Dr. Warren is referring to the mystical bond of friendship, commitment and understanding that almost defies explanation. It occurs when a man and woman, being separate and distinct individuals, are fused into a single unit which the Bible calls "one flesh."

I'm convinced the human spirit craves this kind of unconditional love and experiences something akin to "soul hunger" when it cannot be achieved. I'm also certain that most couples *expect* to find intimacy in marriage, but somehow it usually eludes them.

To those who are anticipating a wedding in the near future, and to couples experiencing their first few years as husbands and wives, let me ask you these tough questions: When the story of your family is finally written, what will the record show? Will you cultivate an intimate marriage, or will *you* journey relentlessly down the road toward divorce proceedings, with consequent property settlement, custody battles and broken dreams? How will you beat the odds?

Fortunately, you are not merely passive victims in the unfolding drama of your lives together. You *can* build a stable relationship that will withstand the storms of life.

Collision with Reality

I heard a story about a young man who fell in love with a pretty young lady. He took her home to meet his mother before asking her to marry him. But alas, his mother disliked the girl intensely and refused to give her blessings. Three times this happened with different candidates for marriage, leaving the young man exasperated.

Finally in desperation he found a girl who was amazingly like his mother. They walked, talked, and even looked alike. *Surely my mother will approve of this selection,* he thought. With great anticipation he took his new friend home to be considered . . . and behold, his *father* hated her!

This young man had a problem, to be sure, but he is not the only one. Finding the right person to love for a lifetime can be one of the greatest challenges in living. By the time you locate a sane, loyal, mature, disciplined, intelligent, motivated, chaste, kind, unselfish, attractive and godly partner, you're too worn out to care. Furthermore, merely *locating* Mr. or Miss Marvelous is only half of the assignment; getting that person interested in *you* is another matter.

The difficulties of identifying and attracting the right partner are graphically illustrated by current statistics on family breakups. In 1986, there were 2.4 million divorces in the United States. What a tragedy! The average duration of those ruined marriages was only seven years—and half of them disintegrated within three years after the wedding. How could this be true?

Not one of those couples anticipated the conflict and pain that quickly settled in. They were shocked . . . surprised . . . dismayed. They stood at the altar and promised to be faithful forever, never dreaming they were making the greatest mistake of their lives. For years I have asked myself why this collision with reality occurs and how it can be avoided.

Part of the problem is that many couples come into marriage having had no healthy role models in their formative years. If 50 percent of the families are splitting up today, that means half of the marriageable young adults have seen only conflict and disillusionment at home. They have felt the apathy and heard the piercing silence between their parents. It's no wonder that today's newlyweds often sputter and fumble their way through early married life.

Among these destructive customs is the tendency for young men and women to marry virtual strangers. Oh, I know a typical couple talks for countless hours during the courtship period, and they believe they know each other. But a dating relationship is designed to *conceal* information, not reveal it. Each partner puts his or her best foot forward, hiding embarrassing facts, habits, flaws and temperaments.

Consequently, the bride and groom enter into marriage with an array of private assumptions about how life will be lived after the wedding. Major conflict occurs a few weeks later when they discover that they differ radically on what each partner considers to be nonnegotiable issues. The stage is then set for arguments and hurt feelings that never occurred during the courtship experience.

For this reason I strongly believe in premarital counseling. Each engaged couple, even those who seem perfectly suited for one another, should participate in *at least* six to ten sessions with someone who is trained to help them prepare for marriage. The primary purpose of these encounters is to identify the assumptions each partner holds and to work through the areas of potential conflict.

Questions to Consider

The following questions are a few of the issues that should be evaluated and discussed in the presence of a supportive counselor or pastor:

Where will you live after getting married?
Will the bride work? For how long?
Are children planned? How many? How soon? How far apart?
Will the wife return to work after babies arrive? How quickly?

How will the kids be disciplined? Fed? Trained?

What church will you attend?

Are there theological differences to be reckoned with?

How will your roles be different?

How will you respond to each set of in-laws?

Where will you spend Thanksgiving and Christmas holidays?

How will financial decisions be made?

Who will write the checks?

How do you feel about credit?

Will a car be bought with borrowed money? How soon? What kind?

How far do you expect to go sexually before marriage?

If the bride's friends differ from the groom's buddies, how will you relate to them? What are your greatest apprehensions about your fiancé(e)?

What expectations do you have for him/her?

The list of important questions is almost endless, and many surprises turn up as they are discussed. Some couples suddenly discover major problems that had not surfaced until then . . . and they agree to either postpone or call off the wedding. Others work through their conflicts and proceed toward marriage with increased confidence. All have benefited from the effort.

Someone has said: The key to a healthy marriage is to keep your eyes wide open before you wed and half closed thereafter. I agree.

Noted counselor and author Norman Wright is perhaps the guru of premarital counseling, having written and spoken extensively on this subject. He discussed his views during a recent interview on my radio broadcast and made several additional observations.

• Couples should not announce their engagement or select a wedding date until at least half of the counseling sessions are completed. That way they can gracefully go their separate ways if unresolvable conflicts and problems emerge.

• Couples need to think through the implications of their decisions regarding children. For example, when an engaged man and woman indicate they intend to have three children, each three years apart, they will not be alone at home for 26 more years once the first child is born! Couples often are stunned at hearing this.

They then proceed to talk about how they will nurture their relationship and keep it alive throughout the parenting years. It is a healthy interaction.

• Spiritual incompatibility is very common in couples today. The man and woman may share the same belief system, but one partner is often relatively immature and the other is well-seasoned. In those instances, couples should pray together silently for three to four minutes a day, and then share their prayers out loud.

After they are married, Wright recommends they ask one another each morning, "How can I pray for you today?" At the end of the day they are instructed to ask again about the issues raised in the morning and to pray about them together. That's not a bad way to handle stress in any relationship!

• Another frequent source of conflict is the continuation of parental dependency in one or both partners. This problem is more likely to occur if an individual has never lived away from home. In those cases, additional measures must be taken to lessen the dependency. Living arrangements are changed so that the person cooks his/her own meals, does the laundry, and exercises independence in other ways. Parental overprotection can be a marriage killer if not recognized and handled properly.

• Many loving parents today are paying for premarital counseling as a gift to an engaged son or daughter. I think this is an excellent idea—and may be the greatest contribution mothers and fathers will ever make to long-term marriage in the next generation.

PART TWO

FOCUS ON HUSBANDS AND FATHERS

7

TEN WAYS HUSBANDS CAN SAY I LOVE YOU

Wayne Oliveira

When a friend asks me if my wife works, I always have a quick reply.

"Yes, she does, and she probably works harder than I do," I say, with a tinge of pride in my voice. Then I wait for the inevitable questions.

"Oh, where does she work? What does she do?"

"Well," I say, pausing dramatically, "she's at home raising our four children."

With our station-wagon load of kids, shaggy dog and pet hamster, my wife has her hands full every day. All wives, whether they work inside the home (as a homemaker) or outside the home (either part- or full-time) need to feel loved and appreciated. A working wife feels the strain of juggling the responsibilities of home and job, even if a second paycheck eases the family's financial burden.

Also, keep in mind that homemakers receive no salary for the enormous task of taking care of a house and children. A homemaker's only payment is the gratitude of her family.

There are many ways to express that gratitude toward your wife—wherever she works! You can take her on a much-deserved vacation to a tropical isle or buy her a new car, but these rewards are often impractical or financially impossible.

There are many inexpensive things you can do, however, to show your love and appreciation, and increase the joy in your marriage. Here are my Top 10:

1. *Provide your wife with some time away from home.* Plainly, a woman needs to get away from the house. A change of scenery will do wonders to refresh her both physically and spiritually. Give her a night out to shop, visit a friend or exercise at the local health club. No employer expects a worker to spend 16 hours every day of the week at the office.

2. *Provide your wife with some time off at home.* Young children or other circumstances may prevent her from actually getting out of the house. Take care of the baby while your wife takes a long nap. Prepare supper while she puts her feet up and spends a little time with her favorite novel. Enlist the children to clean up after the meal.

3. *Back up your wife in front of the children.* When the kids challenge Mom's authority, step in and reinforce her stance. Back her up even if you are privately second-guessing her actions. You can always discuss your wife's decision afterward. If it turns out she was wrong, don't tell the children. Let your wife smooth matters with them so her position will remain strong in the eyes of the children.

4. *Give your wife a gift on an ordinary day.* Every wife expects gifts on Mother's Day, her birthday and other holidays. Buy her something when she least expects it. A small, inexpensive gift or a bouquet of fresh-cut flowers will brighten her day, especially if you include a card.

5. *Praise your wife and tell her you love her.* Everyone needs to feel appreciated. If you ever had a job where the boss never commended you for a fine performance, you would understand the importance of praise. It isn't difficult to find ways to honestly compliment your wife. Everything, from cooking a fancy meal for company to being a thrifty shopper, takes time and effort. Lavish her with praise and words of love, and don't forget to be sincere about it.

6. *Be silent about your wife's shortcomings.* If you must say something critical, say it constructively. Tread lightly. It is easy to start preaching. Leave the room if you have the slightest urge to say "I told you so." Just remember how many times your wife could have hit you with that phrase, but didn't. Above all, don't compare her with your mother, unless you are telling her how much better she is in a certain area.

7. *Give your wife her own tool kit.* It doesn't have to be elaborate; a few basic hand tools will suffice. Your wife may enjoy doing various jobs around the house on her own. Give her the tool kit and stand back. She might even build a new addition for the house!

8. *Find your wife's strong points and use them.* Perhaps your wife is a good organizer or can balance the family checkbook. Let her help you in areas where you need it, such as planning a family budget. She'll enjoy helping you, even if it means an added responsibility, because it will contribute to her self-esteem. Your spouse will feel like part of the management team, not a day laborer.

9. *Keep arguments with your wife private.* Don't belittle her in front of the children, even if you feel you're in the right. Otherwise, the kids may feel that they can challenge Mom whenever they disagree with her. Consider how you would feel if your employer berated you in front of your subordinates. Even if you deserved a reprimand, it would be embarrassing to have your authority weakened.

10. *Put your wife first.* Your love and loyalty to your wife is necessary for her well-being. Second only to your relationship with Jesus Christ, your wife comes first in your life. If you make her number one, she will make *you* first in *her* life. God values marriage so much that He commanded us to love our wives as Jesus Christ loves the church (Ephesians 5:25). This is only possible if we keep Jesus at the center of our marriage and remain in subjection to Him.

One final thought: Galatians 6:7–8 tells us that we are like gardeners. We can sow to the flesh and reap corruption, or we can sow to the Spirit and reap blessings. Plant these small seeds of love and watch the Lord cultivate joy in your marriage every day.

8

HOW TO KEEP FROM BEING ROBBED OF REST

Tim Kimmel

Keeping the average family unsatisfied is vital to our economic system. In order to lure me to a particular product, an advertiser must create a dissatisfaction for what I have . . . or a nagging desire for things that I don't need.

Every time I take a shower I stare at a good example of the persuasive power of advertising. My home came equipped with the standard fixture for a shower. It always managed to get me completely wet and adequately clean. But I kept seeing an ad on TV showing people standing under a special shower head that spun the water around and sent it pulsating over their backs.

The people on the commercial were always smiling and laughing. I thought about the fixture on my shower. It didn't make me smile or laugh. It didn't make my scalp tingle or relax my neck. It just managed to get me completely wet and adequately clean. I had to have one of those shower heads that made taking a bath a holiday.

The new shower fixture cost me about five times more than the one I took off. But my back is worth it, right? I installed this new necessity for happiness about nine years ago. The last time I turned the dial from "Normal" to "Pulsating" was about eight years, 11 months, and three weeks ago. Mainly it has served me as a humble shower. But it does a great job of getting me completely wet and adequately clean.

Essence of Restlessness

Truthfully, I'm grateful to live in a free-market economy. It's a system that offers the greatest opportunities for developing ideas, accommodating needs and enjoying prosperity. But every good thing has a potential down side. If the best way to keep me coming back for more is to keep me unsatisfied, I'm going to fight a problem with restlessness. And so is my family.

I get a kick out of watching parents take their kids through the checkout lines at grocery stores. If it isn't bad enough that they bought more items than they intended to, they are forced to push their children through a narrow stall that has a million things they could live without within the arm's length of a two-year-old. I couldn't figure out why stores created those checkout nightmares until I began noticing how many people actually succumb to the pressure to add to their 4-foot grocery tab. Those racks filled with hundreds of toys, trinkets and candy give even the best parent a literal run for his money. ("Yea, though I pass through the valley of the shadow of impulse, I will fear no temper tantrums, because I left my kids at home.")

What I'm addressing is the very essence of restlessness. When we lose control of our expectations, we are guaranteed to be robbed of rest. Yet the culture in which we live makes losing control a foregone conclusion! If I have any hope of enjoying the rest God intends for me, I have to remind myself that I am in a constant struggle with my environment to maintain a sense of satisfaction.

When people fail to discipline their desires, they feel incomplete. A gloomy cloud of inadequacy follows them around. It's difficult to maintain deep relationships with such people—their feelings of inadequacy drain your emotions.

When people fail to discipline their desires, they place unbearable demands on a marriage. Their partner is quick to realize his or her dissatisfaction, and if the partner can't supply all that he or she wants, the partner feels a sense of failure.

When people fail to discipline their desires, they compound stress in their children. An environment where the best is always in the future breeds an attitude that makes the present look cheap.

When people fail to discipline their desires, they accommodate the powers within the world system that desire to control them. A heart that finds it hard to accept its position in life is putty in the hands of the Powers of Darkness.

When God had Moses carve the Ten Commandments in stone, He used the first and last commandments as the supports for the other eight. They were sweeping statements that served as catchalls for the wandering passions of man. If we view these as guidelines for contentment (which they are), we will see why it makes such logical sense to place them in the order in which they appear in the Bible.

The first commandment says: *I am the Lord your God, who brought you out of the land of Egypt, out of the house of slavery. You shall have no other gods before Me* (Exodus 20:23).

Turning to Him

A focused affection on the God who sets men free is the best way to enjoy a life of balanced love. God is love. He is the essence of its definition. Since love is one of the fundamental needs of man, it stands to reason that we need to begin by loving the Author of love. As we maintain and strengthen our love for Him, we enable our hearts to see the second priority of our existence on earth—people.

The last commandment says: *You shall not covet your neighbor's house; you shall not covet your neighbor's wife or his male servant or his female servant or his ox or his donkey or anything that belongs to your neighbor* (Exodus 20:17).

Coveting has a lot of nasty synonyms: envy, jealousy, lust, greed . . . It starts in our hearts as a seed but gets watered and fertilized by the inevitable pressures on our pride.

Your best friend gets a promotion with a significant pay raise—the seed germinates. The new models for next year roll onto the showroom at the car dealerships—the seed sprouts roots. You go shopping with your best friend, and she fits beautifully into dresses that are the same size she wore when she got married 15 years ago. You stare at the size inside the dress you are holding and notice that it's gone up four digits since your wedding day. Ah, the seed of coveting is now starting to show above the surface of your personality.

Coveting is material inebriation. It's an addiction to things that don't last and a craving for things that don't really matter. It forces us to depend on tomorrow to bring us the happiness that today couldn't supply.

The 'Greener Grass' Syndrome

I'm amazed how often people end up envying the very people who envy them! A pastor sat back in his chair listening to the man seated across from him complain about the cross God had given him to bear. This prominent businessman was regretting that he had chosen the line of work he was in. He knew he should be grateful. After all, since he had bought the majority position in the company, the stock had split twice. The P and L statements for the last three years had supplied him with excellent Christmas bonuses. He and his wife had enjoyed visits to Europe, the Orient, Australia, and most recently, the Iron Curtain countries.

But he fought a lot of guilt.

He had once pursued the pulpit, but took a side road in seminary that placed him in secular work for good. He went on to outline how much he envied the pastor's knowledge of the Bible and his grasp of theology. He wished that *he* had the time to sit around and read the Scriptures all day. Furthermore . . .

The pastor looked past the man's tailored suit to the window through which he could see the two cars parked outside his study. They were the same color, but that was as far as the comparison could go. As soon as this appointment was over, he'd have to take his aging Pontiac home so that his wife could borrow it to do her chores. The odometer broke at 78,000 miles two years ago.

As his counselee rambled on about what a spiritual loser he was, the pastor studied the picture framed on the corner of his desk. His two children smiled so broadly and so proudly. They were too young to be self-conscious. But in a few years, they'd realize what he already knew. Their teeth needed elaborate orthodontic work.

But it wasn't going to happen on his paycheck. He kept thinking of all the times that businessmen had said to him, "Pastor, with your skills, you could have knocked 'em dead in the business arena." They never knew that money was one of the biggest temptations of his life.

Changing places wouldn't solve either one of these men's problems. One man was an ungrateful steward of much, the other was an ungrateful steward of many.

The more we measure our significance by other people's accomplishments, the less we'll be able to feel at rest in our daily lives. A rushed lifestyle is only going to bring more successful people to envy, more unaffordable conveniences to covet, and more failures to regret.

Attitudes That Hinder

One way to check your satisfaction quota is to see how you complete a couple of sentences. The second half of these statements can tell all. Let me help by completing them several ways. I may not hit the areas that you struggle in, but the ones I do offer should give you an idea of how to personalize them.

If only I had . . .
    a job
    a better job
    a more understanding boss
    enough money to retire on
    a bigger house
    a thinner waist
    a better education
    a husband
    a different husband
    a child
    a lifestyle like . . .
If only I hadn't . . .
    dropped out of school
    been forced to get married
    had an abortion
    started drinking

been fired
run up so many debts
neglected my wife
quit that job
sold that stock
If only they had . . .
given me more playing time
recognized my potential
offered me the job
encouraged me to apply myself in school
supported me in my sports
been honest with me
stuck with me
If only they hadn't . . .
abandoned me as a baby
discouraged me
prejudged me
pushed me so hard to achieve
lied to me
been so interested in making money
been ashamed of my handicap

If only . . . if only . . . if only. The starting words for unfulfilled expectations or nagging regrets. No one is immune to their destructive impact. Because we are people and not machines, we can't deny the impact of our past mistakes or disappointments. Nor can we turn deaf ears or blind eyes to the many desires of this world that may be out of reach.

A Disappointing Past

Too many people are unsatisfied with where they are because they don't like the path they took to get there. Often the path to the present was not of their personal choosing.

Most people have had to deal with the pain that comes when they don't meet other people's expectations. But all rejection is not equal. The pain of being rejected by a parent or spouse is far more devastating than being rejected for our ideas or unappreciated for our contributions. Some people can't seem to move out of neutral in the present because their primary "reason for living" let them down in the past.

Others put their life in gear but take off in the wrong direction. A disappointing past can throw our expectations out of whack. We suddenly view acquisitions or status as an antidote for the pain of our past. We think that success will prove we can amount to something, that marriage will prove we are worth loving, that wealth will get people's attention.

I remember an enlightening conversation with a plastic surgeon. Much of what he did brought a healthy transformation to his patients. A rebuilt nose could bring an end to years of teasing. A restructured jaw could restore what the disfigurement of an accident had stolen.

"But you know, Tim," he confided, "many people come into my office for a new look, when what they really want is a new *life*."

A key, then, to experiencing lasting rest in our lives is refusing to allow past disappointments to cause us to pursue unhealthy desires. We need to be disciplined at keeping our past hurts in perspective.

I'm so grateful that we don't have to do this alone. The message of the Bible is that God wants to comfort us in our sorrows, fill our voids and forgive our sins. There is no purchase that will remove the hurt of rejection. There is no activity that will cover the consequences of our negligence. Emptiness and pain need the permanent presence of a God who promised to never leave us or let us down. When our past is handled in a healthy way, we have a better chance of having healthy expectations.

Is It Okay to Dream?

Of course, there is a healthy desire within most of us to improve ourselves and our positions. It is an instinctive quality placed within us by God. To deny it would be foolish, and to ignore it would be sacrilegious.

Certain additions to our lives are capable of giving us a lot of joy. A bigger house could give some badly needed relief from the cramped quarters you presently endure. A graduate degree could offer you a better platform from which to serve people and a better income through which you could accommodate your family needs.

An exotic vacation could allow you to make many beautiful memories with people you love. A spouse could give you an opportunity to love and be loved. There's nothing wrong with these desires.

But if we are going to dream, we need to make sure that we are doing two things at the same time.

First, *we need to make sure that we are pursuing legitimate goals*. What is a legitimate goal? Anything that improves your ability to love and serve God and people is a legitimate goal.

Is there room, then, for acquiring things that accommodate you? Sure. Beautiful possessions have a legitimate place in a balanced person's life. Possessions can never "complete" you, but they can be rewards that come from hard work and conscientious living. They adorn our life—but don't make our life. To pursue possessions in order to fill a void is folly. And if in the process of pursuing them we neglect God-given responsibilities, then they are double trouble. Instead of being rewards, they become treacherous obstacles to healthy living.

Therefore, don't be snookered by "The Lifestyles of the Rich and Famous." Material acquisition cannot fill the void within our lives. Status and influence cannot substitute for our need to love and be loved. You want proof? Trace the trail of broken marriages and troubled children that plague many of the people showcased on that television show.

No, there is nothing wrong with living comfortably, dressing well, driving a nice car, or being famous. These are legitimate rewards that always have responsibilities attached to them. But when they become the things that motivate us, complete us, or sustain us, we're sure to wake up one morning and find ourselves empty. Hollow to the core.

Billy Graham put it well when he said that the smallest package he ever saw was a man wrapped up wholly in himself. Undisciplined desires can make small packages out of big people. Jesus said, "Seek first His kingdom and His righteousness; and all these things [the necessities that sustain and satisfy] shall be added to you" (Matthew 6:33).

Bringing Contentment on Board

Remember that I said we need to be doing two things in order to maintain disciplined desires? The first thing is to make sure that we are pursuing legitimate goals. The second thing is to *make sure that we are making the most of where we are*. You know what I mean. You've seen people who are so busy stretching for the brass ring that they forget to enjoy the merry-go-ride.

We need to make Contentment a member of our internal board of directors. Give him the freedom to ask the hard questions when you start feeling you need something more to bring you happiness. If you do, be prepared to mumble a lot to yourself. He likes to ask questions like:

- Can you afford this?
- Do you have to give up much of the few spare hours that you have left to take advantage of this thing?
- Will this free you up to spend the time necessary to maintain your commitments to family and friends?
- Will this in any way frustrate your relationship with God?

Do you see why people don't want Contentment in the boardroom of their hearts? He demands that we place proper value on the things that bring us joy.

An unsatisfied heart in a life with much blessing is sin. As long as we allow this constant craving to dominate our hearts, we will be denied inner rest. As Calvin Miller wrote: "The world is poor because her fortune is buried in the sky and all her treasure maps are of the earth."

The only way we can keep our expectations and desires disciplined is with God's help. A relationship with God that is personal yields a set of desires that are practical. Knowing that He loves us and has forgiven us keeps us from wanting the wrong things. By following His example when He walked the earth, we develop priorities that sustain our heart both now and through the future.

Excerpted from *Little House on the Freeway*, © 1987 by Tim Kimmel. Published by Multnomah Press. Used by permission.

9

NEW COURSE FOR A NEW DECADE

Bob Welch

T hey were among the written prayer requests received at a suburban church recently, cries for help from a congregation that's probably not a whole lot different than yours.

"My husband says he knows it's wrong, but he's leaving me," one woman had written. "He says he doesn't feel the love he once did for me."

"Please pray for our teenage son, who is having problems with drugs," said another.

"We have a beautiful home and plenty of money, but our family is falling apart. Help!"

The last few decades have not been easy years for North American families. If the '60s opened the door to drugs and rebellion, the '70s marked the "Me Decade," a time of self-absorption. The yuppie years of the '80s continued the trend of materialism and self-indulgence.

In these choppy wakes, America is left with the highest divorce rate in the world, a record number of non-married couples living together, and an attitude among many that children aren't treasures, but trouble.

A New Era Is Needed

"If I had a family, I couldn't do this," a 43-year-old man told me from his bicycle one Sunday morning. He and his wife divorced, he said, because of his passion for physical fitness. "I like to get up and have my freedom to go."

Sure, successful families exist. But the prayer requests I heard in my church suggest there's pain amid the progress, and it's not just secular families who are hurting.

The '90s may well be the last best hope for the American family; never before have the pressures to fracture it been greater. Never before have so many new parents grown up in homes split by divorce, meaning they must navigate without the role-model benefit of having seen a mother and father work in unison. This, then, must be a decade of rededication for Christian families. A decade of taking off worldly ways and putting on godly ways. A decade of back-to-basics recommitment.

For the Christian family, the '90s must not become an extension of the Me Decade, but must herald the arrival of a new era: The We Decade. Families. Together. Not statistical families who share the same roof, but husbands and wives who love each other more than bicycle trips. And children who can turn to a parent, not some toll-free 1-800 hotline when they need to talk.

In order for renewal to occur, families must leave behind many influences of the '80s. Specifically, families need to trade:

Looking inward for looking upward. In the '80s, the New Age movement arrived as an age-old concept dressed in designer clothes. The answer was within, but in fact, the answer is above, within *Him.* "The Lord is my rock and my fortress and my deliverer," wrote the Psalmist. Families need to be built on that foundation. If not, they will continue to crumble.

Secular information for Biblical information. The '80s ushered in the Information Age, heralded as a sort of byte-size savior. The computer gave us access to millions of statistics. Sophisticated polls and surveys measured society's every social hiccup. Self-help books by the hundreds explained that all we needed was self-esteem.

Yet by the end of the decade, all the scrutinizing and philosophizing seemed to have done little good. "Marriage is on the rocks, driven there by divorce, cohabitation and the why-bother attitude of the baby-boom generation," reported *The Economist* magazine.

In the last 20 years, the marriage rate has fallen 30 percent while the divorce rate has risen 50 percent. Two of every five American women giving birth to their first child were not married when they became pregnant, says the U.S. Census Bureau. Divorce and out-of-wedlock births have fueled an enormous increase in single-parent families; nearly one in four U.S. children live with a single parent.

What we need is not more information but the *right* information, which is found in the Scriptures. Proverbs 24:3 says, "By wisdom a house is built, and by understanding it is established."

Quality time for quantity time. Though it has become something of a cliché, this is perhaps the quintessential rationalization of the '80s: Kids didn't need much of our time, just *quality* time. Sure, some parents—particularly single mothers—must work. But for many, the quality-time myth helped alleviate the guilt parents felt about leaving their children in child care all day, or going to the racquetball club three nights a week.

Let's face reality: Our children can't mold their needs around the 7–9 p.m. Thursday time slot we've penciled in for them. Yes, they need quality time—a great quantity of it.

Trends for tradition. Tradition became the bad guy of the '80s. To be traditional was to be out of step. "Leave It to Beaver," though admittedly no documentary on family life in the '50s, became a sort of cult joke. But you wonder if the father of the 15-year-old cocaine dealer I interviewed would trade places with Ward Cleaver. You wonder if the divorced mother who puts her young son on a plane every other Friday so he can fly home to his father would trade places with June.

As the '80s ended, families took on an air of trendiness. Hollywood stars were having babies—many out of wedlock. Films such as "Three Men and a Baby" and "Parenthood" were hot. And a New York firm came out with the 13-minute "Video Baby" so, as one of its creators said, viewers could enjoy "the full experience of parenthood without the mess and inconvenience."

There's a problem with every fad, however. They don't last—but children do. In the '90s, parents must commit to the seriousness of raising a child. Children aren't some sort of Cabbage Patch doll; they're gifts from God. We need to love them as such.

Corporate ladders for family bridges. With an assist from Madison Avenue, success in the '80s was determined by one's position on the company's organization chart. Many working parents were married to their work—and why not? They spent far more time at the office than at home.

It's interesting—and sad—how we'll treat a client with gushing respect, then come home and greet our family with practiced indifference. In the '90s, isn't it time we got our priorities straight? Isn't it time we put as much time into relationships as we do into reports?

Work *is* important; we should do our best. But isn't it time we gave the family some overtime for a change?

Style for substance. The '80s were a decade of seduction. Image became more important than substance. Advertisers sold products that way, politicians ran for office that way, dress-for-success types validated their worth that way, some going so far as to equip their cars with fake car phones to show they had "made it."

In the '90s, we need to see through the veneer of such insidious lies. There's no need to sell ourselves to the world like dish soap; God has already validated our worth. We need to be real people with real needs. Otherwise, we'll be so busy trying to keep up with the Joneses that we won't have time to nurture our own family.

Materialism for relationships. The '80s brought us computerized refrigerators, big-screen TVs and compact disks. The decade also ushered in a rapid increase in one-parent families, child therapy sessions and parents who had decided children just weren't worth it.

"There's just no place for kids," a 27-year-old woman told me recently. "I have a lot of interests and I don't want to give them up. I went to school and I don't want that to go to waste."

Another mother raising three young children was asked by a friend, "I know you have three kids at home, but what are you doing that's worthwhile with your life?"

Because of the baby-boom generation, there are more potential mothers and fathers than ever before. Yet the percentage of couples without children has doubled in the last two decades. Couples who complain that kids are too expensive are probably the same couples who just bought a BMW and portable CD player.

Meanwhile, many of those who are having children—and could live on one income—are perfectly willing to risk their child to a child-care center in order to protect their career. Is it mere coincidence that the increased need for child care has paralleled society's increased consumerism?

In the '90s, we must realize that people, not products, bring us our lasting satisfaction. The American Dream is a mirage. In the final analysis, what's more important—that our house has 2,700 square feet and a big back yard or that the people inside are close to each other? That our kitchen is straight from *Architectural Digest* or that we make time, in our fast-paced world, to eat together? That we have a state-of-the-art intercom system or that we actually communicate love to one another?

A *Reader's Digest* article, "Hard Truths About Day Care," concludes: "What the very young want, and urgently need, child-development experts agree, is not education or socialization, but the affection and unhurried attention of their parents. The deepest problem with paid child-rearing is that someone is being asked to do for money what very few of us are able to do for any reason other than love."

Rootlessness for roots. Ping-pong kids, the children of divorce. Extended families, stretching three time zones. Families on the go, the house becoming more of a transit station than a home. All were signs of the anxious '80s, a decade seemingly stuck on fast-forward. We all seemed to be going somewhere. The question was: Where?

Last year, *The Wall Street Journal* wrote about the strain of divorce, mentioning a seven-year-old Philadelphia girl who shuttles back and forth between her separated parents four times a week. "I wish I could just split myself in half," she said.

It's a sad commentary on our society—and only one example of how the American family has become rootless. In a survey by the *American Sociological Review*, working women said they talk with their husbands an average of 12 minutes each day. How can family members connect with each other if they don't stop long enough to concentrate on each other?

In our clambering up the corporate ladder, has the noise obscured the cries of children in need? I asked a street kid why he got involved in drugs. He did it because he wanted someone to set a boundary, someone to show he had value. Nobody did. "Things like that are cries for help," he told me.

In becoming hurried adults, we've created hurried children, robbing them of time to use their imaginations and simply be kids. Wrote *The Wall Street Journal:* "If Mark Twain penned *The Adventures of Tom Sawyer* today, his barefoot hero would be shuttling between tennis camp and piano lessons instead of dreaming up pranks with his pal Huck Finn."

Rationalization for responsibility. The '80s were a decade when, to avoid any semblance of guilt, a lot of people changed the rules—not their ways. Euphemisms were in; facing facts was not. Living together became simply enjoying a "meaningful relationship." Abortion became "freedom of choice." Adultery became, according to one sociologist who—heaven forbid—didn't want to relate it to evil, a "nonmonogamous relationship." And "safe sex" suddenly became as innocent as an afternoon at the state fair.

Everywhere you looked in the '80s someone was doing plastic surgery on sin. In a *Newsweek* article that pointed out that baby boomers were four times more likely than their parents to live together outside of marriage and four times as likely to get divorced, sociologist William McKinney rushed to the rescue. "That is not to say that the baby boomers are amoral," he intoned. "They just believe that the individual is the final arbiter of what is right and wrong."

Yeah, right.

In the '90s, we need to forego such blatant cop-outs and consider the consequences. Instead of rationalizing that divorce has no more effect on kids than a reshuffling of the family's living room furniture, we need to wake up to the effects of severed marriages. "Almost half of children of divorces enter adulthood as worried, underachieving, self-deprecating and sometimes angry young men and women," said psychologist Judith Wallerstain. Her book, *Second Chances*, details a 15-year study of divorced middle-class families.

Meanwhile, living together has long been touted as a great testing ground for couples. So much for the brave new world; a recent survey of Swedish women showed couples who lived together before marrying had nearly an 80 percent higher divorce rate than those who did not.

And in terms of allowing our children freedom to basically raise themselves, perhaps we should listen to what a *Time* magazine reporter wrote after spending four months with children for a story: "[Children] are looking for someone—parents, teachers, ministers—to set limits and impose discipline," she wrote. "Without walls to bounce against, children seem lost."

Convenience for commitment. In the '80s, convenience became a way of life. We could pop a frozen entree in the microwave, withdraw money from a cash machine, program a computer to carry out our commands—all in seconds. In a sense, such conveniences brought us closer to the yuppieized thirst for instant gratification.

But did they bring us closer together as families? No, because relationships can't be popped into a microwave oven and zapped to life. Good families are the products of years of nurturing, seasons of sacrifice, months of sometimes mundane attention.

At the roots of such nurturing is a commitment, particularly needed from fathers. Lack of spiritual leadership continues to plague many homes. Women still buy three-fourths of all books on the family. They make up the bulk of radio-program listeners on the subject of parenthood. Men too often allow the family to be run on automatic pilot, feigning concern for what's really lack of commitment.

It's interesting how some people in the '80s committed themselves religiously to daily workouts, long hours at the office and weekend bicycle trips. It's sad how few committed themselves to their children with similar zeal or to the spouse with whom they once stood and vowed—for better or worse—a lifetime of commitment.

It's sadder still that Christians, though we like to believe otherwise, are among the uncommitted, many having conformed to the culture and not to Christ. "'The world' is in the church," a woman recently told me. She should know; her Christian husband, after 19 years of marriage, had suddenly left her for another woman.

Don't look now, folks, but our children are watching. "We wonder why we live in so many one-parent homes, why so many parents are abandoning us, why the increase in physical and sexual abuse of children," a Seattle high school girl said at a recent commencement address. "Why the need for drug and alcohol treatment centers? Why has the number of family and adolescent therapists skyrocketed? What has happened to long walks and longer talks, going to church on Sunday and eating dinner at Grandma and Grandpa's house?"

As the '90s unfold, let's hope we find some answers. And, in doing so, not be afraid to look in the mirror and question ourselves.

Children, it's been said, are the one thing we can leave behind us to tell the world what we were like.

What will our children tell about us?

10

SUCCESSFUL FAMILY DEVOTIONS

Denise J. Williamson

A year ago, we asked friends in our church who were raised in Christian homes what was the most important factor in their decision to follow Christ. We were surprised—and troubled, too—that "family devotions" was the most common answer.

The response disturbed us because at that time we were not successfully having daily devotions with our children. As the pastoral family, how could we recommend devotions to our congregation when we were not in the practice ourselves? So, we started a new family routine when Joel was just two years old and Joshua was a baby.

I remember the first couple of nights clearly. Josh cried through my husband Gary's reading of a Scripture. Joel refused to sing with us. After a week of these "quiet times," we considered listening to our friends who advised us to wait until our children were older. Instead, we chose to schedule individual devotional times for our boys, based on our training as educators.

For our baby, Joshua, we found guidelines from secular manuals and tailored them to our objective: sharing the love of Jesus with our son. We found it natural to cuddle, to coo and to have eye contact with our precious baby. Researchers believe that these types of parent-child interactions enhance early development.

I read Scripture, sang hymns and prayed out loud with Joshua in my arms. Verbalizing my faith to him added a new dimension to my private worship time. As Joshua grew, our whole family enjoyed singing praise songs and watching our baby clap and bounce in his own expression of celebration. When he became interested in bright pictures, we began reading sturdy books that focused on Christ-centered themes. Now that Joshua is over a year old, his daily devotions consist of a picture story and a lively song, followed by a short, one-sentence prayer while we hold hands and close our eyes.

An illustrated Bible story, a song and a prayer sometimes make up the content of our older son Joel's devotions, too; but we've learned not to limit his devotion time to sedentary activities. Children between the ages of two and four learn by smelling, tasting, touching and feeling—and using all of the senses makes devotions fun.

Other Sources of Ideas

Sunday school take-home papers are a good source of ideas for activities that complement a preschooler's church-school instruction. We have searched for hidden pennies after talking about the "lost coin" Bible story, played with clay while discussing creation and built a campfire as the setting for recounting how Elijah confronted the prophets of Baal on Mount Carmel. At such events, God becomes the center of some of our most meaningful family times.

Having regular devotions with each child or developing exciting family devotions is time consuming, but it is an important way of communicating to our children that daily time with God is important. Regular worship can help a child know Christ as The Eternal King who deserves reverent praise.

Too often in establishing devotions, parents concentrate only on teaching right behavior or expanding Biblical knowledge. Especially for small children, it is important that devotions be associated with positive, happy feelings. Harsh statements like, "Sit still for just five minutes of prayer!" can make devotions a dreaded time for both child and parent. We do not use our devotional periods for preaching, correction or grueling types of instruction. We sometimes praise our boys for the right behavior they show during worship, but our emphasis is on making each time together an encounter with the living God.

The most attractive family devotions, however, will fall short of encouraging children to worship regularly if the parents neglect their own worship routine. It is healthy for children to see Daddy and Mommy studying God's Word and praying. When my husband and I are having regular quiet times, we see our little ones imitating our behavior. Joel plays "Devotions" with his stuffed animals; Joshua "reads" a devotional book to himself.

Spontaneity is also an important factor in instructing preschoolers. Experts say that children constantly mix secular and sacred thoughts. And, as the parent of a talkative tot, I believe it! Questions like "Did God make mosquitoes?" and "Does Jesus have a bathroom in heaven?" let me know that my son is sometimes thinking about Jesus when I'm not. Children often reveal some astounding ideas that can set the stage for on-the-spot devotions. When I worked at an environmental education center, I was taught to capitalize on the "teachable moment" (expanding on something that catches a child's interest) and on "discovery learning" (hands-on experience). These educational techniques will work well for parents who are attentive to their preschoolers' immediate interests.

Integrating worship into our children's daily lives is an exciting endeavor. I'm drawn to the words of Deuteronomy 6:6-7:

"And these words which I command you today shall be in your heart. You shall teach them diligently to your children, and shall talk of them when you sit in your house, when you walk by the way, when you lie down, and when you rise up."

❦ INSIGHT ❦

Overcoming the Obstacles

On the "Focus on the Family" broadcast entitled, "Effective Family Devotions," Bruce Wilkinson, the founder of Walk Thru the Bible Ministries, dispels some common excuses for not having family devotions:

- **There is never a convenient time.**
  Do it whether it is convenient or not. We find time for football, TV or homework. The Bible instructs us to teach our children diligently, and this implies daily.
- **My spouse doesn't want them.**
  Attack this problem creatively. Choose material that you find stimulating and promote the idea of having devotions, perhaps once a week for starters. But, don't nag your spouse.
- **The children "sabotage" our efforts.**
  Few children say, "I can't wait to make my bed." You have to be committed to establish the discipline. It's incorrect to think that children will have the same values you have.
- **The children's ages are too varied.**
  Plan some devotions for the children at different times, and have some together. In my own home, there were six kids. We learned to give a little when devotions were for the younger children.
- **We've tried before and failed.**
  If I gave up on tennis after trying several times, I would never have learned to play. Like anything, it takes commitment.
- **I don't know the Bible well enough to do devotions.**
  There are many excellent resources to assist you, including, *"Family Walk,"* a monthly publication of Walk Thru the Bible Ministries.

❦ INSIGHT ❦

A Few Things to Remember:

- Devotions should be a regularly scheduled activity.
- Devotions should take place with the majority of the family being present.
- Devotions should be interesting and meaningful.
- Devotions should be centered around the Bible or a relevant life situation.
- Devotions should build godly character and habits.

11

AVOIDING A MONEY MELTDOWN

Ron Blue

My daughter Cynthia called from college to say American Express had sent her an unsolicited application in the mail. The accompanying promotional material said that as a college student she already had a good credit rating. Her question to me was, "Dad, don't I need to have a credit card to get a good credit rating?"

Due to my vocation, she has grown up in a home where money and money management are frequent topics of conversation. Yet even she didn't have a clear understanding of debt and credit.

It's true that most of the common uses of debt don't make much economic or Biblical sense. However, something as simple as cashing a check usually requires two forms of identification, one of which needs to be a credit card. We live in a society that forces us to use credit or to have good credit to transact the daily business of living.

The number of Americans who have absolutely zero debt throughout their lives is extremely small. Almost everyone has, or will have at some point, a home mortgage. In addition, every day you're confronted with the opportunity to borrow money for some purchase. It's essential, therefore, that you understand the different types of debt, the assumptions underlying them, and your own convictions to be able to respond wisely.

I also feel strongly that parents and grandparents should take the responsibility to train their children and grandchildren in the proper use of credit and debt. Children won't receive this training from anyone outside the home. It's not taught in schools or churches, and certainly not by peer groups. The home is the place where kids must get sound, consistent teaching.

Having credit cards does not *cause* one to go into debt. Not only do most of us have some debt and live in a society that compels us to have at least a working knowledge of credit and debt, but all of us, in the daily affairs of life, establish a credit record. Most of us seem to fear our credit rating, but it's really nothing to worry about when credit and debt are managed properly.

Credit Versus Debt

One of the primary points we need to understand is the difference between credit and debt. *Credit is having the right to borrow.* Credit deals with the potential borrower's integrity—his faithfulness and timeliness in paying his bills. Based on that integrity, a potential lender extends credit. That credit may require either the personal guarantee of the potential borrower, as with a "signature loan," or collateral—some type of security interest in something of value. This can be either the item purchased or another asset of the potential borrower.

Thus, credit is not the same thing as debt, but it is used to go into debt. Debt results when the credit extended is utilized for the purchase of some product or service. The Christian who believes having credit cards is wrong should understand that having credit cards does not *cause* one to go into debt. It only means credit has been made available to him. An individual's misuse of those credit cards causes him to go into debt.

It used to be that "being able to afford it" meant you could pay cash for whatever you were purchasing. If you didn't have the cash on hand, by definition you *couldn't* afford it. What a difference time makes! Today "being able to afford it" has nothing to do with whether you have the resources to pay for it. It means strictly "being able to afford the monthly payments."

As such, every borrowing decision can be manipulated simply by extending the length of time of repayment in order to make it "affordable." Prior to World War II, home mortgages rarely went beyond 10 years. Today, 30 years is the standard, and in some cases, it's possible to get a 50-year mortgage. Fifty years may be longer than the home will last. But by extending the terms over half a century, the payments come down to the "affordable level."

This change in the way we view debt is one of its major deceptions. Debt-related deceptions are highly effective because they make borrowing appear to be the wise and logical thing to do. For example, if you believe that "being able to afford it" means being able to afford the payments rather than being able to pay cash, you're certainly not equipped to resist the advertising that offers "easy payments." Nor will you consistently resist the advertising slogan proclaiming "no interest for 90 days."

Credit Card Woes

A women's magazine tells the following tale: "Marcia never gave much thought to how much she was spending with credit cards. 'My friends and I would go to the mall with our babies and spend the day just walking around,' says the easy-going 33-year-old, who lives in a pleasant two-bedroom townhouse in a Chicago suburb.

"'I was always buying things ahead of time: a cute outfit my son could wear next summer; a toy on sale that I could put away for Christmas. There was never anything major; just clothes, meals, gas, birthday gifts—I put them on my charge. Truthfully, when I was charging I didn't feel like I was spending real cash.'

"Marcia takes off her designer glasses ('Charged, of course,' she says, grinning) and continues. 'My husband and I used to pay off our credit card bills completely each year with our income tax refund, so we had a great credit rating, and every year the banks would offer us a higher limit.'

"'Then, of course, there was the Sears card, Montgomery Ward, Lord & Taylor, Marshall Field, Lerner, Wiebolt, Amoco, Shell, Union 76. Oh, yeah, we also had a line of credit on our checking account for $2,000. It was great to know we could go out and get anything we needed anytime,' adds Marcia.

"Marcia and her husband, Ted, are hardly unusual. Today about seven out of ten Americans use credit cards, totaling some 700 million accounts, according to the Federal Trade Commission.

"There's no doubt these ubiquitous pieces of plastic are a tremendous convenience. They enable people to travel without a great deal of cash, they minimize the trauma of robberies (reporting the crime immediately means you won't be held responsible for the thief's bills), they make record-keeping easier, and they allow people to live more comfortably.

"Financial counselors generally say one out of six people who buy on credit is burdened by excessive debt. And all the advantages of credit are easily outweighed by the headaches and heartaches that accompany a mounting stack of unpaid and unpayable bills" (*Ladies' Home Journal*, April 1986).

Marcia and Ted's situation is a classic illustration of how easy it is to fall into the credit card trap. With more than 700 million credit card accounts for a total population of approximately 240 million, there are nearly three credit cards for every man, woman and child in the United States. If you assume half the people don't have credit cards (because they're children), there are more than six credit cards per adult in America today.

Credit card companies aren't foolish, and they don't extend credit in order to lose money. What they've found is that merely putting a credit card in a potential user's hand will lead the person to spend 34 *percent more* than if the individual didn't use that credit card. And because their losses will typically run no more than 5 percent of the outstanding balances, lenders can afford the risk of putting credit into the hands of those who are not creditworthy. Charging an average of 18.86 percent interest, they much more than make up their losses from the millions of cardholders who pay their bills faithfully.

To determine whether you have a problem with debt, answer the following true-false questions (taken from Sian Ballen, *Money*, April 1987).

1. You spend the money in the expectation that your income will increase in the future.

      ☐ True   ☐ False

2. You take cash advances on one credit card to pay off bills on another.

$\square$ True $\qquad$ $\square$ False

3. You spend more than 20 percent of your income on credit-card bills.

$\square$ True $\qquad$ $\square$ False

4. You often fail to keep an accurate record of your purchases.

$\square$ True $\qquad$ $\square$ False

5. You have applied for more than five credit cards in the past 12 months.

$\square$ True $\qquad$ $\square$ False

6. You regularly pay for groceries with a credit card.

$\square$ True $\qquad$ $\square$ False

7. You often hide your credit-card purchases from your family.

$\square$ True $\qquad$ $\square$ False

8. Owning several credit cards makes you feel richer.

$\square$ True $\qquad$ $\square$ False

9. You pay off your monthly credit bills but let others slide, such as doctors' bills and utility bills.

$\square$ True $\qquad$ $\square$ False

10. You like to collect cash from friends in restaurants and then charge the tab on your credit card.

$\square$ True $\qquad$ $\square$ False

11. You almost always make only the minimum payments rather than paying your entire credit card bill.

$\square$ True $\qquad$ $\square$ False

12. You have trouble imagining your life without credit.

$\square$ True $\qquad$ $\square$ False

Now score your responses. How many times did you answer true?

- 1–4 True. You can probably keep going. You don't splurge uncontrollably.
- 5–8 True. Slow down, you have entered the caution zone. It's time to draw up a budget, pay off your bills, and reevaluate your spending habits.
- 9–12 True. You have to stop. You might be wise to consult a credit counselor or financial planner for help in changing your spending habits.

Misconceptions

People typically get into trouble with credit card debt because they fall victim to one or more popular misconceptions about credit. Their fall is hastened by the way these misconceptions appeal to our natural desires or fears, and by the fact that lenders aggressively promote this form of borrowing because they find it so profitable.

I'm going to cover four of the most common misunderstandings here. Three of them are ones with which people delude themselves, and one shows how subtly we can be misled by this form of credit.

1. You can't live without it. This easily accepted notion accounts for a lot of credit card purchases. To a large extent, it also accounts for why people who already have "enough" credit cards will apply for another when they see advertisements using that pitch.

Credit cards are used exclusively, however, to buy temporal and depreciating items—nothing of any permanence. They're often used to pay for entertainment, which is certainly important to living a well-rounded life. But it's not the reason for our existence. People also use them, as one wag put it, "to buy things they don't need with money they don't have to impress people they don't know."

One way to avoid unnecessary use of credit cards is to never make an impulse purchase. Always wait at least a day to buy something you want. If after 24 hours and careful reflection you still want the item enough to make a second trip back for it, you're more likely to be making a good decision.

2. Having a credit card means you're creditworthy. While credit card companies are concerned about creditworthiness, they're much more concerned about their profits. They're willing to take some significant losses while earning almost 20 percent in interest, plus the annual fees they charge.

Don't assume that just because you have a credit card, you can afford to take on debt. The test you took earlier should have highlighted for you whether you have a problem with credit cards. It's really scary, when you think about it, how easy it is to get approved on a credit card application. In some cases, it requires little more than your name, address and telephone number.

3. *You have to have a credit rating.* A third misconception is that you *have* to have a credit rating or you need a credit rating. *There is no such thing as a credit rating.* Various organizations compile credit reports on people who have used credit, but there's no single source to which anyone could go to get your credit rating. There's no scale that evaluates you in relationship to everyone else.

Credit reporting agencies collect data regarding your credit history, payments, delinquencies, amounts borrowed, and so forth, but no central place gives you a credit rating.

The reality is that if you choose to avoid the use of credit cards, then even if there were a credit rating, you wouldn't need it. A credit rating presumes there's risk associated with lending you money. But if you never borrow money this way, there's no risk, and therefore no need for a credit rating.

Establishing a good credit history is simple. Pay all your bills on time, and establish some banking relationships: that is, maintain checking and savings accounts. You don't need to borrow in order to have a good credit report.

4. *All interest is equal.* Another misconception is that there's no difference between an interest rate and an interest charge, when in fact there's a big difference. For example, suppose you borrow $1,000 at 12 percent interest for one year, with the full amount due at the end of 12 months. At that point you would owe $1,120. The interest rate and the interest charge would be one and the same, 12 percent.

However, suppose you borrow the same $1,000 at 12 percent, but instead of paying it back with one payment at the end of the year, you pay it back at the rate of $93.33 ($1,120 divided by twelve months) per month. The stated interest charge is 12 percent, but the *actual* interest rate paid is now approximately 21 percent, even though the total of interest dollars paid remains the same in both cases ($120).

The reason is that as you pay the $93.33 each month, you reduce the amount of principal you still owe by about $83. Yet you're still paying 12 percent interest on the full $1,000 throughout the year, even though the principal shrinks steadily from month to month.

If you borrowed the $1,000 to buy a television set and a VCR, the salesperson would most likely tell you that was the "easy" way to pay for it. At only $93.33 per month, you could well "afford" it. But the fact is that while you could afford to take $93.33 plus interest out of your income each month, it was an extremely costly decision. Twenty-one percent interest, not many years ago, was considered usurious. Now it's considered normal for that type of purchase. This illustration graphically points out the deception of easy payments.

Years ago, the government required all lenders to disclose to the borrower what is known as the APR, a uniformly calculated annual percentage rate of interest. The proper way to evaluate what it costs to rent money is to know the APR—the real interest rate the lender has charged and you have paid.

There are many superficial differences between credit cards. They charge different fees and interest rates and have various ways of calculating the interest rate. They have different repayment terms, and many offer attractive "come-ons." For instance, I recently received a signed $500 check in the mail from a credit card company. I could cash the check, and the amount would be added to my credit card balance. I could then "repay the $500 conveniently over many months."

Other come-ons are free hotel rooms, frequent flier points, merchandise and so forth offered to induce you to either accept or use the credit card. Just remember, however, that credit grantors are not benevolent. The enticement will cost you something.

Recommendations

Most of us have to use credit cards at least occasionally to function within our credit card society. However, we don't have to use them to go into debt. There are three ways to get the benefits of using credit cards without going into debt:

1. Begin with a spending plan.
2. Use a debit card rather than a charge card.
3. Always pay the full balance at the end of the month.

My first recommendation is to begin with a spending plan. Unless you're operating according to that hated word, a budget, you'll never have any real reason to control your spending. To use credit cards to fund your living expenses is to invite temptation into spending decisions. As stated earlier, researchers have shown that you'll spend 34 percent more using a credit card than if you don't.

The way to use credit cards legitimately is for convenience only, staying within your spending plan and paying the balance in full when the bill comes. If you haven't already done so, set up an annual spending plan.

My second recommendation is to use a debit card rather than a normal credit card. An amount charged to a debit card is immediately deducted from your bank or brokerage account balance. It's really no different from writing a check.

My wife and I have a card that lets us earn interest on the total account balance until either a charge comes in or a check written against the account clears the bank. When we use the debit card, we enter the item in our checkbook just as if we had written a check. Then we deduct it from our available balance. In place of the check number in the check register, we put "VISA." Using such a card allows you all the convenience advantages of a credit card, but you never have a credit card bill to pay because, in effect, it's paid the moment you use it.

My third recommendation is that for regular charge cards, never allow a month to go by without paying off the full balance. If you're tempted not to pay the full amount because it will make a big dent in your available cash, you're not using the credit card properly. A credit card can be a great convenience, but it should never be used to go into debt. The cost of credit card debt—12 to 21 percent interest— is always greater than the economic return of whatever the card was used to buy.

My final recommendation is if you can't follow the above suggestions, or if the earlier test shows you have a problem with credit cards, destroy them. Make yourself a colorful decoration that can be hung on your refrigerator as a visual reminder of your problem, and you'll never be tempted to use those cards again.

By the time the credit card companies send you unsolicited replacements, your spending patterns should be reset and the addiction to the use of credit cards broken.

Excerpted from *The Debt Squeeze,* © 1989 by Ronald Blue. Published by Focus on the Family.

12

HOLDING DOWN THE FORT WHILE MOM'S GONE

Bob Welch

I n the beginning were the words. They came from my seven-year-old son, Ryan, shattering my Saturday morning slumber with all the subtlety of a low-flying F–15. For parents of small children, they are the eight most feared words in the English language:

"Don't worry, Dad. I fixed my own breakfast."

Still in my pajamas, I dragged myself to the scene of the crime.

Indeed, my son had fixed his own breakfast—a bowl of Alphabits cereal (which explained why the kitchen floor was strewn with enough letters to spell the entire lineage of David). I sighed. This was going to be an interesting two weeks.

The previous night, my wife, Sally, had left on a short-term missionary trip. Her goal was to bring medicine, encouragement and the Gospel to the needy people of Haiti. Mine was less lofty: to have a measurable pulse when she returned. But now that it's over, I not only have a healthy pulse, but a special message for my comrades:

We have it easy.

I'm not trying to rain on anybody's parade, but given that humility precedes honor (Proverbs 15:33), let's humble ourselves, dads, by admitting that we're spoiled rotten. We take the kid to a ball game; our wives clean Junior's tennis shoes after he's constructed a mud-fortified scale model of Mount St. Helens in the back yard. We get the glory; our wives get the grit.

It starts early, with the birth of the child. The woman has just spent nine months throwing up, gaining weight, craving peanut-butter enchiladas and trying to get out of the car without accidentally honking the horn. Meanwhile, the man's challenge has been in trying to sneak a pillow into the natural childbirth classes.

But when the child is born, guess who's on the phone soaking up the congratulations ("piece o' cake," he tells his friends) while Mom recovers in a sitz bath?

A "Mr. Mom" Experience

The gap widens as Junior grows. We fathers sit in our offices, sneaking a peak at toothy baby pictures. Meanwhile, Mom is home, cutting Silly Putty out of the little tyke's hair while simultaneously lifting the refrigerator to retrieve an overdue library book. And if she's working outside the home, guess who winds up with those duties that evening—after dragging a young Duck-Duck-Goose player home from the child care center?

If you dads want to unspoil yourselves, try being moms for awhile. It's guaranteed to shrink your ego and enlarge your appreciation for the magic worked by your wife—and those single parents out there.

This insight comes after my minor-league "Mr. Mom" experience. While Sally was gone, I lived on Easy Street for much of the time. Friends from our church delivered hot meals most nights. Others watched the two boys—Ryan and four-year-old Jason—until I arrived home from work. But even with such support, I came away feeling as if I'd just been through the W-4 form of parental experiences.

As a single parent, the first thing I learned was that if you don't do something, it ain't gonna get done. And if by some small miracle it does get done, it ain't gonna get done right. Before Sally left, I just assumed that whenever you ran out of soap, the Soap Fairy magically replenished the dish. I also imagined that the Soap Fairy had relatives—the Milk Fairy, the Dental Floss Fairy and the Light Bulb Fairy, among others. As Mr. Mom, I learned the only things in a household that magically replenish themselves are laundry, dirty dishes and junk mail.

I now understand why God said it is not good for a man to be alone. He knew what we needed: a helpmate who knows instinctively how to remove strawberry Jell-O stains from a pet rabbit. One who also knows that you can't make whipped cream out of Half 'n' Half, and that certain anti-static thingamajigs go in the dryer along with the clothes. I learned that after noticing Jason was walking around with something clinging to the back of his sweatshirt—a pair of static-laden Batman undershorts.

I pressed three dress shirts before realizing that the iron was not plugged in. I let so much toothpaste build up in the kids' sink that I could have chipped it off and had a week's supply of breath mints. On one short trip we took, I packed two right-footed boots—and no left—for my oldest son. And somehow, I wound up with nine widowed socks!

But socks weren't the only things that got lost—so did my time with the kids—and my patience. Left unattended, I discovered houseplants don't thrive. And neither do children, who need emotional watering to flourish. But, who has the time when the house looks like Oscar Madison's bedroom?

A Transformation Hits

Too often, I'd plunk the kids in front of a Disney video so I could do more important things, like scraping last night's lasagna from the dining-room table or embarking on a search-and-destroy mission for moldy food in the fridge.

I got grumpy. I was transformed from Guy Smiley to Oscar the Grouch. Early on, I kept my cool. When Ryan locked half the neighborhood in a pup tent, I handled the episode without even raising my voice. But when he used a fork to catapult lima beans at his brother across the dinner table, I became John McEnroe after a bad call.

An uneasy truce ensued, but on Day 12 (after forgetting to give

Ryan his lunch money for the second day in a row), I sensed a smidgen of lost confidence in me. "I want Mom back," Ryan informed me. "Me, too," Jason piped up.

It was time to play my trump card. The kids wanted to paint their wooden sailboats, so I obliged. I made sure the paint was water-soluble. After what I'd been through, the last thing I needed was a set of permanently stained shirts.

How was I to know that my sons were planning to launch their freshly painted boats in the bathtub? "Dad, all the paint washed off," said Jason, sitting in a tub of tomato juice.

I drained the Red Sea and thanked God that bedtime was finally here. While putting the kids to bed, the phone rang. Happily, I thought perhaps things in Haiti had gone so smoothly that my wife's missionary team was coming home a day early.

Not quite. But for a limited time only, I could have my drapes dry-cleaned for a special low, low price.

"Uh, thanks, but—"

The buzzer sounded from the basement. My washer was lop-sided again.

"Dad, you forgot to go over my spelling words with me," Ryan yelled from his bunk.

That's when the pet rabbit knocked over the wooden Noah's Ark puzzle, scattering elephants, zebras and giraffes across the living room, two-by-two.

In retrospect, though, I suppose it's good these things happened. Sometimes we men need to walk a mile in our wives' Reeboks to appreciate everything they do, discover everything we *don't* do and realize how we can be better husbands and fathers.

So this year, when my wife and kids gather around to celebrate Father's Day, I'm going to have a new perspective. If we fathers stand proudly at the helm, it's our wives who keep the ship afloat.

Still, after my pinch-hitting experience, I remain mystified by two things: How *do* mothers do it—juggle family, home and sometimes a job? And, perhaps even more mind-boggling: Just where *are* those missing socks?

PART THREE

FOCUS ON WIVES
AND MOTHERS

13

A MOM'S QUEST FOR QUIET TIME

Margaret Nyman

A friend of mine, who had just published her first book, invited me to lunch one afternoon. As I picked through my chef's salad, she posed several questions: "What would be a good topic for my next book?" "What do mothers like you want to read?"

Mothers like me? With five children between the ages of 10 years and 10 months, I was lucky to find time to open my junk mail, let alone read a book longer than *Horton Hears a Who*. How can a mother of young children find time to have daily devotions when she's on call 24 hours a day?

Moms of preschoolers are rarely "free," and if they are, it's only for a few minutes here and there. Even those little pockets of peace come at unexpected moments. One of my constant frustrations was finding time to meet the Lord regularly, a time I could count as my very own.

No matter how much I tried, failure dogged my steps. One time, I made grand plans to get up before the morning newspaper hit the pavement for 15 minutes of quiet Bible reading and prayer. To accomplish this, I set the alarm clock for 5:15 a.m. Within days, however, exhaustion conquered me.

I tried another scheme—meeting the Lord before I went to sleep at night. This was also a dead-end idea, since I was usually dreaming before verse four.

The kids' nap time was another possibility, but in our house, it's impossible to predict when—or what—would happen. Invariably, one restless preschooler would be unable to sleep while the first napper was sound asleep. And if the kids did sleep simultaneously, the crush of household chores and my lengthy "to do" list pressed so heavily I couldn't concentrate on spiritual things. What's more, I often needed to snatch a quick nap in the early afternoon hours.

Missing Appointments

As I found myself spending less and less time with the Lord, I began playing out this dilemma in my mind. God loves children, I reasoned, meaning our five were gifts sent from His hand. Surely He knew each day was chopped up into small chunks of time, no two alike, no periods of calm to count on. Yet I also knew God desired to meet with me.

I had this constant picture of keeping Him waiting endlessly as I missed our "appointments" day after day. I hated disappointing Him. I also knew I desperately needed a steady stream of His advice to do a good job as a mother.

This problem plagued me for years! As I ate lunch with my author friend, I told her straight out: "Write a book telling moms of little children how to have a daily quiet time."

My suggestion was greeted by a long pause, a thoughtful look and a short comment: "Well now, that's a tough one!" We chatted a while on the subject, coming up with little in the way of solutions. Eventually, we moved on to other things. No book resulted from our conversation.

Five years passed, and my friend progressed to other book topics. I had a sixth baby and was still in the same stew over my devotional life. Then one day, a thought came to mind.

Maybe the Lord could meet me right in the middle of the lively events of my busy days! Didn't He meet Peter out in a boat? Didn't He communicate with two men on the road to Emmaus as they walked? Didn't He get Zacchaeus' attention in a tree? Didn't He share His wisdom in gardens, on mountain sides, during meals, at the beach, in courtrooms and even in cemeteries?

Why couldn't He do the same with me? Of course He could. Maybe He could talk with me while I folded clean laundry or peeled carrots as the children played nearby. Maybe He could minister to me while the kids and I shoveled snow or raked leaves. He could even share His heart in the middle of the night as I rocked a feverish child. Maybe *especially* then.

Finding Time

I started looking for ways to acknowledge Jesus and share some time with Him every single day. I tucked a Bible in a bathroom drawer and read verses one by one as I rolled my hair with curlers one by one. If I was interrupted (which was often the case), the Lord understood. Nor was He offended when I stopped to tie a shoe, answer a math question or bandage a hurting finger. He was still waiting when I returned to my curls and His Word.

I took a spare Bible on errands with me. If I was waiting for a child outside the dentist's office and happened to be alone in the car, I turned to Proverbs. If the children dozed off in their car seats while I waited for a long freight train to pass, I popped open Philippians.

Next I borrowed my son's radio, put it on the kitchen counter and tuned in a Christian station. God met me on the air waves, not just through sermons, interviews and five-minute devotionals, but through glorious music, too.

When I took my prayer requests into the shower, I could pray candidly and openly before the Lord as I washed my hair. I'm sure He didn't mind the running water.

As time went on, the Lord touched me in surprising ways. Often while rocking and feeding the baby, I felt a fresh and real closeness to the Creator. By studying the detail of a little person's face or hand, I somehow felt very near to God's heart; He had formed this precious one so beautifully and intricately. My heart nearly exploded with gratitude and wonder.

Even exercise times—a summer swim or a brisk walk behind a stroller—gave me the chance to sing or hum my favorite hymns and little camp choruses. The Lord was willing to meet me even while I puffed and panted. My times outdoors, enjoying nature, brought me to a new level of appreciation for His greatness. But even pumping an Exercycle in a windowless basement could offer me an excellent prayer time.

Moments of Joy and Peace

Another form of practical help was a small pad of paper, kept handy on a kitchen shelf. When I heard or felt something special, I jotted it down in 30 seconds and tucked it in my Bible to "chew on" later.

The more creative I became in spending time with the Lord, the more I saw that His creativity was much greater than mine! He began solving many of my problems and providing many nuggets of wisdom. I discovered so many moments of joy and peace during my hectic days that I wondered why it had taken me 15 years to figure out the solution to my problem.

The Lord knows our hearts. He knows if we're really trying to get close to Him, to learn the things He wants us to know. He'll meet us where we are. If He sees us wanting to spend time with Him, He'll reach out to us more than halfway. Glitches in our schedules do not limit Him in getting through to us.

These days the endless variety of my new devotional life is like the tossed salad I enjoyed with my author friend: lots to chew on, lots of color, lots of texture and lots of nutrition. And it's never boring.

14

WOMEN OF BEAUTY AND THE ESSENCE OF MYSTIQUE

Jean Lush

What do you do to lift yourself up out of the blues?" I asked a group of ladies in a support group I attended. We'd gathered that day to talk about overcoming depression.

"Oh, I go shopping," said Emily. "I try on all the lovely clothes I can't afford—minks, sequined dresses. Then I treat myself to lunch at Alexander's. The antiques and beautiful table settings and French waiters make me feel . . . elegant. I suppose it sounds silly, but I always go home feeling better."

"No," I said, "I don't think it's silly at all. You are surrounding yourself with beauty, and that makes you feel good. When I'm in a sore mood, I go out and pick or buy flowers. Then, as I arrange them and set them in their place, I admire them. I can almost feel the frustration or anger or depression flow out of me."

"I know what you mean," said Laura, one of the younger women. "I feel the same way when I go for a walk in the woods. I let my mind drift to all the beautiful things God made, and pretty soon I'm feeling at peace again."

Without even realizing it, these women recognized the human need for beauty. In my studies, I realized a fascinating truth: Women of mystique create beauty around them. They somehow recognize the tremendous human need for loveliness.

I think God knows how important beauty is to us. We have but to open our eyes to know He wanted us to be surrounded by beautiful things.

Days of Flower Arranging

During World War II, my husband and I lived in Australia. One of the block wardens, a friend of ours, told us an interesting story. He was concerned because people were resisting his instructional meetings on air raids, blackouts and first aid. He said he'd finally chosen a day when he felt nearly everyone in the neighborhood would be free.

When he announced the meeting day, do you know what the women said? "Oh, no! That's the day I buy my flowers. That's my flower-arranging day."

With Japanese submarines in the bay and danger all around them, these women wouldn't give up their flower arranging. I'm sure they didn't consciously realize it, but in the midst of trouble, those flowers were basic to their well-being.

Think about how you feel when beauty surrounds you, and when it doesn't. Imagine yourself sitting on the steps of a tenement house. You yawn with lazy despair. The ground is nearly bare, with an occasional clump of weeds cut to resemble grass. Garbage oozes over an open garbage can. You bend to pull one of the millions of weeds growing in the cracks of the walk that leads into the litter-lined street. Graffiti covers the fence; the words written in iridescent green make you turn away.

The housing development is only four years old, and already the paint is chipped and peeling on the once-white windowsills. Black soot covers the orange-red bricks. Your attention is brought back to the street as a passing truck driver hurls obscenities at a small child who crouches in the gutter to gather more stones. You wish you could wipe it all away, but it's too much . . . too hard.

Not a pretty sight. Lack of beauty—ugliness—brings grief to the spirit. Shabbiness and disorder drain us.

Now imagine the same place. A woman moves in next door. She scrubs and cleans inside and out, then sands and paints the trim a sparkling white. She waters the parched and patchy yard and scatters grass seed.

Maybe by now you feel a bit guilty and intrigued by the small but effective changes she's made. You ask if she'd mind if you worked together. She laughs and hands you a rake.

Together, you plant flowers and shrubs. You gather discarded bricks and create a garden full of forget-me-nots and candytufts. The child stops throwing rocks and comes to watch. You hand him a packet of seeds, and he smiles.

Can you feel the difference? Beauty creates energy. It lifts the spirit.

Inner Calm and Confidence

I did a survey a few years ago with 150 couples. I asked the men to list, in order, those things about their wives and home life that upset them the most. More men complained about bad housekeeping than about cooking, sex or their wives' appearance. Men also have a need for a beautiful and tidy environment.

Contrary to what you may be thinking, it doesn't take a lot of money to create beauty. I have never been a woman of affluence. For some years during the Depression, we were quite poor. Yet my children recently told me they'd never realized it. I always set the dining room table with a linen cloth and china and nearly always arranged a centerpiece of fresh flowers on the table.

Perhaps because of my British upbringing, I stressed proper table manners. Even though we had little money, I tried to give my family a lovely environment whenever possible.

As for a woman of mystique, she has an inner calm and confidence. She loves herself and her body and portrays the essence of God, in whose image she was created.

This is perhaps the aura of mystery that is missing in so many women. A true woman of mystique has within her being a spiritual realm, filled with a loving God who gives her strength to cope with any situation.

She is constantly changing and growing. She is a mystery to men and women because she involves herself deeply in the things of God.

Her days are spent in learning God's ways and carrying out His will for her life through Bible study and prayer. She is in love with life, celebrating each moment, each day, as if it were her last. She is vital, growing, alive and filled with the Spirit of God.

Our woman of mystique is by no means perfect. She is fully aware of her flaws and weaknesses, yet she is strong enough to admit them and not be embarrassed by them.

Perhaps a good illustration of a woman of mystique would be the virtuous woman in Proverbs 31. The woman acclaimed as a great wife and mother worked hard and was skilled in many areas. She managed her home and finances well. Her husband was proud of her, and her children called her blessed.

I know it sounds like I've painted a picture of a woman who is impossible for us mere mortals to live up to. I share all this information on mystique not to make you feel overwhelmed or guilty, but to help you grow. I know it looks unattainable, especially when you see all these virtuous attributes in one place. But I'd encourage you to go back to the beginning. Work on one thing at a time. Ask God to help you grow in the way He has chosen for you.

Possessing the qualities of the woman of mystique isn't going to magically transform your life. There are no assurances that even with mystique you'll have a devoted husband and happy-ever-after life. Nothing can guarantee that. But mystique can make you feel better about yourself, make you a more appealing, more interesting, more exciting person to yourself and to others around you.

Reprinted from *Emotional Phases of a Woman's Life*, © 1987 by Jean Lush and Patricia H. Rushford. Published by Fleming H. Revell Company. Used by permission.

15

CORRALLING THE CHAOS

Emilie Barnes

One Sunday after church service, my husband, Bob, and I were visiting with some friends. When one woman asked me about my "More Hours in My Day" ministry, I told her about some of the recent seminars I had conducted around the country.

All of a sudden, a man who was listening to our conversation grabbed my arm. "Emilie, our family lives in a cesspool," he complained. Thankfully, his wife was not within earshot.

"My wife doesn't work. We have three children, two of them are in school. Yet she says she doesn't have time to clean the house."

Do you think that is an isolated case? It isn't. In today's hectic society, men and women are so busy that often there is no time left to plan and execute the daily routines of life.

For many, life is lived in a constant panic, trying to stay on top of the house, family and career. With more women in the work force, there has never been a greater need for basic organizational skills in our homes.

Establishing the Target

If you don't have a goal for organizing your home and life, you can never know if you have hit or missed the target. Much time is wasted because we don't know where we're going.

Early in our marriage Bob and I felt it was important to set goals. We dreamed of the type of home and family we wanted. We realized that in order to achieve those dreams we needed a plan. That plan became the "Barnes' Family Life Goals."

We talked often of those goals, and periodically we adjusted them as our lives changed. The biggest change came as we began to mature in our Christian faith. That's when our goals became more Christ-centered.

Goal-setting doesn't just happen. You must take time to think long-range in order to effectively plan for the next few years. And your goals must be important enough to work at making them happen.

Bob and I have set 10-year goals, and then we've broken those down into smaller goals. Where do we want to be in five years if we're to fulfill our 10-year goals? What about three years? One year? Six months? Three months? One month? Today?

See the progression? How can we plan today if we don't know where we're headed? Sure, we can fill our time with activities; that's easy. But by goal-setting, everything we do is directed toward a purpose that we've set.

Priorities—What Comes First?

Jean had set her goals and organized her days according to those goals. But she never was able to complete her daily "To Do" list.

I asked Jean to show me a typical list of her day's priorities. Of the 16 activities written on her list, Jean realized she could not possibly do every one of them. She needed to divide these options into three categories:

Yes: I will do this.
Maybe: I will do this if there is time.
No: I will not attempt this today.

Notice the last option? You must learn to say "NO!" Too many women assume that their only options are "yes" and "maybe." If we can't say "no" to some things, we become overcommitted and wind up carrying heavy loads of guilt because of unfulfilled commitments.

Making Decisions Using Priorities

Just how does a Christian proceed with decisions when the answers are not obvious?

Priority #1—God: According to Matthew 6:33, our first priority is to seek and know God. This is a lifelong pursuit. When God has first place in your life, deciding among the other alternatives is easier.

When I feel hassled or hurried, it's often because this priority is out of order. Usually I need to adjust my schedule in order to spend time with God. When I allow Him to fill my heart, I can relax and have a clearer perspective on the rest of my activities.

Priority #2—Family: In Proverbs 31 we read about the woman who "watches carefully all that goes on throughout her household, and is never lazy. Her children stand and bless her; so does her husband."

How does a woman receive such praise from her family? The answer is by providing a home setting full of warmth, love and respect.

Priority #3—Church-Related Activities: Hebrews 10:25 tells us to be involved in our church, but that is not at the expense of the first two priorities.

Priority #4—All Other Areas: This includes job, exercise, classes, clubs and other activities. Some people are amazed that there is time for any of these items. But there is.

God wants you to live a balanced life, and that means you need time for work and time for recreation—time to cut some flowers, drink a cup of tea, or go shopping with a friend. These activities can revitalize you for the responsibilities of home and church.

With these priorities in mind, Jean attacked her list of activities, beginning with the junk mail. "I think I'll just toss the whole pile," she said. By eliminating three more activities and putting four in the "Maybe" category, Jean was immediately more relaxed.

I encouraged her to cross off the "Yes" activities as she completed each one to give herself the satisfaction of seeing the list shrink during the day. If time permitted, she could do the "Maybe" activities, but if she didn't, some of them might become "Yes" activities on another day.

Of course, not all decisions can be made swiftly—some require more time and consideration. I've made Paul Little's five-point outline from his booklet *Affirming the Will of God* my criteria when I have trouble establishing my priorities.

1. Pray with an attitude of obedience to the Lord. God's promise to us is, "I will instruct you and teach you in the way you should go; I will counsel you and watch over you" (Psalm 32:8).

2. What does the Bible say that might guide me in making the decision? "Be diligent to present yourself approved to God as a workman . . . handling accurately the word of truth" (2 Timothy 2:15).

3. Obtain information from competent sources in order to gain all the pertinent facts. "A wise man's heart directs him toward the right" (Ecclesiastes 10:2).

4. Obtain advice from people knowledgeable about the issue. It's best if our counselors are fellow Christians who can pray with and for us. "Iron sharpens iron, so one man sharpens another" (Proverbs 27:17).

5. Make the decision without second-guessing God. ". . . he who trusts in the Lord will prosper" (Proverbs 28:25).

The purpose of establishing priorities is to avoid becoming overextended. If you know you are always doing the most important activities first, you can relax even when you cannot complete everything on your "To Do" list.

Family Conference Time

Probably the number-one question women ask me when I give a seminar is "How do I get my husband and children involved?" That's a tough question to answer because each family is different.

One mistake many women make is that they assume every family member understands his or her role. They never discuss their expectations with their husband or children. With many mothers

r was responsible to complete his assignment. Mom and
drew their chores from the basket—this was a team effort.
children range widely in their ages, you may want to use
ets—one for smaller children and one for the rest of the
this way, the younger children do not draw jobs that are
cult for them.

also important that Mom and Dad inspect the work to make
ores are being done properly. Occasionally, give a special re-
or a job well-done.

ase note that I am not suggesting that children assume the
maintaining a house. As parents you must allow your chil-
to participate in their own activities. They need time to get in-
d in sports, music, homework, and other school and church
ities.

Balance the Priorities

u also need to recognize your priorities in relating to your
ate. When my children were still at home, I often remembered,
ou were a wife to your husband before you were a mother to your
hildren." Our children will grow up and leave home (hopefully).
However, we will still have our mate after the nest is empty.

A couple needs to spend quality time with each other without
the children. You must not use the excuse that you can't afford it.
You can't afford *not* to. Bob and I plan times together and reserve
those days on our calendar just as we would any other appointment.
We protect those times and don't cancel unless there is an emer-
gency.

For single parents who are raising children alone, the pressures
are even more intense, especially when the children are young. I
believe the family conference time and division of responsibilities
can help relieve some of the pressure. However, sometimes as a
parent—whether married, single or widowed—you may have to
leave some things unfinished rather than continue to tax your spirit.

There are no rules on how a home should be run; each family
needs to set its own standards. My family enjoys working together
as we set joint goals, but it is a process that takes time.

In his first letter, the apostle Peter wrote that wives could influence their husbands: ". . . even if any of them are disobedient to the

working, it is often necessary for o
some of the responsibilities that on
an's. The family needs to understand

Mom is not the only player in the f
able part. So I first recommend that m
team. That only leads to tired, burned-

It did not take the Barnes family long
regular time to discuss important topics.
goals was to raise independent and respon
felt one way to achieve this goal was to all
part of the decision-making process.

Yet how could we set aside more time w
ready busy with many activities? Our solution
chronic problem in our home.

Probably the most hectic time for our family
ing before church. Mom and Dad often had a fev
cause we were late. By the time we drove into the ch
we were rarely in a mood for worship.

In order to solve our two problems—stressful Su
need for family meetings—we decided to start going
fast on Sunday mornings before church. Overnight
provement.

This eliminated the problem of food preparation an
and it gave us time to discuss various aspects of our fam
established Sunday breakfasts as part of our regular
budget, and all of us looked forward to this time together.

Our family activities and conference times played a valua
in establishing harmony, respect and pride within our famil
every meeting and activity was a success, but we usually ga
greater respect for one another.

ily membe
Dad also
If you
two bask
family. I
too diffi
It is
sure ch
ward f
Ple
load i
dren
volve
activ

Yo
m
"
c
l

Family Work Planner

One idea that helped our family better distribute the housework was
to establish a "Daily Work Planner." We would write the weekly
chores on separate slips of paper, place them in a basket, and every
Saturday each of us drew one or more slips to learn our duties for
the upcoming week.

As each assignment was drawn, it was recorded on the Daily
Work Planner, which was posted in a conspicuous place. Each fam-

word, they may be won without a word by the behavior of their wives" (1 Peter 3:1).

Even though the context of this verse deals with salvation, Peter provides an excellent principle. In our society, the mother sets the tone for the family and home. Many times, Dad and Junior are not as excited about the home as Mom is. If you are aware of this truth, you will be disappointed less often because you will not have as many expectations.

We need to remind ourselves that it is not our role to change our husband and children. God will do that in His time. We must be faithful to the Scriptures and love our family even when they may not return that love.

It is important to realize that there are many areas of stress that you *can* relieve. I have attempted to give some practical helps in many of those areas. Implementing these organizational techniques can help you enjoy more hours in your day and experience more joy in your home.

16

WHY WOMEN NEED OTHER WOMEN

Ruth Senter

I was talking to a woman one day about friendship. "My husband is my best friend," she declared. "I don't need other friends." While I would not discredit or seek to invalidate her experience (in fact, I rejoiced with her in the strength of her marriage), I, for one, need women friends.

Today, my doorbell will ring, and a friend who works nearby will share her lunch break with me. We will eat sandwiches and catch up on the past two weeks since we've been together.

Last Saturday morning, a friend called from North Carolina to chat. "How are Mark and the kids?" she asked. "Any new writing projects?" And another close friend from my high school days recently dropped me a note. She was coming through Chicago on vacation with her family and wanted to get together.

Women friendships—long and meaningful relationships. Are they threats to my marriage or happy, comfortable additions?

Looking back on 23 years of marriage, I am struck by how much my friendships have enriched my relationship with my husband. Having close friends, for example, has meant that Mark—although he is my friend—doesn't need to be everything to me. I am less likely to try to squeeze from him all the emotional and spiritual reinforcement that I need when I can draw upon other confidants as well.

An Example of Encouragement

Over lunch with a friend, for example, I can work through some disappointment I am feeling with the children. By the end of the day, when Mark comes home from his hour-long commute after teaching at the seminary, I have already been encouraged by my lunch-time acquaintance. I am able to listen to Mark talk about his day, or walk around the yard with him and notice the growth of the Norway maple we just planted. There will be plenty of other days when I will need Mark to listen to me.

Having close women friends also relieves Mark of the pressure to "always understand." He will not always understand. In fact, if he *always* understood, he would be a woman. The important thing is that there is someone who can look me in the eye and say, "I know, I've been there, too."

Last summer, my hands kept going to sleep at night, and my patience with our 14-year-old seemed at an all-time low. I had moments of emotional bleakness I'd never had before. Perhaps it was the home-decorating project I had undertaken for the summer. Maybe a bit of homesickness for our 17-year-old who was thousands of miles away working at a missionary radio station for the summer. Mark suggested I call Dr. Parker and schedule my annual physical a few months early.

In the meantime, I met my North Carolina friend at a weekend retreat. The first night, as we sat over a late-night cup of coffee, I felt like I was hearing myself talk. Nelda was listing the exact symptoms I had described to Dr. Parker just five days earlier. We looked at each other and said the word together—"menopause!" We laughed. She understood. How could Mark ever have known? I suddenly loved him even more for our differences.

Women friendships have also filled the holes for me when Mark has not been home. In our days of youth ministry, Mark was frequently away with the youth group, and we did not want to drag two preschoolers through the woods to a rugged camp somewhere. It was much easier to see Mark leave for the weekend when I would be taking the children and visiting a dear friend at her farm, just a short drive away.

Although there were times during those 12 years of youth ministry that I felt lonely and possessive of my husband, I have no doubt that I was less lonely because friends provided havens of warmth and happiness in Mark's absence. I have no doubt also that Mark felt freer to leave because he knew I would enjoy spending time with my friends.

His Idea of Relaxation

Mark and I were not far into our honeymoon when I learned that his idea of relaxation was not browsing through antique shops in quaint New Hampshire villages or looking for just the right gift in the country store at Old Sturburg Village. He would rather be climbing Mt. Washington or white water rafting down the Swift River. Although there have been, and still are, times when Mark shops with me (and I go hiking with him), I am less prone to try and coax him into antique store expeditions when friends will gladly accompany me.

While I advocate women friendships, I am also the first to admit that establishing friendships has not been easy. Friends do not generally float into my life on a happy cloud of serendipity. I have had to pick up the phone and schedule a lunch, sit at my desk and write a note, or plan a day's outing to the city.

Maintaining a friendship also takes work. I have known the agony of having to admit to occasional insensitivity or negligence . . . to talking when I should have been listening . . . to comparing myself with my friend rather than giving her the praise she was due.

Another drawback is that I can only cultivate and sustain a limited number of close friendships. Careful thought and prayer are essential, lest I go rushing headlong into relationships that drain me, rather than enrich my life. A friend should never become competition for my family.

If my husband and kids make statements like "You're going out with her again this evening?" or "How many times have you talked to her on the phone today?" they may be feeling squeezed out by my friend. If so, I need to reconsider the relationship and attempt to restructure my involvement with that friend.

Friends, too, must understand my family priorities and must respect my husband and children. I know of a situation where a woman constantly cut down her friend's husband in his presence and behind his back. Fortunately, the friend was wise enough to confront the woman and when the put-downs did not stop, she terminated the friendship.

While I am not overly jealous, I am on the alert if a friend always needs to touch my husband when she talks to him, or if she carries on a conversation only with him when we're both present, or if she always calls to ask his advice. On the other hand, friendships that grow out of mutual respect have their own unique rewards.

Peggy and I have been friends since we were high school sophomores. Several months ago, she and I drove from Chicago to the Pennsylvania town of Manheim—the place where our friendship began. Her mother had died, and Peggy needed to go east to take care of business. So she invited me along for company. As we drove for 15 hours each way, we talked of where we've been, where we are today and where we'd like to be 10 years from now. We laughed and cried together.

Nearing the end of the trip, the lights of the city were low on the horizon and Peggy was asleep in the passenger seat as I drove. I had a sense of well-being, of continuity with my past and of anticipation for the future. Peggy had been part of my life for 30 years. She would be there tomorrow when I hopped into my car for the 30-minute ride to her house or when I picked up the phone to chat.

I almost laughed aloud as I thought of God's joyous grace. Peggy and I had gone our separate ways after high school. We both married ministers. Years and miles later, our husbands ended up teaching at the same seminary. To top it off, we both married men who like to go white water rafting. And best of all, they like to do it together while their wives go shopping!

❦ INSIGHT ❦

Tips for Cultivating a Friendship

- Ask about and remember little details of your friend's life. Write them on your calendar or in a notebook.
- If you did not grow up together, try to meet her parents or visit her home town.
- Look at her high school yearbooks and scrapbooks.
- Send her a cheery card for no reason at all.
- Plan events that include both of your husbands.
- Drop her a note when you are out of town, or bring her something that smells, tastes, or feels like the area you've visited.
- Take her children to a special event.
- Watch for opportunities to celebrate her successes.
- Keep a list of her favorite things and the colors she uses in her house. Think about her when you shop.
- Keep her on your prayer list. Ask frequently what you can pray for her about.

17

HOW TO MANAGE PMS

Sharon Sneed, Ph.D.
and Joe McIlhaney Jr., M.D.

I (Sharon) spent many years not knowing why I had strange feelings at various times of the month. I spent sleepless nights wondering about intermittent aches and pains. I anguished over angry words spoken to a child, knowing that I was temporarily out of control and overwhelmed with tension and irritability.

I am also a research scientist and have worked for years in a laboratory learning to be objective. From observing myself and other patients, I am convinced that premenstrual syndrome (PMS) is absolutely real.

As practicing clinicians who have helped numerous PMS patients, we firmly believe that treatment is crucial. And as Christians, we recognize treatment is also important for your spiritual life. So much anxiety and tension accompanies PMS that many Christians equate its symptoms with a weakened relationship with God. We do not believe that is true.

We certainly don't have all the answers why PMS affects almost all women to some degree. We do, however, feel that diet, exercise, certain medical treatments—and prayer—can help women deal with it more positively.

Most physicians now agree that PMS is a real problem. A good definition has been written by Dr. K. Dalton: "A wide variety of regularly recurring physical and psychological symptoms which occur at the same time in the premenstrual period of each cycle."

Symptoms of PMS

Some of the following symptoms affect almost all women at some time, while others may be rare, even among PMS patients. Since so little is known about the syndrome, and the specific cause is undiscovered, this list is probably incomplete.

Physical Symptoms

- abdominal bloating
- generalized swelling of the body
- carpal tunnel syndrome (numbness of the hands related to swelling in the wrists)
- breast tenderness
- headaches
- skin rashes
- irritation of the eyes (conjunctivitis)
- backache
- muscle spasms—pain in the arms and legs
- fatigue
- dizziness
- clumsiness
- heart palpitations
- increased problems with hypoglycemia

Emotional Symptoms

- tension
- irritability
- depression
- anxiety
- mood swings
- forgetfulness
- self-blaming

- desire to withdraw from people
- change in sexual interest (usually increases at the time of ovulation and decreases afterward)
- sleeping disorders
- inability to accomplish work at the usual pace
- indecisiveness (or the making of poor decisions)
- marital conflict
- increased appetite

In order to attribute any of these symptoms to PMS, they must occur only in the 14 days before—and at the start of—the menstrual period. You must be absolutely free of the symptoms as soon as your period is over.

If they occur at any other time, the culprit isn't PMS. Seek medical help for some other condition that may or may not be serious. Don't let PMS become a catchall diagnosis for your ailment.

Treatment Options

Many researchers and laypersons disagree about which treatments really work. Nonetheless, the treatment of PMS at specialized clinics and through private physicians is all very similar.

Beware of so-called miracle promises. The miracle may be how *quickly* your wallet empties and how *little* your health improves.

Things You Can Do Yourself

- education
- pursue a regular exercise program
- maintain correct body weight
- choose a correct diet
    —PMS diet plan (for days when you have PMS symptoms)
    —Regular diet plan (for other days of the month)
- educate family and friends about PMS
- make lifestyle changes to accommodate PMS days
- control your stress
- take vitamin and mineral supplements

treatment Requiring a Physician's Supervision

- correct diagnosis
- elimination of other medical problems

- referral to other professionals
  —for psychological help
  —for nutritional help
- prescription medications as needed
  —non-hormonal medications, such as diuretics and anti-anxiety preparations
  —hormonal therapy
- over-the-counter medications (get medical advice beforehand)

How Exercise Can Reduce PMS Symptoms

Every major publication about PMS that we researched included exercise as an important part of the program. Specifically, aerobic exercise was recommended. Some of the long-term benefits:

More energy. Tiredness is a common complaint of many women who suffer from PMS.

Greater productivity. The inability to make decisions and the presence of fatigue can dramatically lower productivity in school, the work place or home.

Decreased appetite. Increased appetite and various food cravings are very common symptoms of PMS.

Reduced stress. A moderate amount of stress in our lives is normal and healthy. However, if we are in poor physical condition, even a small amount of stress may feel excessive.

A more positive attitude. This may be attributed to endorphin secretion, which can accompany an aerobic exercise program. Some researchers feel PMS may be caused by the endorphin deficiencies that may occur premenstrually.

Improved ability to handle sugars. Exercise enables the body to handle sugar in a healthier way, with fewer peaks and valleys in the blood-sugar level. This can decrease hypoglycemic feelings.

Decreased body fat and improved weight maintenance. Normalizing body-fat levels seems to normalize levels of certain hormones, which may improve PMS.

Diet and PMS

In a 1987 paper, Abraham and Rumley evaluated the clinical, bio-chemical and endocrine effects of a total dietary program in patients with PMS. After PMS patients had kept to a healthier diet for three to six months, their symptoms improved noticeably.

Though three to six months is a long time to wait, your rewards will be long-lasting. Stay with it. Find new recipe books that make good-for-you foods also taste great. Think of this as a new life-time attitude toward food—not something you do temporarily to make yourself feel better. You should practice good nutrition habits throughout the month, not just during the last seven to ten days before your period. You probably should lose some weight, too. Being at your correct bodyweight will not only help you control PMS, but it will also improve your general health.

Premenstrual Dietary Guidelines

Avoid sugars. This includes table sugar, brown sugar, honey, molasses, jams, jellies and sugary drinks. Hidden sugars are present in ketchup, sweet pickles and relish, many breakfast cereals and sweet mustard. Avoiding sugar will help you control the hypoglycemic reactions that are common in some cases of PMS.

Avoid caffeine. Tea, coffee, many sodas, chocolate and some aspirin-type preparations contain caffeine. Most PMS specialists agree that caffeine avoidance seems to reduce such symptoms as tension, anxiety and insomnia.

Avoid salt excesses. Limit salty snacks, salty spices and salty prepared foods. Beware of such condiments as soy sauce and Worcestershire sauce. Controlling your salt intake will help you control water retention and bloating during the premenstrual days.

Eat at least 1,200 calories per day. Hypoglycemic reactions—tiredness, fatigue and lack of energy—may be worse if you severely restrict your calories.

Do not overeat. More specifically, do not consume too many high-fat, high-calorie foods during the premenstrual time. This can lead to lethargy and bloatedness.

Eat more frequently. Try eating five or six small meals during the days leading up to your period, rather than three traditional meals. Save something from each meal and eat it two hours later as a snack.

Avoid alcohol. Women are more sensitive to the effects of alcohol during their premenstrual phase.

Family and PMS

If you have a diagnosed case of PMS, you owe it to yourself to discuss it with your family. They will almost immediately realize the cyclical pattern of your irritability. They will also recognize that you do have good days—times when you are a different person. This will enable them to accept the "whole" you and even offer encouragement as you start your new PMS treatment program.

Lifestyle and PMS

What might normally be a slight problem may become a huge, anxious dilemma during PMS time. Carefully schedule your activities.
   Here are some practical ideas:

- avoid demanding social commitments that require you to make elaborate preparations.
- be more productive during other parts of your cycle so you'll have time to relax during PMS.
- schedule vacations during the first two weeks after your period.
- if possible, arrange car pools and other such commitments on a rotation that frees you from responsibility when you are premenstrual.
- if you have young children at home, arrange for occasional babysitting during your menstrual time.

Prayer and PMS

All of life's situations need prayer, including PMS. During the PMS time, you may feel God doesn't hear your prayers and is far from you. In fact, He hears you and is close by. Prayer is a tremendous tool. Pray often and in faith.

Pray regularly. Be sure to continue your prayers and fellowship with God when you are premenstrual. This may seem unnatural at first, especially before the treatment program takes effect. Many women feel out of fellowship at this time and thus avoid prayer time. Don't fall into this trap.

Pray for the right physician. Pray that God will lead you to a physician who will meet your needs.

Pray for perseverance in your treatment program. Pray that God will give you the inner strength to continue indefinitely. This includes careful attention to diet and exercise.

Pray for your family and friends. Pray that with education and acceptance, your loved ones can come to understand this problem more clearly.

18

HAVING IT ALL—AT HOME

Beth Spring

When our son, Jonathan, arrived after more than 12 years of marriage, I had a decision to make: abandon my solid career as a journalist, or stay home and raise Jonathan.

It really wasn't a tough call. All along, my husband, Jeff, and I were planning to live off his income if and when our first child came along. Now, with Jonathan entering the toddler years, I've resumed my writing career—on a part-time basis, working out of a spare bedroom. Occasionally, to meet a deadline, a neighbor watches Jonathan or I hire a teenage baby-sitter.

But then, housework tends to get neglected until my house looks like a toxic waste dump. Other days, I'm too exhausted to face my word processor. Adjusting from two incomes to Jeff's steady salary means we'll have to drive our trusty 1981 Honda Civic until it dies. Once again, Jeff and I won't be vacationing in the Bahamas this winter.

But we have something far more valuable: precious time with Jonathan during his most formative, changeable years. I've come to enjoy a spontaneous, flexible schedule, which suits a toddler best. It's been sheer delight to watch Jonathan feed chunks of day-old bread to the ducks at a nearby pond, or listen to his squeals of happiness as he goes higher and higher on the park swings. In my mind, I'm "having it all."

At first, my open-ended days frightened me. Would I use time well, or slowly sink into soap-opera oblivion? Being disciplined became a necessity, for Jonathan's sake and my own. What helped most was discovering that I am not alone. In fact, there appears to be a trend toward mothers staying at home when they are able to do so financially.

Naturally, single mothers, widows, and those whose husbands are disabled or ill have no choice but to join the work force. For the rest of us, however, staying at home deserves serious thought. I believe it is, at its heart, a common-sense choice that places the best interests of the child above the career aspirations of the mother.

A support group—Mothers at Home—encourages mothers who choose (or would like to choose) to stay at home with their children. Mothers are responding—this group has seen its membership mushroom from 648 members in 1984 to 8,000 today.

The national organization, which is based in Washington, D.C., publishes a monthly 32-page newsletter, *Welcome Home*. A recent issue cited a survey of 50,000 women conducted by *Family Circle*. The question put to working moms: "If it were possible, would you quit your job to stay home with your children?" More than two-thirds responded "Yes."

"Mothers are not in the market for bigger and better day-care facilities," according to the newsletter. "They are in the market for spending as much time as possible with their children."

Making a Choice to Stay Home

Women who find ways to stay home as much as possible see it as a positive choice for themselves and their families—not a drudgery of changing diapers and warming bottles. A friend of mine, Virginia Vagt, says her decision to stay home was a choice that took her by surprise. She was director of research and planning for a publishing firm near Chicago, and she intended to work part-time after Susanna was born in 1987.

"For eight weeks after Susanna's birth, I worked from home and went into the office on weekends," she recalls. "But things started falling through the cracks. One big mistake happened, and it was because I wasn't there. It made me panic. Then, the week I was going to go back part-time, the child care I had arranged didn't work."

Virginia resigned and hasn't looked back: "I realized after eight weeks that I already had a job." Changing her identity overnight required an adjustment, since she had worked full-time for 15 years before her baby was born. "Sometimes I have to pinch myself, because I can't believe I'm doing this. I ask myself, *Is taking care of a baby supposed to be this much fun?* At this point, going back to any job at an office holds no appeal for me."

Another mom, Jeannette Lee, approached motherhood wanting to stay home as much as possible. "As soon as I knew I was pregnant, I planned to quit," she remembers. But her company, the National Easter Seal Society, valued her work as its marketing manager. They proposed a part-time arrangement that allows Jeannette to work five to 10 hours per week at home, with occasional trips to the office.

The flexible schedule works well. "I was tired enough as a full-time professional that I could not see raising a young child in the time left over," says Jeannette. "We wanted to have children and thought we could not, so our daughter is a very precious gift. I want to be the one to raise her. My priority now is to build a sense of security into my little one. I don't want someone else to do it. I thoroughly love being at home, seeing her develop and change."

The 'New Traditionalists'

Unfortunately, mothers like myself, Virginia and Jeannette are not heard from when Congress debates issues such as child care and parental leave. But we have not escaped the notice of national marketers. Consider an advertising campaign by *Good Housekeeping* magazine, long a stalwart companion of homemakers.

The full-page ads—placed in major newspapers and national magazines—tout *Good Housekeeping* as the magazine of choice for America's "New Traditionalist." This woman, according to the ads, "has made a new commitment to the traditional values that some people thought were old-fashioned." The ad cites social research identifying new traditionalism as the "biggest social movement since the '60s."

Putting family first, particularly for mothers and fathers of young children, is not a new concept to Christian and pro-family advocates. What makes it suddenly newsworthy is reliable secular market research identifying a yearning for a return to home, hearth and long-held values. Ann Clurman, who first used the term "new traditionalist," is senior vice-president of Yankelovich Clancy Schulman, a firm that surveys Americans to identify their values. The results determine, among other things, what kind of advertisements manufacturers will use to sell their products.

Then came an article in the *Harvard Business Review* by a seasoned advocate of business opportunities for women, Felice N. Schwartz. Directing her comments toward U.S. corporations, Schwartz said upper management should be aware that while some women will make their jobs their top priority, others will take a detour from their careers to spend time raising their children.

Derisively billed as the "mommy track"—a term Schwartz never used—the idea that working women might choose homemaking over career at some point in their lives fueled debate in the national media. Schwartz's supporters said her advocacy of more flexibility and attention to family is sorely needed in the workplace. Critics lambasted her for attempting to turn back the clock and undo the gains of working women.

The definition of a working mother is rather fuzzy. William R. Mattox Jr., editor of the *Family Policy* newsletter, points out that women with children are often categorized as either "working" or "staying home." Using these rigid categories, statistics show 65 percent of mothers "work" outside the home. But when the numbers are refined a bit, a different picture comes to light.

"Many employed mothers work part-time—some for as much as 34 hours a week year-round, others for as little as a few hours a week during the Christmas season," says Mattox. "And many of those who are considered full-time workers do not work full-time year-round. In fact, a recent study found that only 29 percent of all married mothers work full-time year-round."

Because Jeannette Lee and I report annual income on our tax returns, we would be counted among "working mothers." But both of us are full-time stay-at-home moms.

Contending with Cultural Change

The "new traditionalist" trend is no surprise to Connie Marshner, a leading pro-family activist in Washington, D.C., who coined a similar term—"new traditional woman"—in 1982. Being traditional does not mean forsaking higher education or the unique gifts a woman may have. But it does mean putting into practice the Biblical idea of considering others before self—specifically, children and spouse.

Seven years ago, Marshner wrote, "The New Traditional Woman is not the vicious cartoon that the feminist movement has made of wives and mothers. The New Traditional Woman is not the syrupy caricature that Hollywood of the 1950s beamed into our living rooms. She is new, because of the new era, with all its pressures and fast pace and rapid change. She is traditional, because of unremitting cultural change. She is oriented around the eternal truths of faith and family. Her values are timeless and true to human nature."

Today, Marshner cautions that two major obstacles stand in the way of "new traditionalists": the divorce epidemic and the lure of consumer goods. "Whether this trend continues depends on whether people can break their dependency on what liberals used to call conspicuous consumption," Marshner says. "So much of the idea that mothers have to work means that they have to have material things. That is going to continue. We have to become radical about simplifying our lives."

What Stay-at-Home Moms Need

Mothers at Home is trying to clear up several misconceptions that may prevent some mothers from being home as much as they would like. Members appear before congressional hearings, advocating "family-friendly" employment practices such as flex-time, job sharing and benefits for part-time workers.

Above all, Mothers at Home tries to debunk myths about what women really want and what children really need. In its *Welcome Home* newsletter, the group notes, "Legislators under pressure to end the nation's child-care woes may be rushing to give America's mothers something they do not want . . . [Mothers] are looking for creative work options that allow them time to rear their own children."

The Family Research Council, the Washington-based affiliate of Focus on the Family, advocates tax relief for parents. As Congress debates the merits of several child-care bills this fall (including the "ABC" bill, which creates a huge, federal government child-care bureaucracy), our nation's lawmakers need to hear from families who want to raise their own children.

Pro-family advocates are pushing for a significant increase in the dependent tax exemption (the amount of money a parent may write off his or her taxes for each child). In addition, a tax credit, which would better assist low-income families, would not discriminate against families in which the mother cares for her own children at home. Parents could use the tax credit to purchase child-care services or to help them make ends meet without a wife's income.

Another solution involves an "attitude adjustment" on the part of mothers themselves. Our role models (at least in much of the nation's media) are full-steam-ahead careerists who stop at nothing to move up the corporate ladder. Actually, many women are jumping off the career track to rear their children, and then returning to work at a later date.

Research by Edith Fierst, a Washington, D.C. lawyer, points out that many successful women, including Supreme Court Justice Sandra Day O'Connor, interrupted their careers for as long as a decade to rear their children. Then they returned to the work force, either full- or part-time.

In the past, feminists have called for public policies to treat men and women exactly alike, or in their words, to be gender-neutral. Those policies and that ideology fail to take account of the realities of childbearing and child rearing, and American society appears to be ready for a new framework that puts children—and flexibility—first.

Whether a promising social trend will make itself felt in the halls of Congress and in corporate boardrooms remains to be seen. But advocates of the family believe they may have a new window of opportunity to make their case.

❦ INSIGHT ❦

Do You Need that Second Income?

If you and your spouse both work outside the home, you may wonder whether you can get by on just one income after a child arrives. Sometimes it is just not possible, but in other cases, it may be. Here are some questions for evaluating your true needs:

1. What do you do with that second income now? Is it spent on essentials or extras? Is it being saved?

2. What can your family do without? Could you make do with your current car for several more years? Can low-cost vacations be planned?

3. Do you have large debts to repay, such as college loans? Do you anticipate being financially responsible for an elderly parent?

4. Is the family's first income secure? Does the employer provide adequate health coverage and retirement benefits?

5. What goals do you have for your marriage and your family? What sort of home life do you want your children to experience?

6. Do you stick to a monthly budget? If not, financial planning might make a difference.

7. Have you read books on financial planning and talked with friends who live on one income?

8. How much of the second income is lost on job-related expenses such as child care, transportation, clothing, away-from-home meals and convenience dinners?

9. Could you re-enter the job market in your field after your children are in school? Could you use your time at home to learn new skills and develop new interests?

10. Have you explored alternatives such as part-time work, working out of the home, or job sharing?

19

THE LASTING LEGACY OF MOTHERHOOD

Dale Hanson Bourke

There was no getting around it. I was feeling deeply, profoundly sorry for myself as I shuffled on to the airplane that would take me home from a brief trip. Four months pregnant, I had outgrown most of my clothes, but my maternity dresses looked as if I were playing dress-up. So I made do with baggy sweaters and pinned skirts and tried to fight the fatigue and morning nausea that was still following me into my second trimester.

I found my aisle seat quickly. Sitting down with a sigh, I loosened the seat belt enough to accommodate my growing middle. The seat next to me was empty except for newspapers that the man one seat over was discarding in a growing pile.

Maybe reading something would take my mind off my troubles.

"Mind if I look at the front page?" I asked the man.

"Help yourself," he replied, as he continued to pore over the business section.

I glanced at him briefly above the billowing newspaper. Horn-rimmed glasses, neat haircut, button-down shirt, small print tie. *Must be a lawyer,* I thought to myself, as I mentally checked off all of the telltale signs.

"Interesting day for news," he said cordially. I smiled, but said nothing. I just wasn't in the mood for idle chatter.

"Coffee?" the flight attendant offered. It smelled wonderful.

"No, thanks," I said, looking at the pot longingly.

"I'd love some," the man with the newspaper replied cheerfully. "I just need a little help with my tray table." I glanced over to see why his table wasn't working. He dropped his newspaper and as I stared at him for a moment, I realized the problem. His table was fine. But the man's left arm ended at his elbow.

The flight attendant helped him with his tray as he folded the newspaper up. "Thank you," he said, reaching for the cup with a right hand that looked almost like a child's. I tried not to stare. But as I glanced in the man's direction I saw him drinking his coffee and reading the paper with surprising grace and ease.

He seems so normal, I thought, and then I was chagrined by my own prejudice.

Catching my eye, the man smiled warmly. "I thought the coffee would never come," he said, saving me from embarrassment.

"It smells great," I replied. "I wish I could have some, but I'm pregnant, and it's against the doctor's orders."

How foolish, I thought. *Here I am complaining about not being able to drink coffee, and I'm sitting next to a man who doesn't even have a good hand.*

But he didn't seem to notice my selfishness. "When are you due?" he asked. We talked for a few minutes, and I realized how skillfully he turned the conversation toward me. He seemed genuinely interested in my pregnancy.

"By the way, my name's Dan," he said as he held out his misshapen hand. My own hand completely enveloped the partial fingers. I hoped he hadn't noticed any hesitation as I introduced myself.

"What type of business are you in?" he asked, again easing me through an awkward moment.

"Publishing," I said. "How about you?"

"I work for a news service," he said. "I've been on the road the last week covering some stories."

I tried not to show it, but I had so many questions. *How could he possibly travel? How could he write stories? Could he really hold a pencil or use a typewriter with partially formed fingers?*

"Is it difficult for you?" His question interrupted my thoughts. Difficult for *me*? What did he mean?

He saw my confusion and asked the question again. "I mean, as a woman, is being in the publishing business difficult? I know some of the women in my office feel that they have to work a lot harder than the men."

I stumbled as I answered. "I guess it's harder at times. But then I think I have an advantage at other times. So I guess it all evens out."

"I think I know what you mean," he said. "Sometimes people feel so awkward around me that they find a reason not to give me a job. But then other people seem to go out of their way to give me a chance." Once again he had found a way to put me at ease.

Smiling sheepishly I asked, "Do you always have to be the one to bring up the subject of your disability?"

"Most of the time," he acknowledged. "Except with children. They always come right out with the questions the adults are thinking. I love to be with kids because they're so open with me, and I can be honest with them."

Sharing Interests

For the next hour, Dan and I talked about everything from our shared belief in God to our common interest in journalism. He told me funny stories about how people treated him because of his disability, like the man who shouted at him, for some reason believing his hearing was impaired.

He talked about the difficulty of having friends who sometimes felt sorry for him. He talked about his career and his hopes of finding an even more challenging position.

Finally I asked him the questions that had been forming the entire time we talked: How was it that he was such a whole person despite his physical handicap? Why was there no bitterness or self-pity in what he had told me?

"I think, in some ways, I am luckier than most people," he began. "I grew up in a wonderful, loving, godly home. My mother always told me that I was special. I never realized what an advantage that was until I met people who had no physical handicaps, but were scarred forever on the inside."

"Tell me about your mother," I said, wondering what kind of a woman could raise such an extraordinary child.

"She was very wise and very loving. She never complained, but taking care of me must have been emotionally and physically difficult. Just teaching me the simplest things took months of effort."

Dan smiled as he recounted boyhood memories of coming home after playing softball, crying because he had lost a game. "She was kind and caring," he said. "But she never let me use my disability as an excuse. She told me to go out and try harder the next day. As a child I thought that being the way I am was like being left-handed: It was different, but not necessarily worse.

"It couldn't have been easy for her, I realize now," he continued. "The doctors recommended that I be institutionalized. But my mother insisted on caring for me at home.

"Some people criticized her for pushing me too hard, but she used to say, 'If I do everything for him now, who will take care of him when I am gone?'

"She must be very proud of you now," I said.

"She passed away a few years ago."

"I'm so sorry," I said. "She must have been an incredible woman."

"Yes, she was."

Looking at Dan, I knew that his mother had accomplished more than most people dream of in a lifetime. Dan was a living testimony to the power of a mother's love.

As our trip came to an end, Dan picked up his bags and ran to catch another flight. I stood watching him, my hands unconsciously resting on my growing stomach. I wondered what kind of mother I would be to this child. As Dan waved to me, I felt tears in my eyes.

"Thank you, God," I prayed, "for trusting me with this child. And thank you for helping me understand just how important a mother's love can be."

Excerpted from *Everyday Miracles*, © 1989 by Dale Hanson Bourke. Word Books. Used by permission.

20

A GOOD MOM NEVER YELLS
(and other motherhood myths)

Stephen and Janet Bly

I shouldn't even be here. The thoughts kept pounding in my head. *I'm a busy person. It's a work day. I'm sure someone needs me at the office.*

But someone else needed me, too. That someone was my five-year-old son, Aaron. The occasion was a trip to the doctor's office to treat a serious infection.

Following in the Bly tradition, Aaron hates shots. And the anticipation of what was coming loomed before him for almost an hour as we sat in the waiting room. He alternated between tears and relative calm while I fumed. *What am I doing here? This is a job for his mother.*

Finally we shuffled into an examination room, and things got serious. The whole office looked and smelled like a shot. At last the doctor entered—smiling. He examined the patient and left—smiling.

"A shot of antibiotic will clear this up in no time," he chirped on the way out the door.

Aaron gasped for breath and tried to hold back the sobs. "I want my mommy!" he managed. I couldn't have agreed with him more.

After what seemed an eternity, two nurses and a huge hypodermic needle entered the room. Aaron looked for a place to hide. In between efforts to talk to him and comfort him, I kept mumbling, "Never again. This is his mother's job."

He sat quietly in the car as we headed for home. "You know, Dad," he said in his mature reasoning, "Mommy is better at this than you are."

Aha! I thought, I knew it. *This is one of the things moms are supposed to do!*

But is it? We all have our opinions of what moms should do. Society collects these ideas and sketches a vast composite of "ideal motherhood."

But what makes a good mom anyway? Doing everything exactly right? Producing good kids?

Here are some common assumptions we've gleaned from our acquaintances:

A Good Mom:

- Never bakes biscuits from little cardboard tubes that go "pow!"
- Appears instantly whenever any family member yells, "Mom!"
- Knows exactly what garment each child wants to wear to school each day and has it washed, mended and hung in the closet.
- Is always home when you call.
- Uses coupons to save a minimum of $15 on each visit to the grocery store.
- Never raises her voice.
- Never dreads teacher conferences.
- Attends every T-ball and soccer game in hose and heels (fresh from the office, of course, or some other world-expanding venture).

- Never leaves kids with runny noses in the church nursery.
- Never says no to the PTA.
- Keeps a regimented family schedule of daily tooth flossing and Bible memorization.

We each have our composites of good moms—or poor ones—but mothers of all kinds and types still hold an honored place in our society.

The number one holiday in America for restaurant business is not Father's Day. It's Mother's Day. In fact, Mother's Day boasts a flourishing bonanza for greeting card companies, florists, candy companies, and most other retailers.

But never have we heard complaints about the disparity of celebrations between these two holidays. That may be because most of us carry around a nagging realization that prods, "You haven't done enough for Mom!" We hold to the "balanced ledger" concept of relationships: If a relationship is to be strong and healthy, an equal amount of give and take is needed from both sides.

But, it's a lousy theory, simply because it doesn't work. For one thing, it's too hard to keep score. For another, mothers have many years worth of a head start on us. With such an impossible task, the least we can do is send flowers or candy once a year in May.

However, moms struggle with guilt burdens of their own. They may give little thought to the "balanced ledger," but few mothers can ignore comparisons to "ideal motherhood."

In the contest of ideal motherhood, the emphasis is "do everything right." If the children turn out well, she is deemed "a good mom." If they don't, she lives under the strain that somewhere, somehow, she must have "done something wrong." This prevailing theory is supported in psychology classes that pronounce, "If you're messed up in any way, it's because of faulty parental influence."

No wonder moms feel, at times, like failures. Television banters out one image of motherhood. Women's magazines list the "four easy steps." Your kids tell you about a mother down the street, and your husband tells you "that's not the way I was raised."

Many of today's moms find themselves under the gun of unreachable ideals. In response to the pressure, some drop out. Four basic misconceptions account for most of the pressure:

Mothering Is Easy

No job on earth takes more physical, mental, social, emotional and spiritual strength than being a good wife and mother. If a gal's looking for the easy life, she might try teaching tennis, cutting diamonds, or joining a roller derby team. There is nothing easy about good mothering. It can be backbreaking, heart wrenching and anxiety producing. And that's just the morning.

Mothering Is Natural

By nature, all of us are self-centered, prideful and petty. Our nature tells us, "Let Nick make the bed for a change." "Tracy can sew up her own skirt." "Clayton can walk home from school. A little rain won't hurt him." "If Jerry's folks don't bother letting us know they are coming to town until 10 minutes before they arrive, then they can live with "thingies" on the rug and write their names in the dust on the table."

There's no innate quality in a mother that gives her delight in cleaning the vomit off the antique quilt. In fact, part of the struggle to be a good mom is to overcome some natural, even sinful inclinations. Perhaps that was a part of what God meant when he told Eve, "In pain you shall bring forth children" (Genesis 3:16).

Mothering Is Always Fun

Let's face it, if housework was so fulfilling, if being cooped up in a house all day with little people was such sport, then why do we have such a difficult time finding anyone to take on either of these chores even for small stretches when we so desperately need a break?

Traipsing off to a dress shop with a $100 bill in your purse, now that's fun. Having a candlelight dinner at that exclusive restaurant overlooking the harbor . . . that's sheer delight. Putting another log in the fireplace, relaxing in the recliner, and reading a novel . . . pure joy.

Mothering does have its many pleasurable moments, but those come only with a total commitment of the will to weather all the sticky times in between.

A Mother Is Repaid for All She Does

Ruth stayed up until 2 a.m. to complete Shirley's cheerleading outfit because no one remembered to tell her that it had to be ready for pictures today. Then she got a call at noon. "Mom, I've got to have the matching jacket too! Really, Mom, I'll just die if I'm the only one without a jacket."

So, Ruth set aside her own plans, ran down to the yardage shop, and plunked back down into the sewing room. Years of performance under pressure came through for her and the jacket, complete with monogrammed name, was ready for the 4 o'clock pictures. "Mom, can you wait to give me a ride home?" Shirley pleaded.

Then it was time to chop the chicken meat, stir-fry some veggies, toss a salad, and call everyone to dinner. At 7 p.m. Ruth groaned as she remembered the PTA meeting. She longed to collapse in a chair or a warm bathtub, but this was the meeting to discuss who would be in charge of the annual carnival. Last time she missed a meeting like that, she was chosen as chairman. She wasn't about to have that happen again.

As Ruth ran a comb through her hair, smoothed on some lipstick, and grabbed a sweater, she hollered at Shirley, "Honey, I need you to do the dishes for me tonight."

The meeting dragged on and on because no one would volunteer to be carnival chairman. She wasn't quite sure how it happened, but about 10 o'clock a blurry-eyed Ruth agreed to do it another year. Back home again, she dragged herself into the kitchen. All the dishes remained exactly where she'd left them.

Oh, sure, Shirley would receive a proper reprimand by morning, but Ruth was looking for even more than obedience. Gratitude, maybe?

Any kind of interaction with another human, whatever the context, requires dealing with disappointment and irritation. However, the family context offers some rich additional dividends that other groupings can't provide. Here are just two of the rewards that make the whole mothering process worthwhile:

Companionship. There is a deep human joy in being intimately involved with another person's life. We are created to be social people. We are to communicate with others. Our ability to laugh, cry, struggle, feel, succeed and even fail with others is an important part of what it means to be human.

But we can't jump into just anybody's or everybody's life at that level. We only have the capacity for that level of intimacy with a few folks. Families provide the built-in structure for nurturing that kind of companionship.

Satisfaction. None of us can escape the inner drive to have meaning and purpose in life. Few of us purposely choose a shallow, insignificant existence. A tree or a butterfly doesn't worry about what impact it has left on its turf when it is gone. We would like to think we've helped this old world be a little more loving, a little more generous, a little more peaceful. At the least, we want to be a part of preserving the same quality of life that we have enjoyed.

Satisfaction comes from having a lasting, positive impact on the lives of others. Nobody on earth even comes close to a mother for having the potential for that kind of influence.

Setting aside the misconceptions, and all the array of varying standards, where does a woman turn to find a sane list of expectations for being a good mother?

The only consistently reliable source available is the Bible. Psychology systems come and go; they're too temporary. Advice columnists are too hit-and-miss, and require much discernment. Even friends don't always see the total picture.

One general outline for being a wife and mother is found in Proverbs 31. Many Christian women, familiar with the passage, will cringe at this suggestion. They view this chapter as living proof that they have failed to be The Perfect Ideal wife and mother God expects them to be.

Let's focus in on the overall spiritual principles of the passage and set aside the cultural details of "wool and flax," "merchants," "maidens," "spindles," "vineyards," "lighting lamps . . ."

The Proverbs 31 Woman:

Is trustworthy (v. 10): Reliable. To be counted on. Consistent. Secure. Realistic.

Is virtuous (v. 11): Morally excellent. Learns from past mistakes. Keeps to her principles. Works to understand the difference between what's good, and what's not.

Is industrious (vv. 13, 14, 28): Hard working. Diligent. Active, busy, persistent. She hangs in there with tough tasks when her body and mind tell her to quit.

Is generous (v. 15): Unselfish. Considerate. Kindhearted. Ungrudging. Willing to give or share.

Is wise (vv. 16, 27): Perceptive. Intuitive. Thoughtful. Shrewd. Uses well the knowledge she has. Aims for practical, God-honoring goals and uses the highest course available to achieve those goals.

Is strong (v. 17): Stable. Sure of herself. The ability to withstand pressure. That could imply physical, emotional, as well as spiritual stamina.

Is compassionate (v. 19): Tender. Sympathetic. Responsive and warm. Willing to offer constructive help.

Is dignified (v. 28): Stands tall with grace. Poised.

Is spiritual (v. 30): Knows some things are sacred. Fears God. Has experienced some of the greatness of God first hand. Reverences her relationship with God above everything else.

Make a note of the qualities above that you and your family already recognize as part of you. Thank God for his part in establishing these merits in you. Ask Him for specific help in an area that makes you wince. We all have one (or more), so you're not alone. But, we're aiming for a pretty high goal: to be a good mom. We need lots of those around if we're going to heal our families and our society.

21

WHEN YOU FEEL LIKE SCREAMING

Pat Holt and Grace Ketterman, M.D.

In preparation for a mothers' seminar some time ago, we asked 150 nine to twelve-year-olds to anonymously answer two questions:

- What do you like most about your mother?
- What do you dislike most about your mother?

Although the answers to the first question varied, the answers to the second did not. We were amazed by the results. Almost every child used the phrase "her screaming." Over and over again we read, "I can't stand it when she screams."

Then we went into a half-dozen fourth, fifth and sixth grade classrooms and told the children we needed their help. We wrote the phrase, "Mommy, Please Stop Screaming!" on the chalkboard. Giggles and sighs of understanding followed.

Mothers already know children "can't stand" screaming, and yet we continue to scream. Why? What drives us to lose control?

Although the "screaming habit" breeds guilt in mothers, it can be difficult to break. Why? Because many mothers are comfortable with the results of screaming: It usually guarantees a measure of success. Screaming moms tolerate the guilt that follows.

Changing behavior always involves risk. In the case of screaming, mothers are apprehensive to exchange a familiar habit (which brings predictable results) for the unknown benefits of quiet control.

However, alternatives to screaming can give such a high rate of success to the mother that her confidence level will soar. Strong, controlled and confident mothers are capable of raising confident and controlled children. We believe true strength is expressed only through gentleness and self-control.

How to Control Yourself

That woman who is cool and collected, who is master of her countenance, her voice, her actions and her gestures, will be the mother who is in control of her children, and who is greatly beloved by them.

—Old Inscription

Like it or not, mothers set the tone of the home. As a mother, you have probably noticed that when you are in control, the children are much easier to keep under control. But when you are upset, the children are usually "off the wall." Children are sensitive; they respond dramatically to the emotional pulse of the mother.

Let's look at some positive ways to gain control.

Planning Ahead

A controlled mother is organized. Remember—you need to be the *master* of the day, rather than the *victim*. It is vital to have a strategy that anticipates potential problems and plans how to deal with them.

Rita, a newly organized mother, tells this story:

I used to just get up and let the day happen. It happened all right, and most of it was bad. Everyone else was controlling my life—my children, my husband, my friends. I began to feel used, abused and resentful. I decided to make a change. I wanted to feel that I had some control over my life.

To help myself get organized, I began to make lists on little scraps of paper that I would misplace and lose. Oh well! I felt I was on the right track. Later on, I bought an organizer and actually began to enjoy writing down my plans for the day, the week and the month. It became a game to see how many things I could actually get done.

Little by little, my family and friends began to have some respect for my time and plans. I am even learning to say, "No!" to foolish requests.

Flexibility

A controlled mother is flexible. Some moms tend to make following a schedule more important than meeting the needs of their children. This rigidity will result in loss of control and, ultimately, screaming bouts.

Life is full of interruptions, emergencies, crises and urgent happenings. A mother must learn to go with the flow, even if it means temporarily abandoning her plans.

Although Kate struggled with flexibility for months, she found it reaped great benefits in her family life.

> When my daughter was a toddler, she reached that stage where she wanted to touch everything. She knew what "No!" meant, and she heard it often.
>
> I had big plans for this particular Saturday and needed to leave the house, but my daughter was exerting her strong will. She reached out to touch something. I said, "No!" but she touched it anyway. I slapped her hand. This did not deter her, and she touched the object again and again.
>
> I was irritated and perplexed. Should I stay home and reinforce the correct behavior, or should I carry on with my plans? I really felt we were at a crisis point and needed moment-by-moment consistency. I reluctantly canceled my plans and stayed home, spending much of the day saying "No!"
>
> I'm glad I did. She learned that "No!" meant "No!" and that she needed to respect property and not touch everything in sight.

A Sense of Humor

A controlled mother has a sense of humor. The mother who can laugh at herself, with her children and at the impossible situations of life is far ahead on the road to personal control. Having the wisdom to step back and see the humor of her situation helped Sharon gain control.

It was the night of the school Christmas Pageant—the first program our two older children had ever been in. At the time, I had a four-year-old girl, a three-year-old girl and a baby of nine months. My husband was gone, and the children were constantly at each other. Besides that, so many little things went wrong. Socks were missing, the children had spilled food all over themselves and their clothes, their hair was extra unruly, and I was exhausted with the ordeal of getting them ready and out the door.

Then I discovered the car keys were missing. I felt frustration plus. Believe me, I was literally ready to tear my hair out.

Suddenly, I realized how funny the whole situation was! I was in the midst of a situation comedy that no one would ever see but me! I sat down in the middle of the floor and began to laugh. I laughed so hard that tears came to my eyes.

My children didn't know what to think. They sat down on the floor with me and put their arms around me. But you know what? We found the keys—under a pillow, of all places—and just barely managed to get to the program in time.

Balance

A controlled mother strives to keep balance in her life. A mother is often frustrated and weary at the end of the day—not because of her work load, but because she did not have time to pursue activities that were important to her personal growth and development.

You may feel like each new day is a juggling act. You have to balance commitments to your husband, your children, your home and your work, yet leave some time to pursue special projects and maintain friendships. Whew! What a task!

Achieving balance can change your attitude toward your children. It did for Carol.

I almost went crazy being a mother. I had three children in five years and was under a daily load of laundry, dirty dishes, a house strewn with paraphernalia and sticky fingerprints decorating my walls. I had been an art designer and longed to spend time alone in my studio, which was now a catchall room!

I was so frustrated with never having time for my art that I began to wish I'd never had children. Then I would feel guilty and miserable.

For a while I assumed I was the only mother who had ever felt trapped. I confided my feelings to another mother of three. She felt the same way. We thought of a plan to baby-sit twice a week for each other for half a day. We've been doing it now for almost a year. Having that time alone to pursue my art work has made all the difference to me and my children. I can now enjoy them, knowing I'll have some well-earned time for myself.

To find balance in your life, we suggest learning to say "No!" to tasks you may be asked (and even *wish*) to do. When your children are more independent, you can take on additional jobs.

A Prescription for Change

A controlled mother has a prescription for change. Now we'd like to offer you some clear and proven steps that will enable you to change:

Motivation. Breaking any habit is so much trouble that one must truly want to do it. Few habits are harder to break than screaming. Some ideas that may motivate you are these:

- happier, better adjusted children;
- a desire to be a better mother;
- enjoying good feelings, rather than the shame or remorse you experience after yelling;
- the approval of your spouse, parents or friends because of your changing;
- confidence that you can learn better, more successful parenting skills.

Permission to change. This idea may sound foolish at first, but think about it. Chances are you yell because you were taught to yell. Perhaps your mother screamed, or you accidentally discovered that screaming brought short-term results.

Decide firmly to change. How often do we think about breaking a habit? Do these phrases sound familiar? *I ought to go on a diet?* Or, *I really should learn to control my spending.* And, *I need to organize my time better.* All of these words (*ought, should* and *need*) are emphatic and indicate intentions to change. But change does not happen automatically.

We recommend that you think clearly along these lines: "I know my screaming does more damage than good. I am choosing to stop screaming, and I *will* begin to break that habit today." It takes a definite decision and commitment to effect change.

Formulate a plan. Outline a goal that is *possible* for you to reach. Can you scream one less time each day? Can you avoid screaming on one occasion that you would normally yell?

Consider what upsets you so much. On the surface, of course, it's something your child has said or done—or *not* done. But when you consider a situation closer, you will often discover some underlying memory or deep fear of losing parental authority.

Knowing *how* you feel and *why* you feel that way will enable you to make a pivotal decision. "What will I do about this situation that will really cure it?" You should take a "time out" and plan your response. During this time, your children can ponder their misbehavior and become a bit anxious. That uncomfortable feeling may help them decide to overcome problem habits.

Find some help. We want to remind you that God is always on call. Don't forget to contact Him for the patience and wisdom you will need.

We know you can do it!

Excerpted from *When You Feel Like Screaming,* © by Pat Holt and Grace Ketterman, M.D. Published by Harold Shaw Publishers. Used by permission.

PART FOUR

FOCUS ON CHILDREN

22

"MOM, I'M BORED. WHAT CAN I DO?"

Kathy Peel and Joy Mahaffey

Summertime finds many a mother checking airline schedules for the next flight out of town. Escaping the blaring TV, the empty pantry, the messy rooms and those screaming kids is her persistent dream.

Summer vacation often becomes a test of endurance rather than a special time to enjoy her children. She impatiently marks off the calendar and counts the days before the kids go back to school. Hot, tired and out of ideas, many mothers capitulate and allow their children a steady diet of television.

It's our desire to help you turn summer vacation into a memorable, rewarding adventure, rather than a boring ordeal. We've included some tried-and-true ideas to help you transform tedium into joy—without a lot of work on your part.

Fun for Every Week

We suggest you not only plan major events like family vacations, but also take time each week to schedule special activities.

Here are some helpful steps for planning your activities:

• Make a list of ideas that would be fun anytime you can plug them into the schedule.

• Check and see which activities need advance planning and make the necessary arrangements in plenty of time.

• Make a list of any supplies you will need for the week. Collect or purchase them beforehand.

• Make sure the activities you plan are age-appropriate and safe.

• Stay flexible. Plans you make on Saturday may not look good when Wednesday, the day of the event, arrives. Be ready with an alternative.

• Plan group activities with other dads and moms from your neighborhood or church. For example, sponsor a group picnic and have family games for all ages.

• Keep in mind the many children's programs in your city. Check on summer classes offered through your local library, museum, YMCA, boys or girls clubs, community colleges, or parks and recreation departments.

• Enroll your kids in a summer sports program.

• Send your youngsters to summer camp. Everybody needs a break—including your kids. Going away to camp teaches children flexibility and responsibility.

• Finally, check with your children weekly to get a feel for their moods. What are they tired of? What are they excited about?

Help for Working Mothers

If you are a parent who works during the summer, you can make the most of your children's vacation by employing special planning and effort. When interviewing prospects to look after your children, be sure each individual understands your commitment to providing meaningful activities for them.

Discuss your summer goals with your baby-sitter, then plan activities and excursions. Together, fill out a weekly planner, including plenty of opportunities for creativity, exercise and reading. Instruct the sitter that "tubing out" in front of the TV most of the day is not an option.

If the kids are old enough to stay alone, communicate clearly what you expect of them while you are gone. Assist them in setting goals each day that will contribute to their growth.

Super Summer Jobs

Listed below are ideas for great summer jobs for older children. Some jobs—such as selling food—require a business license or permit. (Check with your local city or county government offices.)

- Baby-sit.
- Bake and sell homemade bread and cookies.
- Clean houses or move furniture.
- Clean swimming pools.
- Paint house numbers on curbs with stencils.
- Start an odd-job or yard-work service. Advertise by distributing fliers in the neighborhood.
- Take care of pets or walk dogs.
- Water plants for vacationing neighbors.
- Teens can provide a party service for parents who need help giving birthday parties for little ones.
- Teens can tutor younger children.

Things to Do When Kids Say, "I'm Bored!"

Younger Children:

- Colorful creative salt: Add 5–6 drops food coloring to ½ cup household salt. Stir well. Cook in microwave for 1–2 minutes or spread on waxed paper and let dry. Store in airtight container. Use as you would glitter.
- Have a dress-up party. Invite friends to come dressed in Dad or Mom's old clothes, such as hats, jewelry, scarves, suits or ties. Serve tea and cookies.
- Have your children create books about themselves. They might want to include their date of birth, handprints, footprints and drawings of themselves and the family.
- Create a submarine from a large appliance box. Cut portholes and make a periscope.
- Decorate empty syrup bottles; tag with each child's name and use them as water jugs in the refrigerator. Keep the bottles on the bottom shelf so your children can get their own drinks.

- Ask at a furniture store if you can purchase damaged table leaves. These are often available for a nominal cost and make wonderful ramps for small cars. You can also go to the lumber yard and buy plywood.
- Conduct a neighborhood tricycle wash.
- Create a portrait screen. Paint characters or animals on a tall box. Cut holes where the characters' faces should be for the kids to stick their faces through. Take snapshots.
- Construct a zoo. Put stuffed animals in box cages.
- Cover a wall in your children's room with plain brown paper. Let them design their own wallpaper.
- Make macaroni jewelry. Mix 1 tablespoon food coloring with 2 tablespoons rubbing alcohol in a bowl. Make several different colors. Stir macaroni into the colored solutions. Spread on newspaper to dry. String on a shoelace for bracelets or necklaces.

Older Children:

- Baker's clay: Mix 2 cups white flour and $1/2$ cup table salt in a bowl. Add $1/2$ cup water and stir for a few minutes. Slowly add $1/4$ cup water while turning dough in bowl. Form dough into a ball and work in any remaining dry flour and salt. Knead for five minutes. Shape dough into desired shapes, adding a little water to join pieces together. Use cookie cutters for preschoolers. Bake your creations at 250 degrees for 15–30 minutes until hard. Time will vary according to thickness of dough. Let cool completely. Dough can be painted with acrylic paints and finished with clear lacquer.
- Visit a bakery and ask the bakers to show you how they decorate cakes or prepare the pastries for the oven.
- Go to a dairy farm.
- Make an appointment to see a newspaper or magazine printing plant.
- Check your automobile tour guide book for directions to local historical sights.
- Go on a nature hike and try to identify birds, leaves and wild flowers. Make a nature book of the things you've studied.

Other Fun Things to Do

- Build an ant farm. Find a large jar and a smaller jar that fits inside the bigger one. Place moist dirt and ants in narrow space between jars. Cover with lid and include small air holes. Keep soil moist and feed ants bread crumbs, dead insects and small pieces of meat or vegetables. Study about ants in the encyclopedia.
- Create rice art. Draw a simple picture on cardboard. In butter tubs, use food coloring to dye rice different colors. Dip a toothpick in white glue, then pick up one grain of rice. Dip it in the glue again and place the rice grain on the picture. When the picture is completely covered with rice, brush a coat of glue over entire surface. It will dry clear.
- Write crazy commercials and perform them for each other.
- Make a big bowl of popcorn and look at old family movies, photos or slides.
- Put on a backyard carnival. Build booths from refrigerator boxes. Have face-painting and pie-throwing (whipped cream on paper plates) contests. Make a ring toss using old coat hangers as the rings and soda pop bottles as targets. Sell tickets to the neighborhood kids and give out small prizes.
- An old tire is a great creative toy. Make an obstacle course, sandbox, tire swing or a target for a football or Frisbee.
- Have the children record interesting sounds in the neighborhood on a cassette tape player. Ask them to play it back to you and have you guess the sounds.
- Set up a bicycle obstacle course. See who can ride through it the fastest without falling.
- Have a smile contest. See who has the biggest smile; measure them with a ruler.
- Start an herb garden in an egg carton and later transfer to small pots. Your kids will love seasoning their meals with herbs they grow themselves.

Excerpted from *A Mother's Manual for Summer Survival,* © 1989 by Kathy Peel and Joy Mahaffey. Published by Focus on the Family.

23

LISTEN TO YOUR CHILDREN!

C. Joanne Sloan

Luke won't talk to his parents. When he comes home from school, he goes straight to his room without bothering to say hello. His parents know nothing about his high school friends, and they have no idea what he does when he's away from home. His family never discusses problems, and their few talks usually end in shouting matches.

Luke can't remember the last time his parents really took the time to *listen* to him. They're always busy—his father with his job and his mother with her part-time work and various social activities. Even if they did make an attempt to listen to him, Luke wonders if they could understand his problems at school.

Luke's family is typical of many families today. His parents do not realize it, but Luke doesn't talk to them because they have never listened. Even as a child, he would not confide in his parents because they were always doing the talking. They never recognized the crucial role that listening plays in communication.

Experts say that if you don't want your children to talk to you, never listen to them. But parents who want open communication lines—who want their children to come to them rather than strangers in a crisis—need to make listening a high priority. Here are some simple practices for developing listening skills.

Desire to Listen

To be a good listener, you must *want* to hear what your child has to say. You have to believe that your youngster's thoughts and feelings are important, and that he gains tremendous benefits from your listening.

In his book *Ask Me to Dance*, Bruce Larson tells of a church secretary who had a sign on her desk which read: "I love you enough to listen." Parents need to wear an invisible sign that conveys this message. And it's best to start listening to a child when he is small—not when he is 16, and communication barriers have become difficult to bridge.

Make an Effort to Listen

Although listening seems simple, it's actually a complex and challenging art. To learn to listen effectively, you must be self-disciplined and willing to sacrifice your time. It means putting everything else out of your mind to concentrate on what your child is saying.

Being a good listener requires that you examine your priorities. What is more important to you than your relationship with your child? You may have to make some sacrifices—putting down the newspaper, turning off the television set, giving up a golf game—to give your child a thorough hearing.

Try to make listening an integral part of your family's routine. Create a time to be alone with each child on a regular basis. Sit down with your nine-year-old after school and hear about his day. Take your teen out for dinner and get to know one another. Use every opportunity to listen.

My husband and I have found that the best time to share happenings and concerns is at the dinner table. Since meals provide the only time for some families to be together, parents might plan to discuss specific topics so that dinner conversations don't result in idle talk or stony silence.

Commit to Listening

In a recent survey, young people were asked what they wanted most from their parents. The overwhelming response was that they desired that their parents take time to listen to them and understand them.

Dr. Paul Tournier, a gifted Swiss psychiatrist, writes in his book *To Understand Each Other:* "It is impossible to overemphasize the 'immense need' humans have to be really listened to, to be taken seriously, to be understood."

Parents who are committed to meeting this "immense need" must become willing and sensitive listeners.

Listen Actively

Listening is more than just hearing. Whereas hearing is physical, listening is psychological. It should not be a passive process.

Unfortunately, much of our listening is done passively. We hear words and sounds, but we do not absorb them. Passive listening can become a habit.

Vicki Grossman, a family therapist in Bothell, Washington, and co-founder of the Youth Suicide Prevention Center, says in a recent issue of *Parents* magazine that if she could give one piece of advice to parents, it would be to "listen actively." Here are five guidelines for active listening:

Hear Your Child Out

Don't rehearse in your mind how you will answer your youngster. Listen carefully and evaluate his requests when he is through talking.

It takes self-control and humility to avoid making judgments, especially when your child's views contradict your own. But, hear him out and then give your honest appraisal. Proverbs 18:13 says it well: *"He who answers before listening—that is his folly and his shame."* (NIV)

Keep Your Eye on Your Child

Have you ever had a conversation with someone who rarely looked you in the eye? Did you have the impression that the person wasn't interested in what you had to say?

Look at your child while he's talking to you. Gazing around the room or out the window is distracting and implies that you aren't listening. If circumstances do not enable you to maintain eye contact, let him know he still has your attention.

Create an Atmosphere of Acceptance

When children don't feel threatened, they are more likely to share their anxieties and joys.

Establish a supportive climate. Don't interrupt or contradict your youngster. Make your children feel comfortable by giving them all the affirmation you can. Positive gestures like smiling and nodding will often prompt youngsters to continue speaking.

Your son may feel more at ease talking about school while shooting a basketball. Your daughter may be able to share her dating concerns while you are biking together.

Force Yourself to Be Interested

How many times have you tuned out your children because it was too tiresome to listen to all the details of their activities?

When you make yourself listen to them, you may be surprised at all the delightful things you can learn. You may also perceive emotional, social and spiritual needs that you may not have discovered if you hadn't listened.

Listen to Feelings

Listen to feelings—not just words. Feelings may be shown through body language and tone of voice. Sometimes a shrug of the shoulders means more than a hundred words.

Notice the tone of your child's voice or a change in attitude. If a child stops talking altogether, he may be having serious difficulties.

Benefits

Many times family members assume they know how parents, children or siblings feel when they really don't. When loved ones care enough to listen, there are many rewarding benefits.

Listening intently and asking questions to clarify a point of view help to eliminate misunderstandings that often arise from trying to "read your child's mind."

Your children, if they model your example and become skillful listeners, will learn to "hear you out," as well. You will then have the opportunity to share with them your knowledge, experience and insight.

Finally, when you listen to your children, you are paying them a compliment. By listening, you increase their feelings of self-respect and self-worth.

If you would like to give your children a lasting gift, give them a listening ear.

Excerpted from *Together at Home*, © 1989 by Dean and Grace Merrill. Published by Focus on the Family.

24

EIGHT IS ENOUGH?
The Advantages of a Large Family

Bob Welch

Families are smaller today than ever before—many would fit comfortably in a Volkswagen Rabbit. This is a story about two families that would have trouble squeezing into a Chevy Suburban. Meet the Millers, a rural family from Halsey, Oregon, and the Cliftons, a suburban family from Bellevue, Washington. Each has six children. Each faces the prodigious challenge of making a large family work.

The Miller Family

The whistle from an afternoon train blows in the distance. A light breeze tickles the curtains in the century-old farmhouse. On the front lawn, a handful of new pups gather for dinner.

Here in the heart of Oregon's farm-rich Willamette Valley, there's something cathartic about spending an afternoon at the home of

Dewey and Sara Miller and their six children. The directions were simple to their rented house in Halsey, population 700: "Come into town, take a right at the Goodyear store and go until the street ends," Dewey Miller told me. "We're the last house you'll come to."

But if the setting has a certain rural romance to it, the Millers have known the struggle of hard times. "The most challenging part, I suppose, has been making the paycheck reach till the last of the month," says Dewey, 43, who has worked as everything from a millworker to a welder. A short, stocky man, Dewey has also known the pain of unemployment.

His quiet counterpart is Sara, a homespun woman of Mennonite background. The Millers, who now attend Grace Bible Fellowship in nearby Albany, include Duane, 21, Linda, 19, Bonnie, 16, Loren, 13, Wendell, 11, and Annalise, 6. All but Duane live at home.

With a tightly knit spirit, a rural home and no TV, the Millers still remember the bleak Christmas when Dewey and Sara told the kids there wasn't much money for presents. "So we each chose a name of another family member and went to the Salvation Army and picked out $2 gifts," said Sara. "The kids thought it was great. Some of our friends have talked about how unappreciative their kids are and wonder why ours aren't that way. I suppose it's because we couldn't lavish a lot of gifts on them."

Questions from Friends

The Millers occasionally run into people who are amazed at the size of their family. "Six kids," they'll say. "How in the world do you do it?"

The answer is a grassroots, back-to-basics approach to life: Build a strong husband-wife relationship. Talk instead of watching television. Pray instead of worrying. Laugh instead of languishing in life's problems. And work together as a team.

When one child didn't have the money for a school field trip, for example, the rest of the kids pooled their dollars and cents. "Things like that draw you together as a family," said Sara.

For the Millers, the kitchen is the heart of the home. "That's where a lot of conversation takes place," said 19-year-old Linda, who'll soon leave for Prairie Bible College in Alberta, Canada. "It's almost a competition as to who can tell the most exciting thing that happened that day."

Conversation never has to compete with cartoons or "Cosby"—the Millers ditched the TV years ago. "There's not a lot wrong with TV, but it's an attractive nuisance," says Dewey. "I'd much rather have the kids outside on their bikes, doing things children should be doing."

The Millers' openness with one another fosters a closeness that's missing in many families. "One of the most important things around here is our faith," says Dewey. "We spend a lot of time talking about that. The 'why' and 'why nots' of life."

The family has also found security in numbers. Once, Sara applied for a housecleaning job and didn't get it. "I felt really bad, but the boys heard about it and were upset. The girls were, too. Just knowing they felt awful about it helped me get through the disappointment. It's neat to have that support."

It's also neat to have so many people around on a game night. "It's like having a party by ourselves," said Sara. "You don't need to invite people over."

Perhaps that's why chores often evolve into "family fun" activities. After canning snap beans or apple sauce, it isn't surprising to find the Millers returning to the kitchen table for a new round of Bible Trivia.

But for this Oregon family, life has not been all fun and games. In 1982, Dewey lost his business—and shortly afterward the family car broke down on the way to church. At the service, someone said he had just inherited a car he didn't need; could the Millers use it? "On several occasions things like that have happened," said Dewey. "Times when we've found a check in the mailbox because the deacons knew we had a light bill we couldn't pay."

Committed to a Christian Upbringing

In other families, a new house is reason for celebration. For the Millers, a new wood stove once was; it and another stove were all they had to heat their home in the winter. "With Christ, there's not much we couldn't get through," said Sara. "He's helped us through a lot. We've grown through the experience."

Despite the economic hardships, the Millers are committed to sending their children to a Christian school. At one point, they had five children in the same school, but thanks to the school's cheaper-by-the-dozen philosophy, they had to pay for only three. Still, it's been expensive.

To cut down on school costs, the entire Miller clan cleaned their church on Saturday nights—and served as custodians at the Christian school as well. "Sometimes, we'd try to make a game out of it," said Linda. "We'd see who could get the work done fastest."

Laughter, says Dewey, is an important ingredient of a large family. "We don't take ourselves too seriously around here," he said. "We tend to roll with the punches. Fun is real important to us. There's enough stress in life."

Around the house, the biggest stress point is the family's single bathroom. In the morning, it's first-come, first-served. And no reading while on the porcelain throne.

With one bathroom, Sunday mornings definitely get wild at the Miller household—but there's a happy ending. "When we're all through screaming and hollering at each other," said Dewey, with a smile, "we pile into a couple of cars and try to calm down by singing praise hymns all the way to church."

The Clifton Family

Walk into the Bellevue, Washington, home of Jim and Rachel Clifton, turn to your right and you'll see what helps this family of eight tick. It's a job chart so detailed and complex you wonder what kind of software they used. Each week, for example, one child makes school lunches for the other five—that's 30 lunches a week.

"The system starts out well in the fall, but by January, everyone hates the lunches being made for them," said Rachel, whose family goes through 20 gallons of milk and a couple of three-pound tubs of peanut butter each month.

To your left is "The Question Box." At dinner, everybody draws a question and answers it as a means of promoting discussion. For example: "What's your greatest fear?" or "If you could be anyone for a day, whom would it be?"

Just when you're thinking to yourself that this family is so well organized they're a born-again version of the Brady Bunch, Rachel reveals the other side. "The other day I counted all our unmatched socks," she confided. "There were 72."

Widowed socks notwithstanding, it's obvious the Cliftons are doing something right. They are a lively, fun-loving bunch capable of doing the impossible: sitting still during a church service on un-padded chairs.

The family consists of Jim, a lanky 46-year-old cardiologist at Providence Hospital in Seattle; blonde-haired Rachel, 44; and the children: Julie, 16, Amie, 13, Stevie, 11, Joe, 10, Tom, 9, and Melissa, 7. That's right, the Cliftons once had six kids age 9 or less. "I look back and wonder how I did it," groaned Rachel. But there have been no regrets; in fact, the Cliftons are discussing adopting a seventh child.

With six children, you just can't drop in on friends. You don't take vacation trips across the country. "And in the winter," reminded Rachel, "you have 16 socks to wash every single day."

On the other hand, with each child having distinct interests, Jim and Rachel take in all sorts of new vistas—from opera to baseball cards, soccer to school band.

"You have a lot of people to play with," said 13-year-old Amie. "You don't get lonely."

"And there are more toys for us to play with," piped in nine-year-old Tom.

Faith is the foundation of the Cliftons' success as a family. "If we weren't Christians, we probably wouldn't have six children," said Jim, who met Rachel in 1968 when he was interning—and Rachel nursing—at a hospital in Southern California.

One night a week, Jim and Rachel try to get out by themselves. "Remember," said Rachel, "even if friends take four of our kids for the evening, we still have two. It's hard to find time alone."

Added Jim, "We believe the best way to relate to our children is to have a good relationship ourselves. That provides great security for the kids."

So, too, does individual time with each child, they say. Sometimes that means allowing each child to pick an activity to do with one parent for a day, such as going on a tour of baseball card shops. Sometimes that means simply running an errand alone with one of the kids. And sometimes that means Rachel and Jim saying no to outside activities.

Looking Out for the Kids

Because she's around the children more, Rachel is better at pinpointing the needs of each one. "I'll say, 'Hey, you know, Jim, you haven't been out with Stevie alone for a while.' My mind's continually assessing how each child is doing. It's not just how they're doing academically that we're concerned with, but how each of them are doing socially and spiritually, too."

Like any mom with kids constantly underfoot, Rachel battles going bonkers. Recently, the kids were fighting, and she found herself yelling. This, as she stood wearing her "Best Mom on Earth" T-shirt.

On a typical school morning, chaos reigns. "Someone can't find a shoe, another took someone's jacket, a bike tire is flat, and someone is trying to do some memory work," said Rachel. "On mornings like that, when they're out the door, I just pray, 'Take them, Lord, and bring someone to encourage them.'"

The Cliftons have gifted children and some with learning disabilities; some are perfectionists, others happy-go-lucky. At times, Jim and Rachel have actually sat down and listed their children's strengths and weaknesses on paper—all with the idea of improving their parenting.

"We're real concerned that the children learn to serve," says Jim. The kids realize they come from an affluent home; the challenge, he says, is making them realize their need to help others. The family has put together food and clothing packages for people in Seattle's poorest district. This Christmas they are planning to serve meals at the Union Gospel Mission.

"It's important to instill spiritual values in them," says Jim. At the dinner table, the Cliftons often discuss sermons they've heard at Antioch Bible Church in nearby Kirkland. They hold "wisdom searches" through Proverbs. They try to worship together as family.

"I like sitting together," said 16-year-old Julie. "It makes us feel like we're a unit."

The Cliftons drive a van with a personalized license plate that reads JOY OF 6. On Sunday mornings, that van used to be traditionally late to church. But like the Millers, the Cliftons improvised a new plan: If everybody were ready 45 minutes early, they could all go out for doughnuts before church.

"Only three times in the last eight years have we been late," said Jim.

"Yeah," said Rachel, "even if their Sunday school teachers sometimes complain they're on a sugar high."

25

HOW TO TALK TO YOUR KIDS ABOUT SEX

Connie Marshner

How can we talk to our kids about sex? In a word, simply. Talk is only one part of it, though. The bigger part is giving our children the *desire* to be chaste, and then giving them the practical help they need to follow it up.

Sex education begins in the parent's mind, long before the baby is born. It begins with the mother's and father's attitudes: Do we respect the human body as part of God's creation? Do we believe that God called his creation "good"? Are we comfortable with being a woman? A man?

If we are comfortable with our own sexual nature, we can be comfortable with our children's—and with our job as our children's primary sex educator.

Baby Talk

The doors of communication start out open, but where sex is concerned, they can bang shut before toddlerhood is over.

Imagine the scene. You're at Proper Aunt Priscilla's tea table, and Junior chirps up in wonderfully clear diction: "Why doesn't Susie have a pee-pee like I do?" Mother turns purple, and Aunt Priscilla looks like she just swallowed her crumpet.

"Jason!" his mother screams. "We don't talk about things like that!" The boy is silenced—probably for good. He has just learned that bodies are not to be talked about with adults, not even with Mommy. That's precisely the wrong lesson.

To Jason, his question was no different than "Why is it raining?" Bodies and weather are all part of the world he is discovering, and he's interested in both. Of course, he popped that question at an embarrassing time, but how was Jason to know that Aunt Priscilla's dining room table was not the place?

Far better for Mom to have begun sooner, in the bathtub, telling Jason all the parts of the body. She should use correct, clinical terms, not silly, baby words that will embarrass him later on in front of his friends. In such an environment, Jason's questions could come out spontaneously and be easily answered.

Jason can be taught, too, that we only talk about our bodies when we're in private, or in our own home with Mom or Dad. At the same time, he can be taught where other people are *not* allowed to touch him.

First Impressions

Attitudes are formed early, early on. Before most parents even know kids are noticing things, children are already forming attitudes. We mustn't forget that *we* want to be the adults who guide and form our children's attitudes. If it isn't us, then who should it be? The TV? Teachers? Classmates? Friends in the neighborhood?

These influences may not be bad, but we can do a lot more to keep our children wholesome and *reinforce* proper attitudes about sex.

Suppose you're walking in the park with your three-year-old. Two teens are doing some serious necking on the park bench. You have two choices: hurry past and hope your youngster won't notice, or you can say something. If you do the former, and your child *does* notice, he may think necking on park benches is an okay thing to do.

So what do you say? Something like, "I sure hope those two are married. People shouldn't kiss and cuddle like that unless they're married. And even then, they should do it at home." Yes, you may start a conversation, but so much the better. That's when you can build on that foundation of instilling correct behavior.

Expectations are very important, and we have to make them clear before they're controversial. Our expectations often unfold gradually to our children, sometimes without anything being said. When we take our daughter, Mandy, to ballet lessons, we implicitly tell her that we expect her to learn how to plié, just as we expect Nick to play with the baseball and bat we bought him for Christmas.

Expectations of modesty can be conveyed just as easily: a gentle correction to a pint-sized streaker running through the house naked; an observation to a pre-teen that a pair of shorts are too tight to be worn any more; and a quiet explanation to a high school-age child why you don't want him to see a "teen sexploitation" film.

The 'Talk'

When should your child know the differences between males and females and the facts of reproduction? Generally speaking, if your child hasn't learned the "birds and the bees" by the time he is 10 years old, you have no time to lose. Why? Because he will soon hear it from somebody else. And if he hasn't heard your values, he will probably accept somebody else's attitudes about sex.

To help you talk about sex with your child, I will address some of parents' most common queries in a question-and-answer format.

How can I be an approachable parent?
The first thing you need to do is read some adult-level books that fill in any gaps in knowledge you may have. Read up on the subject to more than your heart's content. The idea is to know the topic to the point that it isn't strange or mysterious to you.

But what should I do if I don't know the answer to one of my kid's questions?
Tell them you'll find the answer. Then, at an appropriate moment, bring up the subject again. "Oh, Kimberly, remember last week we were wondering how twins are made? I found out the answer for you."

When parents say, "I don't know," children usually assume

that's the end of the subject. If *you* bring up the topic again, they'll be really impressed. They'll know your "I don't know" was genuine. This will indicate your sincere desire to answer their questions and to have open lines of communication. That's why it's important to follow up and deliver an answer later on.

I'm embarrassed by sex. I just know my discomfort will show when I try to talk to Ryan. I'm not very good at pretending. What should I do?

The younger your child is, the easier it will be, because he won't read anything into your embarrassment. Just tell him straight out: "I want to talk to you about something very special and very holy. I've never talked about it before with anybody, so if I seem a little nervous, that's why. Grandma and Grandpa never had a conversation like this with me, so this is the first time I've talked about it with anybody."

Plunge right into it and get the focus of attention off you and onto the subject. The next words out of your mouth should be "Do you know how babies are made?"

If your child is close to puberty, she's going to be embarrassed about the subject. She's probably agonizing in private over the physical and emotional changes she's noted in herself. Wherever she is right now, she may be wondering, *Where were you when I needed you?*

You might start out by saying, "Sally, I can tell your body is well on the way to womanhood by now. I probably should have talked to you sooner, but you know the saying, 'Better late than never.' Before you grow up anymore, I want to make sure you understand why God made your body the way He did." Then proceed candidly.

Again, focus on the information you are imparting; in this case, emphasize God's plan for sexuality. Even if Sally is a senior in high school and you can reasonably expect that she studied human reproduction in 10th grade, she'll be interested in hearing the biological information again. She may not show it, though.

In fact, Sally may frown and say, "Mom, I've known all that for years." Your reply should be, "Well, good. I wanted to make sure you knew. I want to be certain you have accurate information. Your future happiness will depend in part on how you use that information, you know. And I truly want you to be happy. Your Dad and I have lived through 20 years of marriage, and we've learned a few things. If any of our knowledge can help you, we want you to ask."

My children are six and seven. They seem too innocent. I don't think they need to be burdened with all this yet.

What is "all this"? Is knowing that God made every part of their body for a special purpose a burden? It shouldn't be. Is knowing someday they will probably get married a burden? It shouldn't be, and they should be absorbing some basic principles.

For example, they can know that marriage is forever, that one of its major purposes is to take care of the children God causes to be born, and that a lot of self-sacrifice is involved in marriage. Children need to learn these truths from the very first time they start thinking about marriage and the differences between mothers and fathers. They start noticing those differences by age four, whether they tell you about it or not.

You are not "bothering" them when you tell them they are temples of the Holy Spirit, created by God for a special purpose. In fact, if they get to 15 or 16 and don't know that yet, they will have a real burden in trying to understand why they are the way they are.

I know my child is hearing things on the streets, but he hasn't approached me. I don't know how to bring up the subject, but I want to. Any suggestions?

Create a situation involving both you and the child, such as watching a wildlife program on TV that includes reproduction. You could also rent a video. Or take the child with you as you pay a social call on a new mother. Driving there and back alone with your child, start a conversation about where babies come from. Discussions like this can be helpful in telling you what your child already knows.

If you know somebody whose cat has kittens, ask if you can come see them. I've never known a child who didn't think kittens were adorable, and the sight of nursing kittens gives the child a reassurance about the subject of reproduction. I was always grateful to the neighbors who convinced my mother that we should see kittens being born.

My mother was visiting us and heard me answering my four-year-old's questions in the bathtub about the different parts of the body and what they do. I was giving simple but frank answers. My mom hit the roof. She says I never knew anything until I was a teenager, and why should I do anything different with my daughter. What do I say?

The first thing you need to say is "Mom, I love the way you raised me," or something positive about your upbringing. Continue this way: "But Mom, the world I grew up in was so much simpler. My husband and I have talked about how dangerous it is today, and we've decided to answer all of our child's questions. We think this is the best way to protect her against getting wrong ideas."

If the subject isn't laid to rest easily, point out that children whose parents talk to them are *less* preoccupied with sexuality than children whose parents stay mum on the subject.

I'm divorced, but my ex-husband sees the children regularly. My 10-year-old son seems to get along much better with his father. I'm afraid that if I try to talk to my son, he'll reject me. Should I go ahead anyway?

Assuming your husband has the same values—chastity, self-control—as you do, then there's something to be said for asking your husband to bring up the subject. On the other hand, if your husband has worldly ideas, you might try gently introducing a book to your boy, such as Jamie Buckingham's *Let's Talk About Life*. When he reads it, say you're willing to discuss the subject further. Use a light touch, but be straightforward. Explain that because you love him, you want him to have the facts, both about his body and the moral consequences of premarital sex.

My daughter is 13, and I think some of the girls in her crowd are pretty fast. Every time I try to talk to her about Christian values, she pooh-poohs me. She says the "new morality" gives women what men have always had—equality in sexual behavior—and that she's not going to be bound by some medieval standard of morality. How do I respond?

With prayer to begin with—incessant prayer that the Holy Spirit will touch her heart. But you also need some practical tips.

Such a girl seems to be a victim of women's lib and the Planned Parenthood agenda—that the individual can decide his or her own values. Somebody needs to tell her that the sexual revolution is the worst joke ever played on women by men. Even some prominent feminists agree.

Go to the public library and thumb through some back issues of *Ms.* or *Cosmopolitan* magazine. Find an article making the same statement. Bring home a photocopy, but don't present it to her with a flourish and say, "I told you so." Wait for the right moment, then present the article in love, without being pushy. She'll probably want to talk to you right away.

Is there anyone in your circle of acquaintances whom she respects? Maybe one of them can talk to her. Does she associate with the youth group at church? If so, talk privately with the youth pastor and clue him into the situation. He might arrange to stage a conversation on sexuality when she's present.

One point he might mention is it's far easier for a man to repent and change a promiscuous lifestyle than it is for a woman. Why? Because women become much more emotionally involved in sex than men, and once she has tarnished her reputation, her self-esteem takes a nosedive. When a young girl has a certain "reputation," she practically has to move to another state to change it. It's extremely difficult to live down gossip in the peer grapevine.

I just found out the school nurse gave my daughter's fifth-grade class a lecture on "safe sex" last week. My daughter is wondering why I never told her about family planning.

"Family planning" for children is a euphemism for giving a false sense of security to fornication. Sex education advocates imagine (or pretend to imagine) that by giving out contraceptives and encouraging young people to use them, they are protecting children against the consequences of their actions.

Nothing could be further from the truth. Armed with a false sense of protection, young people plunge into promiscuity, and we end up with the highest teen pregnancy rate in the world.

Did you know this lecture on "safe sex" was coming to the fifth grade? If you didn't, you might want to talk to the school principal and your school board to protest this invasion of parental rights.

I think it's unrealistic to expect our kids to wait until marriage before having sex. Fact is, I wasn't a virgin at my own marriage. Why should I expect my son or daughter to wait until marriage?

Because you love them, and you want them to have a better, happier, more virtuous life than you. Children can become self-fulfilling prophecies—they will act as they believe you acted. Listen to what one mother told me:

"When I was about 15 years old, I was having a conversation with my mother. She told me no one was a virgin when they got married and I wouldn't be either. Up until that time, I thought my mom, who was a Christian, expected me to be a virgin until I was married.

"To me, her comment was like a license to go ahead and lose my virginity—and I did, a short time later. I'm not putting the entire blame on my mother. The main thing I want to convey is that parents must be careful what they say to their kids."

Bearing Fruit

One thing is important: our children need to know that we, their parents, care passionately about their character and lifestyle. We care through our instruction, our love and our actions. They may rebel, but deep down, kids have a way of expecting of themselves what parents expect of them.

Some may reject our teaching and depart from the path of righteousness. But sooner or later, they will find themselves unhappy. And then, in a dark moment, the Spirit of the Lord will be able to bring to their mind our words, our example and our love.

They will know where they need to turn. And in that moment, though it may be years later, the rebelliousness will be forgotten, and the teaching and the caring will bear their fruit.

26

SEND YOUR CHILDREN TO ANOTHER WORLD THIS SUMMER

Ray Seldomridge

Pulcifer had a problem. Despite the efforts of his parents, teachers and the local librarian, he simply could not stop reading books, so he never had time for TV.

"When I was your age, you couldn't pry me away from the television set," said Pulcifer's disappointed father. "I'd always hoped that my own son would follow in my footsteps."

What finally happened to Pulcifer? You'll have to read *The Problem with Pulcifer* by Florence Parry Heide to find out. (*Groan.*) This is a trick to send you off to the public library, where you can find out about the summer reading program for your children. Unless Pulcifer is your child, you may need to offer a little encouragement to your young readers. Before stores start advertising "Back to School" sales, you still have time to show your kids that reading can be fun.

More parents and children than ever before are turning to reading as a good summer pastime. Last year, 750 boys and girls in a small town not far from Los Angeles, California, read 12,000 books over an eight-week period. Enrollment in the library's reading club had doubled in just three years, and a lecture by Jim Trelease (author of *The Read-Aloud Handbook*) drew a packed auditorium of interested parents.

So don't believe it when you hear someone say this is the age of video, and all kids do nowadays is sit in front of the TV. Children's books are rolling off the presses in record numbers, and parents are snatching up armloads of them faster than compact disks.

Few of these parents have ever read an essay or article on why books are important—ponderous prose from an educator saying things like "books teach children basic moral values" or "reading will broaden your child's perspective and give him a zest for life." Those statements are as boring as they are true. Instead, parents understand the value of reading because they themselves are readers.

"It doesn't take an educational study," writes Betsy Hearne in *Choosing Books for Children*, "to show that children do what you do, not what you tell them to do. If you like to read to yourself and your children, they will like reading to themselves and their children."

On a similar note, Jim Trelease tells his predominantly female audiences that if Dad always picks up a ball instead of a book, his children may be getting the message that athletics are more important than reading.

Suppose you *are* a bookworm, and the local library has a summer program that promises glittering prizes to kids who will read. What if your son or daughter still hasn't heard the siren call? Well, there's a number of ways you might successfully beckon a child into this world of unimaginable delights. Here are a few ideas:

Capitalize on your child's other interests. If your eight-year-old son wants to do nothing but play computer games, show him a book or two on BASIC programming. Maybe he'll create his own games and learn a lot while doing it. Or if your 12-year-old daughter spends most of her time trying on clothes, a book like *Just Victoria* (published by David C. Cook) will catch her interest as she relates to another girl who's becoming boy-conscious.

Offer to extend bedtime for the purpose of reading. During the summer months, it won't hurt to have even a five-year-old go to sleep a half-hour later than usual. But the child has to be in his or her bed, quietly reading or looking at the pictures during that time. If your son or daughter takes you up on this offer, be ready to provide a bedside lamp and lots of good print materials.

Reward book reading with . . . more books!. Tell your kids that for every five (or two, or 10) books they read, you'll let them pick out a new one for purchase at the bookstore. If you aren't terribly rich, you may need to limit their selection to quality paperbacks. But children who have a chance to build their own libraries are more likely to become lifetime page-turners.

Read aloud as a family. Whether your children are infants or high-schoolers, reading aloud together is indispensable. And everyone is doing it! Professors at Oxford University read literature to their students, just as Ezra the scribe got the nation of Israel off to a fresh start by reading aloud the law of Moses for six hours straight (Nehemiah 8:1–3).

Try to read aloud every night. You will find it an easy habit to stick to, as long as you select books that appeal to you as much as they do to your kids.

Leave books lying around the house. What do you suppose would happen if you put boxes of chocolates by the telephone, in the bathroom and on the kitchen table? Presto, they'd get eaten. Likewise, colorful, interesting books left in these places will get read. Try it, and don't forget to change the books (from the library, of course) every week. Also be sure your home has at least one good reading area and a book rack full of assorted temptations.

Build reading into your family traditions. Already many families celebrate Christmas Day by reading the Nativity story in Luke 2, and even Dickens' *Christmas Carol*. But family life is full of other settings that need a good book for a crowning jewel. Try sharing *Charlotte's Web* together at the time of the county fair, or *Mr. Revere and I* on July 4th.

All these ideas are worth your attention if you want books to play an important role in your children's development. But two bits of advice should also be mentioned:

- You will probably have to limit TV viewing hours. Children who eat junk food aren't as likely to touch their dinners, or to read books, if they've been lulled into passivity by Pandora's electronic box.
- Don't hurry your children into reading. If encouraged by read-aloud parents and enticed by available books, they will read when they are good and ready. One distraught mother told Jim Trelease that her four-year-old had failed to become a reader. He quickly replied, "Obviously a case of brain damage."

  "Really?" she asked with furrowed brow.

  "Yes," he said, keeping a straight face. "*Yours!*"

Just suppose that motivation is no problem. You and your eager child would rather go to the library than to Disneyland. But neither one of you knows which books are worth reading. Sound familiar? Then here are some pointers.

Let each library trip become an adventure. Wander the aisles together and familiarize yourselves with the types of books available. Are you looking for picture books for the very young, beginning readers for your six- to eight-year-old, or short novels for the later lementary grades? Does your son or daughter want suspenseful mysteries, sports stories, hobby books, fantasies, classics, biographies, historical fiction, poetry, animal tales, folklore, factual science books, or a mixture of these?

Let your children decide. You can help guide them in their reading tastes, but ultimately only *they* know what they want. Encourage a variety of reading so that they learn what's available.

Trust your judgment. "Taste" a page or two. If a book seems to be lacking, put it down and try another. Dabble a lot.

Go for whatever is good and uplifting. Naturally, your first impulse will be to look for books from Christian publishers. If so, search for those that are well-written and have interesting, believable characters (rather than being "preachy").

Try such tales as *The Tanglewoods' Secret* by Patricia M. St. John or *A Horse Named Cinnamon* by Jeanne Bovde. Also, don't forget the many creative Bible story books, including Tomie de Paola's *Queen Esther* for younger children.

Much so-called "secular" literature also abounds with Christian moral values and theological truths. Don't miss this treasure trove, which includes *Little House on the Prairie, Robinson Crusoe, Anne of Green Gables* and dozens of other gems.

Moreover, don't fear such fantastic tales as C. S. Lewis' *Chronicles of Narnia* or Robert Siegel's *Alpha Centauri*. As you may know, much of today's fantasy literature is abhorrent because it dwells upon evil and glorifies ungodliness. But Christian fantasy parallels Scripture itself in the effective and proper use of "good vs. evil" imagery. Such stories help young readers grasp at a deeply emotional level the fact that evil cannot ultimately triumph. (Some well-meaning Christian parents avoid anything to do with fire-breathing dragons, forgetting that this symbol for evil is used in the Bible itself—in Revelation 12:7. What matters is that the dragon is defeated!)

Get recommendations. Ask your friends about the books they've read. Scan the library's recommended reading lists. You may even want to obtain a copy of *Books Children Love* by Elizabeth Wilson (Crossway, 1987), a fine annotated bibliography written especially for Christian parents.

Okay, okay. Here's what happened to Pulcifer. He was sent to a special corrective remedial class for non-TV watchers, and then to a psychiatrist. Neither ploy worked.

"We've done all we can," said his mother. "No one can say we haven't tried."

Assured by his father that they loved him anyway, Pulcifer "settled down comfortably with his new stack of library books."

End of story. But not a bad beginning for you and your children this summer.

27

WHO'S MINDING THE KIDS?

Beth Spring

B ehind the one-way mirror, a team of psychologists is taking notes. Peering through the glass, they watch a mother place her one-year-old son on the floor in the middle of the room. After a few minutes, another woman, who is a stranger to the infant, enters from a side door. The mother quietly exits, leaving her baby with the stranger. She returns a few minutes later, but then she and the woman leave the room together.

During the entire experiment, the psychologists are studying the baby. Does he crawl quickly toward the mother when she comes back in? Does he wish to be comforted right away? Does he avoid the mother? Does he crawl toward her, and then veer away?

All of these responses mean something to child psychologists, who use this procedure known as "Strange Situation" to measure the attachment of infants to their mothers.

According to Dr. Jay Belsky, a Penn State University psychologist who has been researching the effects of infant child care for 10 years, a baby forms an attachment with the person who provides his main care—typically the mother—during his first year of life. This relationship helps the infant learn what to expect from people.

If a mother responds promptly—and in the same manner—every time her infant cries for food or comfort, she cultivates what Belsky calls a "secure attachment." The infant trusts the mother and is assured by her predictability and availability. She functions as a "haven of safety" from which the infant can confidently move out and explore his environment.

Studies have shown that secure infants tend to greet Mom after being separated, and they are comforted by her. Insecure babies, however, actively avoid eye contact and physical contact with the mother. Some will even push her away after first seeking her out. Insecurely attached babies are also more likely to cry or push away a toy offered in comfort.

According to Belsky, numerous studies show that these babies "generally look less competent as they grow older." As toddlers and preschoolers, they tend to be less cooperative, compliant and self-controlled than the secure infants. As five- and six-year-olds, they appear to run a greater risk of developing behavior problems. Some research indicates this is especially true for boys.

A Growing Concern

It's little wonder that parents—especially those who both work—are keenly interested in the effects of child care. Since 1972, married women with children under three years of age have been the fastest-growing segment of the job market. Surveys show that most working parents have difficulty finding good care. They also indicate that mothers who are dissatisfied with their child care arrangements are more prone to employee absenteeism and unproductive work time.

Overnight, child care has become the hottest family issue of the '80s. Unlike topics such as national defense or trade policy, child care is an emotional issue that strikes millions of voters where they live—the home.

For many families, Mom's paycheck keeps home and hearth together. Couples with children have been steadily losing economic ground to the rest of the population, says a recent Congressional Budget Office report. A stagnation in real earnings for young men between 1973 and 1985 sent millions of wives into the work force to defend household living standards.

Many young couples have either postponed childbearing or reduced family size to maintain their standard of living. Those who have young families have turned to substitute care arrangements, such as a local day-care center, a relative's home or non-accredited (and cheaper) care at a neighbor's house. Sooner or later, though, working mothers ask the inevitable question: Does my care arrangement help or harm my child?

Specialists who research this topic are deeply divided. They tend to agree, however, that America faces many unknowns about the next generation.

Studies, such as those conducted by Professor Belsky, do indicate differences between children in day care and those raised "traditionally" at home. The findings are not encouraging for working mothers. One study reported that children under 18 months old who spend 20 or more hours a week in day care lose their sense of security. Another revealed that children in full-time day care may have poorer study skills and lower self-esteem when they reach the primary grades.

Various Circumstances

But other social scientists say that child care, per se, is not to blame for bad behavior or a poor attachment with the mother. Instead, they point to low-quality care and the high turnover prevalent among day-care employees who move on to better-paying jobs. The behavior of the day-care children, when compared with those raised at home, does not indicate maladjustment, these experts say. Rather, it simply indicates that children learn to cope with their circumstances in different ways.

Because the opinions are so divided, it's rare for any professional in this field of research to say that it is best for children to be raised by their mothers. However, even the studies that advocate day care say that centers should strive to come as close as possible to a cozy, secure, stimulating environment with a low child-teacher ratio. In other words, the day-care center should provide the kind of care a child would receive at home.

"Pressures to expand the supply and depress the costs of child care have consistently shortchanged efforts to improve the quality," says Dr. Deborah Phillips, a University of Virginia psychologist and strong advocate of day care. Child care outside the home is here to stay, Phillips and her colleagues maintain. So the question must be: How can we make child care better?

Early Studies

Child development theory indicates that young children require a close, loving and sustained relationship with one or two people—usually their parents—to ensure a normal upbringing. An early landmark study by John Bowlby in 1951 said that every infant and young child needs "a warm, intimate, and continuous relationship with his mother, in which both can find satisfaction and enjoyment."

When women began entering the work force in earnest in the '60s and '70s, studies about the effects of day care were scarce. Substitute care was viewed as a necessity for mothers compelled to work because of financial need.

Public opinion about day care began to shift in the 1970s, as more middle-class and professional mothers returned to work. At the same time, the rights of women to equal pay and equal job opportunities became an overriding public policy issue. Pressure to accommodate working women by providing child care colored early attempts to study the impact of day care, and it continues to cloud the issue today.

Psychological studies about the immediate effects of day care on young children were summarized by Professor Belsky and Lawrence Steinberg in 1978. Belsky and Steinberg concluded that day care neither helped nor harmed the intellectual development of the child. They found that day care did not appear to disrupt a child's emotional attachment with his mother.

At the same time, this report contained several cautions. Studies awarding day care "clean bills of health" were often those conducted in high-quality, university-based centers with experienced staff members. These centers did not accurately reflect the typical care choices of working mothers.

Ten years ago, Professors Belsky and Steinberg drew this conclusion: "To even say that the jury is still out on day care would be, in our view, premature and naively optimistic. The fact of the matter is, quite frankly, that the majority of the evidence has yet to be presented, much less subpoenaed."

A Change of Heart

The caution lights flicked on by Belsky a decade ago have not gone away; in fact, further research has illuminated new problems with child care. Belsky grew increasingly uncomfortable with his early convictions each time he updated his day-care files. "Evidence kept crossing my desk which was directly at odds with conclusions I had reached in my original analysis," he said. "New findings showed that children of day care were at risk for heightened aggression, noncompliance and possible social withdrawal."

In 1986, Belsky broke with his cautiously neutral message in the 1978 study. It is virtually impossible, he pointed out, to isolate the effects of day care from all other influences in a child's life. He stated: "A relatively persuasive circumstantial case can be made that early infant care may be associated with increased avoidance of the mother, possibly to the point of greater insecurity in the attachment relationship, and that such care may also be associated with diminished compliance and cooperation with adults, increased aggressiveness, and possibly even greater social maladjustment in the preschool and early school-age years."

No Easy Answers

It is clear that American families have embarked on an immense social experiment in the last two decades. By the time the experiment has proceeded long enough for researchers to draw conclusions about long-term effects, it will be too late to change the circumstances of the children enrolled in day care.

Perhaps the most realistic advice is that parents ought to exercise extreme caution when making decisions about how to best raise their children. Ultimately, it is up to parents to do all they can to raise secure, stable offspring. The choices they make about employment and child care are critical in that process.

❦ INSIGHT ❦

Tips for Parents Who Must Work

Statistics about working mothers often leave an all-or-nothing impression. When it is reported that more than 60 percent of women with children under age 18 are in the work force, there is a tendency to view them as 40-hour-a-week wage earners with little choice other than institutionalized day care for their preschoolers. In fact, a substantial number of working mothers find ways to achieve a balance between working and staying home with their kids.

Many work part-time, or full-time for only a portion of the year. Some trade off child care with their husbands, taking advantage of flexible hours on the job. Others work at home while caring for their children.

The Bureau of Labor Statistics shows 54 percent of all preschool children have mothers home full-time. Among the rest, 11 percent are cared for by a relative, 10 percent are in a family day-care home, and 3 percent have baby sitters in their homes. Only 11 percent go to community day-care centers.

If both parents must work outside the home, here are some guidelines to consider:

- *Try to remain at home with a child for as long as possible during his infancy*. Studies repeatedly show that emotional attachment to the mother takes place during a baby's first 12 months of life. Being in substitute care will not replace or destroy the child's bond with his mother, but it may weaken it so that a child will avoid or resist contact with his mother after being separated from her.

   Being at home during the crucial early months of a child's development benefits parents as well. The National Association for the Education of Young Children points out that it takes time to begin to feel competent as a parent. Learning a baby's routine, reading his signals, and knowing what he likes and dislikes will help parents choose substitute care more confidently.

- *Avoid placing a baby in child care for the first time when he or she is between eight and 12 months of age*. This is the period when separation anxiety is the strongest. It is a milestone point in child development when the baby has established an emotional attachment to Mom and is keenly aware of her absence.

- *Consider all the child care alternatives:* a sitter who comes to the home or even lives there; care in another person's home with or without other children present; and a community or church-run day-care center. Each type of care has advantages and drawbacks.

Care in the child's home is apt to be the most expensive, and it requires good communication and a high level of compatibility with the family. It has the advantage of offering a child familiar surroundings, continuity, and a more flexible schedule.

The quality of care in another person's home may vary greatly. If only one adult is present, it is difficult to discover abuse, neglect, or routines which may not benefit the child, such as sustained television viewing. The care provider may or may not be licensed and meet state regulations.

This type of care, however, can be more convenient. Often, an elderly neighbor or a woman down the street with one child of her own will take in extra kids. If she is loving, creative and interested in the child, his development can be nearly the same as if he were raised solely at home.

Finally, group care in a day-care center is the fastest growing option for working parents. Centers can provide safe, interesting environments for children to explore, with plenty of appropriate toys, games and activities. Situations in which each adult cares for no more than four children, especially for infants, are ideal.

- *Spend time with the care provider being considered.* Observe how she (or he) responds to the child's smiles, conversation and activities. A good sitter enjoys being with the child, talks cheerfully and initiates games. Assess the person's values, interests and energy level. Most importantly, choose someone who is willing to commit themselves long-term. Switching from one arrangement to another is very unsettling for young children.

- *Contact other parents whose children have been, or are, in the care of the sitter you are considering.* Ask them about her reliability, flexibility and maturity. What sort of discipline does she use? Has she ever lost her temper on the job?

- *Insist on being able to visit the sitter's home or the day-care center without notice.* Pay several surprise visits there before and after placing your child.
- *Take a good look at the surroundings.* Is the home or building clean and safe for children to explore? Do the children go outdoors regularly? Are there appropriate, unbroken toys for various age groups? Does the center meet state standards? Is it licensed, and if not, why not?

  Many church-based day-care centers may be exempt from licensing because government cannot regulate ministry activities. Still other church centers may refuse licenses on theological grounds.
- *If a neighbor or relative cares for the child, the agreement should still be approached as a business contract.* Agree ahead of time on payment, as well as arrangements for holidays, vacation and sick leave.
- *Maintain close communication with the care provider, exchanging observations about the child's progress and interests.* Children in the care of substitute moms can thrive if their situations resemble ordinary, busy, enthusiastic households.

  Child care appears to work best when the parent and sitter consider themselves partners in child rearing. Let the sitter or teacher know that their work is appreciated.

28

AND A LITTLE CHILD SHALL LEAD THEM

Mark Cutshall

S he was only three years old. Beaming smile. Eyes alive. There in the rest home, the little girl stood with her grandmother next to the man in the wheelchair.

He was in the twilight of life. Everette Rao had not smiled in weeks. Eyes that once sparkled now stared into space. The girl, Jennifer Turnidge, could not see that a brain tumor was slowly ushering life out of his body. "Brother Everette, I've brought someone to see you," said the grandmother.

Slowly, the 55-year-old terminally ill man turned his head. Hoping he still had a glimmer of vision, Florence Turnidge pointed down to a small, cherubic face. Everette's eyes responded. A grin crept across his face. All around the room, the feeling was contagious.

"The nurses told me they hadn't seen him smile like that in weeks," said Florence. That day at Seattle's Crista Nursing Center, a child had done what medicine, nurses and even a trickle of caring visitors had not been able to accomplish—bring a flicker of happiness and hope to a lonely, dying man.

For 70-year-old Florence, Brother Everette represents thousands of ailing or elderly people in America's nursing homes who are living out their remaining days alone. And though many of the nation's aging—including those living in rest homes—enjoy fruitful relationships with friends and relatives, others are forgotten by their families. They are often left to wander in a world of empty halls and quiet rooms.

Love Being Shared

Today, the hallways and the faces at the Crista nursing home are shining brighter because a little child and her grandmother are busy spreading an infectious brand of love.

"The first time Jennifer reached out and took Brother Everette's hand," recalls Florence, "I saw his face come alive. I said, 'Lord, there's a ministry here for children who can bring hope to the elderly, and I want to be a part of it!'"

For years, many people have assumed that "rest home" rhymed with "keep out." Florence, however, believes otherwise. Every Thursday afternoon she unites laughing children with lonely elderly people as she walks with Jennifer and her eight-year-old brother, Jason, the two blocks from her north Seattle home to the nursing center. It is a weekly pilgrimage of joy that began, ironically, on a rocky path of personal grief when Florence's mother died in 1983.

"We were inseparable prayer partners," remembers Florence. "She was my spiritual mentor, and next to my husband, my dearest friend. When she died, I thought I would be very brave. But after two years I still felt terrible waves of loneliness come over me. 'Lord,' I said, 'I've got to do something about this.'"

The Lord prescribed a large dose of generosity for Florence's hurting heart.

"My grief was too great to handle alone, so I decided to walk over to the nearby rest home. There I met older, widowed women like Mother, who somehow didn't have a loving family to look after them. I thought to myself, 'This is where I belong.'"

At Crista, Florence visited Everette Rao, a Bible scholar from India with whom she had led prayer groups for 12 years. "For a long time he was able to converse. Eventually, though, his health worsened. It got to the point where his hollow eyes looked straight through me. One day, I walked back home and said, 'Lord, I'll keep going to see Brother Everette, but it's going to be terribly hard. I've got to have grace, because I can't stand it.'

"As I walked on, the Lord whispered to my heart that Brother Everette loved children. That was it! I came right home and phoned my granddaughter. I said, 'Jennifer, I have a friend at the rest home, and you can make him happy. And if you make him happy, you'll make Jesus happy.'"

Since that first trip to Brother Everette's room, Jennifer and her brother, Jason, have brought joy to scores of residents at the nursing center.

"Often, you can feel an immediate emotional bond between the kids and the elderly," says Florence. "There is something about children that brings new life and enthusiasm to the elderly."

Walk down the hall with Jennifer and Jason, and see how that hope comes to life:

- Mrs. Gladys Rowe, an 89-year-old widow from Middlebury, Ind., sits on her bed and greets the two children who run into her room. "They get up on my lap and hug me, and I love them. It's greater than being a millionaire—I'm just crazy about them."
- Miss Evelyn Danielson, a retired bookkeeper, can't recall any children other than Jennifer and Jason who have visited her in the past nine years. "They were very cute. They sang me a song, and I enjoyed it very much."
- Jennifer and Jason knock on the door of Olga Hagstrom. She has a photo album filled with a sea of young relatives, yet her calendar is filled with blank days. "I have 11 grandchildren, but I don't see my own two children as often as these two kids. I love it," said Olga.
- The children walk outside and find a man they've come to know as "Little Paul." He proudly tells them he is 101 years old. Since his wife died five years ago, Paul's only permanent companion is a wooden cane. On this one afternoon, however, his "family" is made larger by two new members who hold his hand and sing him a song:

Don't try and tell me that God is dead,
He woke me up this morning.
Don't try and tell me that God is dead,
He lives within my heart . . .

Not all the visits are pleasant ones. This spring, Mr. King, a favorite grandpa of Jennifer and Jason's, died of cancer.

"Confronting death is the hardest of all," says Florence. "The kids could see him getting sicker and sicker. They know, however, they'll be with him forever in heaven. And they know they still have Mrs. King to visit."

Through her own family crisis, Florence Turnidge knows that even death cannot stand in the way of a child who wants to reach out in love.

"When Jason was born, his mother developed gangrene. The doctors said Diane might make it. However, they said there was no hope that Jason would survive."

For 16 days after Jason's birth, both mother and child stood at death's door. Miraculously, Jason and his mom made it. Today, both live healthy, active lives. Among the many people who interceded for the two was Brother Everette, who stayed awake one entire night praying that Jason and his mom would live.

Jason's dad told his son the events surrounding his birth. Within a few days, the young boy came to his grandmother. "Grandma, can I go thank Brother Everette for praying for me?" Grandma said yes by taking Jason to see the man whose prayers had contributed to the boy's miraculous healing.

❦ INSIGHT ❦

How can you make your first visit to a nursing home with children a positive experience? Liz Neufeld, former volunteer coordinator for the Crista Nursing Center in Seattle, offers these common-sense answers to four often-asked questions.

1. How young can a child be? Kids can be as young as two. Age is not as important as the child's readiness. Hyperactive children, for instance, present more of a risk. They may overreact to an older person watching them and become nervous. It's important to create an atmosphere in which both child and older adult feel comfortable.

2. *How long should our visits last?* Ten to 15 minutes is reasonable. Think quality, not quantity. A child and a nursing home resident can experience love and natural acceptance within moments after meeting. Likewise, establishing a meaningful rapport often takes only minutes.

3. *How should we prepare for our visit?* If the child is old enough to understand, explain where and when you'll be going, as well as why you're visiting. Wheelchairs and walkers may seem threatening to small children. Share with them that the Lord has provided these helps so that older people can live with dignity and purpose.

4. *What if I don't have a child or grandchild?* Ask a little friend from your neighborhood or church to be your special partner. If he or she doesn't have grandparents, then the visit will be all the more meaningful because of the grandma or grandpa they are bound to "adopt."

PART FIVE

FOCUS ON TEENAGERS

29

SURVIVING YOUR CHILD'S STORMY TEEN YEARS

Dr. James C. Dobson

In my second film series entitled, "Turn Your Heart Toward Home," I offered this advice to parents of teenagers: "Get 'em through it." That may not sound like such a stunning idea, but I believe it has merit for most families—especially those with one or more tough-minded kids. The concept is a bit obscure, so I will resort to a couple of pictures to illustrate my point.

When parents of strong-willed children look ahead to the adolescent river, they often perceive it to be like this:

9   10   11   12   13   14   15   16   17
Ages

195

In other words, they expect the early encounter with rapids to give way to swirling currents and life-threatening turbulence. If that doesn't turn over their teenagers' boat, they seem destined to drown farther downstream when they plunge over the falls.

Fortunately, the typical journey is much safer than anticipated. Most often it flows like this:

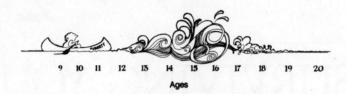

What I'm saying is that the river usually descends not into the falls, but into smooth water once more. Even though your teenager may be splashing and thrashing and gasping for air, it is not likely that his boat will capsize. It is more buoyant than you might think.

Yes, a few individuals do go over the falls, usually because of drug abuse. Some of them even climb back in the canoe and paddle on down the river. In fact, the greatest danger of sinking the boat could come from . . . *you!*

This warning is addressed particularly to idealistic and perfectionistic parents who are determined to make their adolescents—*all* of them—perform and achieve and measure up to the highest standard. A perfectionist, by the way, is a person who takes great pains with what he does and then gives them to everyone else. In so doing, he rocks a boat that is already threatened by the rapids.

Perhaps another child could handle the additional turbulence, but our concern is for the unsteady kid—the one who lacks common sense for a while and may even lean toward irrational behavior. Don't unsettle his boat any more than you must!

I'm reminded of a waitress who recognized me when I came into the restaurant where she worked. She was not busy that day and wanted to talk about her 12-year-old daughter. As a single mother, she had gone through severe struggles with the girl, whom she identified as being *very* strong-willed.

"We have fought tooth and nail for this entire year," she said. "It has been awful! We argue nearly every night, and most of our fights are over the same issue."

I asked her what had caused the conflict, and she replied, "My daughter is still a little girl, but she wants to shave her legs. I feel she's too young to be doing that, and she becomes so angry that she won't even talk to me. This has been the worst year of our lives together."

I looked at the waitress and exclaimed, "Lady, buy your daughter a razor!"

That 12-year-old girl was paddling into a time of life that would rock her canoe good and hard. As a single parent, Mom would soon be trying to keep this rebellious kid from getting into drugs, alcohol, sex and pregnancy, early marriage, school failure and the possibility of running away. Truly, there would be many ravenous alligators in her river within a year or two. In that setting, it seemed unwise to make a big deal over what was essentially a non-issue.

While I agreed with the mother that adolescence should not be rushed into prematurely, there were higher goals than maintaining a proper developmental timetable.

I have seen other parents fight similar battles over nonessentials, such as the purchase of a first bra for a flat-chested pre-adolescent girl.

For goodness sake! If she wants it that badly, she probably needs it for social reasons. Run, don't walk, to the nearest department store and buy her a bra.

Plenty of Real Issues

The objective, as Charles and Andy Stanley wrote, is to *keep your kids on your team*. Don't throw away your friendship over behavior that has no great moral significance. There will be plenty of real issues that require you to stand like a rock. Save your big guns for those crucial confrontations.

Let me make it very clear, again, that this advice is not relevant to every teenager. The compliant kid who is doing wonderfully in school, has great friends, is disciplined in his conduct and loves his parents is not nearly so delicate. Perhaps his parents can urge him to reach even higher standards in his achievements and lifestyle.

My concern, however, is for that youngster who *could* go over the falls. He is intensely angry at home and is being influenced by a carload of crummy friends. Be very careful with him. Pick and choose what is worth fighting for, and settle for something less than perfection on issues that don't really matter. *Just get him through it!*

What does this mean in practical terms? It may indicate a willingness to let his room look like a junkyard for awhile. Does that surprise you? I don't like lazy, sloppy, undisciplined kids any more than you do, but given the possibilities for chaos that this angry boy or girl might precipitate, spit-shined rooms may not be all that important.

The philosophy we applied with our teenagers (and you might try with yours) can be called "loosen and tighten." By this I mean we tried to loosen our grip on everything that had no lasting significance, and tighten down on everything that did. We said "yes" whenever we possibly could, to give support to the occasional "no." And most importantly, we tried never to get too far away from our kids emotionally.

You Need to Be There

It is simply not prudent to write off a son or daughter, no matter how foolish, irritating, selfish or insane a child may seem to be. You need to be there not only while their canoe is bouncing precariously, but after the river runs smooth again.

You have the remainder of your life to reconstruct the relationship that is now in jeopardy. Don't let anger fester for too long. Make the first move toward reconciliation. And try hard not to hassle your kids. They *hate* to be nagged. If you follow them around with one complaint after another, they are almost forced to protect themselves by appearing deaf.

And finally, continue to treat them with respect, even when punishment or restrictions are necessary. Occasionally, you may even need to say, "I'm sorry!"

My father found it very difficult to say those words. I remember working with him in the back yard when I was 15 years of age, on a day when he was particularly irritable for some reason. I probably deserved his indignation, but I thought he was being unfair. He crabbed at me for everything I did, even when I hustled. Finally, he yelled at me for something petty, and that did it. He capsized my canoe. I threw down the rake, and quit. Defiantly I walked across our property and down the street while my dad demanded that I come back.

It was one of the few times I ever took him on like that! I meandered around town for awhile, wondering what would happen to me when I finally went home. Then I strolled over to my cousin's house on the other side of town. After several hours there, I admitted to his father that I had had a bad fight with my dad and he didn't know where I was. My uncle persuaded me to call home and assure my parents that I was safe. With knees quaking, I phoned my dad.

"Stay there," he said, "I'm coming over."

To say that I was apprehensive for the next few minutes would be an understatement. In a short time Dad arrived and asked to see me alone.

"Bo," he began, "I didn't treat you right this afternoon. I was riding your back for no good reason, and I want you to know I'm sorry. Your mom and I want you to come on home now."

He made a friend for life.

Maintain a Reserve Army

A good military general will never commit all his troops to combat at the same time. He maintains a reserve force that can relieve the exhausted soldiers when they falter on the front lines. I wish parents of adolescents would implement the same strategy. Instead, they commit every ounce of their energy and every second of their time to the business of living, holding nothing in reserve for the challenge of the century. It is a classic mistake which can be disastrous for parents of strong-willed adolescents. Let me explain.

The problem begins with a basic misunderstanding during the preschool years. I hear mothers say, "I don't plan to work until the kids are in kindergarten. Then I'll get a job."

They appear to believe that the heavy demands on them will end magically when they get their youngest in school. In reality, the teen years will generate as much pressure on them as did the preschool era. An adolescent turns a house upside down . . . literally and figuratively. Not only is the typical rebellion of those years an extremely stressful experience, but the chauffeuring, supervising, cooking and cleaning required to support an adolescent can be exhausting.

Someone within the family must reserve the energy to cope with those new challenges. Mom is the candidate of choice. Remember, too, that menopause and a man's mid-life crisis are scheduled to coincide with adolescence, which makes a wicked soup! It is a wise mother who doesn't exhaust herself at a time when so much is going on at home.

I know it is easier to talk about maintaining a lighter schedule than it is to secure one. It is also impractical to recommend that mothers not seek formal employment during this era. Millions of women have to work for economic reasons, including the rising number of single parents in our world. Others choose to pursue busy careers. That is a decision to be made by a woman and her husband, and I would not presume to tell them what to do.

But decisions have inevitable consequences. In this case, there are biophysical forces at work which simply must be reckoned with. If, for example, 80 percent of a woman's available energy in a given day is expended in getting dressed, driving to work, doing her job for eight or ten hours, and stopping by the grocery store on the way home—then there is only 20 percent left for everything else.

Maintenance of the family, cooking meals, cleaning the kitchen, relating to her husband and all other personal activities must be powered by that diminishing resource. It is no wonder that her batteries are spent by the end of the day. Weekends should be restful, but they are usually not. Thus, she plods through the years on her way to burnout.

troops into front-line combat. She is already exhausted, but there is no reserve on which to call. In that weakened condition, the routine stresses of raising an adolescent can be overwhelming.

Highs and Lows

Let me say it again. Raising boisterous teenagers is an exciting and rewarding but also a frustrating experience. Their radical highs and lows affect our moods. The noise, the messes, the complaints, the arguments, the sibling rivalry, the missed curfews, the paced floors, the wrecked car, the failed test, the jilted lover, the wrong friends, the busy telephone, the pizza on the carpet, the ripped new blouse, the rebellion, the slammed doors, the mean words, the tears—it's enough to drive a *rested* mother crazy.

But what about our career woman who already "gave at the office," then came home to this chaos? Any unexpected crisis or even a minor irritant can set off a torrent of emotion. There is no reserve on which to draw. In short, the parents of adolescents should save some energy with which to cope with aggravation!

Whether or not you are able to accept and implement my advice is your business. It is mine to offer it, and this is my best shot: To help you get through the turbulence of adolescence, you should:

- Keep the schedule simple.
- Get plenty of rest.
- Eat nutritious meals.
- Stay on your knees.

When fatigue leads adults to act like hot-tempered teenagers, anything can happen at home.

The Desperate Need for Fathers

It is stating the obvious, I suppose, to say that fathers of rebellious teenagers are desperately needed at home during those years. In their absence, mothers are left to handle disciplinary problems alone. This is occurring in millions of families headed by single mothers today, and I know how tough their task has become.

Not only are they doing a job that should have been shouldered by two; they must also deal with behavioral problems that fathers are more ideally suited to handle. It is generally understood that a man's larger size, deeper voice and masculine demeanor make it easier for him to deal with defiance in the younger generation.

Likewise, I believe the exercise of authority is a mantle ascribed to him by the Creator. Not only are fathers needed to provide leadership and discipline during the adolescent years, but they can be highly influential on their sons during this period of instability.

Someone has said, "Link a boy to the right man and he seldom goes wrong." I believe that is true. If a dad and his son can develop hobbies together or other common interests, the rebellious years can pass in relative tranquillity. What they experience may be remembered for a lifetime. Let me address the reader directly: What common ground are you cultivating with your impressionable son? Some fathers build or repair cars with them; some construct small models or make things in a woodshop.

My dad and I hunted and fished together. There is no way to describe what those days meant to me as we entered the woods in the early hours of the morning. How could I get angry at this man who took time to be with me? We had wonderful talks while coming home from a day of laughter and fun in the country.

I've tried to maintain that kind of contact with my son, Ryan. We're rebuilding a Model A Ford together now. We've also hunted rabbits, quail, pheasant and larger game since he turned 12. As it was with my father, Ryan and I have had some meaningful conversations while out in the fields together.

Last year, for example, we got up one morning and situated ourselves in a deer blind before the break of day. About 20 yards away from us was a feeder which operated on a timer. At 7 a.m., it automatically dropped kernels of corn into a pan below.

Ryan and I huddled together in this blind, talking softly about whatever came to mind. Then through the fog, we saw a beautiful doe emerge silently into the clearing. She took nearly 30 minutes to get to the feeder near where we were hiding. We had no intention of shooting her, but it was fun to watch this beautiful animal from close range. She was extremely wary, sniffing the air and listening for the sounds of danger.

Finally, she inched her way to the feeder, still looking around skittishly as though sensing our presence. Then she ate a quick breakfast and fled.

I whispered to Ryan, "There is something valuable to be learned from what we have just seen. Whenever you come upon a free supply of high-quality corn, unexpectedly provided right there in the middle of the forest, be careful! The people who put it there are probably sitting nearby in a blind, just waiting to take a shot at you. Keep your eyes and ears open!"

Ryan may not always remember that advice, but *I* will. It isn't often a father says something that he considers profound to his teenage son. One thing is certain: This interchange and the other ideas we shared on that day would not have occurred at home. Opportunities for that kind of communication have to be created. And it's worth working to achieve.

Excerpted from *Parenting Isn't for Cowards,* © 1987 by Dr. James C. Dobson. Published by Word Books. Used by permission.

30

HELPING YOUR TEEN SAY NO TO SEX

Josh McDowell

Dear Mr. McDowell,

Having premarital sex was the most horrifying experience of my life. It wasn't at all the emotionally satisfying experience the world deceived me into believing. I felt as if my insides were being exposed and my heart left unattended. I know God has forgiven me of this haunting sin, but I also know I can never have my virginity back. I dread the day that I have to tell the man I truly love and wish to marry that he is not the only one—though I wish he were. I have stained my life—a stain that will never come out.

Monica

I would be encouraged if Monica's situation were the exception to the rule and that most of our youth from Christian homes were not struggling with premarital sex, but it's not.

Consider our 1987 "Why Wait?" study on teen sexual attitudes and behavior in the evangelical church. We scientifically surveyed 1,400 kids and learned that by age 18, 43 percent of churched youth have engaged in sexual intercourse, and another 18 percent have fondled breasts or genitals. Additionally, 36 percent of the youths said they were *not* able to state that sexual intercourse was morally unacceptable before marriage!

Definitive Steps Are Needed

My wife, Dottie, and I are the proud parents of four children. We don't want them to suffer the pain that Monica and thousands of others have experienced. Yet, unless we take definitive steps to reverse the trends, the moral convictions of our children may also be eroded.

At every turn society tells our kids: "If it feels good, do it" and "Life only comes around once, live it to the fullest, now!" The radio screeches out songs like "Tonight's the Night" and MTV vividly illustrates lewd and suggestive lyrics. By and large, secular broadcast media do little to reinforce moral values or demonstrate the consequences of irresponsible moral behavior. When was the last time you saw a secular TV program show a person contracting a sexually transmitted disease or portray a broken teenager suffering through an unplanned pregnancy?

Society's false and distorted messages on love and sex are having a devastating effect on the basic moral convictions of our young people. Those basic moral convictions once held by a previous generation are apparently not being passed on to our present generation. And a generation without moral convictions is a generation crumbling under the pressures of a secular world view.

History shows that when a generation fails to know *why* they believe what they believe, their convictions are in danger of being undermined. Today, perhaps more than at any other time, we lack a "sexual apologetic"—a sound defense for our moral convictions. As one 18-year-old told me, "I was asking questions about Christianity and not having them answered. I was seeking reasons not to have premarital sex, and couldn't find any." If your child and mine don't learn why God said to wait until marriage to enjoy sex, they will lack the foundational basis for their moral convictions.

The Bible is quite clear on this subject. For when Paul admonished, ". . . this is the will of God, your sanctification; that is, that you abstain from sexual immorality" (1 Thessalonians 4:3), he did so in the positive. One of the greatest truths you can share with your child about saying no is that inherent within every negative command in the Bible there are two positive principles: 1) it is meant to protect us; and 2) to provide for us.

God knows that if sex is going to be meaningful, it must be experienced within a loving commitment of marriage. His laws, restrictions and commands are actually for our good (Deuteronomy 10:12-13). They establish the boundaries and guidelines that define maximum love, relationships and sex.

As much as possible, explain to your children this basic truth behind the restrictions God places upon them. Be sure to communicate that both you and God want only what is best for them. Eventually the point will get through: You love them and your loving limits—that come from a loving God—are to protect and provide for them.

Here are effective arguments—from spiritual, emotional and physical perspectives—that you can use to describe the reasons why God wants your child to wait until marriage to enjoy sexual relations.

Protection from God's Judgment

Fundamentally, there is only one primary reason to abstain from premarital sex—because God says so. There are many reasons He gives for prohibiting us, but His "Thou shalt not's" should be sufficient when we believe His restrictions are for our best interests. Hebrews 13:4 says that "marriage should be honored by all, and the marriage bed kept pure, for God will judge the adulterer and all the sexually immoral."

When the Bible says we reap what we sow, it would certainly apply to immoral acts. Judgment will surely fall on the disobedient—a good reason to follow the commands that God has given to us.

Protect the Mind from Sexual Comparisons

Some of the most beautiful relationships I have seen were destroyed through the programming of the most important and sensitive sex organ—the mind. One of the fallouts of premarital sex is the continual fear of sexual comparison—comparing the sexual performance of one against the other. A mind programmed with unhealthy sexual experiences can come back to haunt us as "sexual ghosts."

Scores of young people have told how they battle with the fear of sexual comparison. In many cases, it has actually been the cause of breaking up relationships. Give an example to your child from your own life or the life of another of how "reruns in the theater of the mind" cause problems before and after marriage.

Protect from Suspicion and Provide Trust

Most marriage counselors will tell you that one of the key factors to a fulfilled marriage and sexual relationship is *trust*. And premarital sex, to varying degrees, erodes the trust factor in a relationship.

When a husband or wife knows the other has waited to have sex until after marriage, it strengthens that trust factor. And one of the best motivations for continued fidelity in marriage is again *trust*. If you waited in your own relationship, share with your child how waiting secured trust in your marriage.

Share all these truths convincingly within the positive context of God's provision and protection. But while the reasons to wait are important to helping your child say no to sexual pressures, they only address one side of the problem. The flip side involves a close relationship between you and your child.

Protect from Fear and Provide Peace of Mind

Today, perhaps more than any other time, there is widespread fear of contracting a sexually transmitted disease. In the next 24 hours, more than 35,000 Americans will get a sexually transmitted disease—that's 13 million people in the next year! A few years ago, there were just five of these diseases—today there are more than 34. And with the advent of the killer AIDS virus, medical doctors are becoming prophets of doom.

Surgeon General C. Everett Koop and others predict that unless cures are found or lifestyles are changed by the year 2000, our plague-stricken generation could be sterile or give birth to more infected or deformed children.

God wants to protect us from the nightmare of being infected with diseases and provide us with peace of mind. God certainly had our children's best interests at heart when He said that we should abstain from sexual immorality (1 Thessalonians 4:3).

Rules Without a Relationship Equal Rebellion

Danny was from a Christian home and had come to me for advice.

"Sometimes I feel so alone—like no one cares," he said. "My folks live in their adult world, and I live in my teenage world. It didn't always seem to be that way. I know it sounds crazy, but I want them to leave me alone, and yet I want to be a part of their lives."

Danny looked up and gazed past me as he spoke more slowly. "Most of the time, they do leave me alone, and it gets pretty lonely."

I'm afraid Danny's feelings, representative of so many today, are a contributing cause of sexual involvement. Studies show that of those teens that are sexually active, 58 percent feel they have never gotten to know their father, and 40 percent believe they have never gotten to know their mother.

This sense of feeling alienated from the family is one reason why many young people are extremely susceptible to sexual involvement. Yet it is not sex they are seeking. A young lady wrote me recently and in three succinct sentences identified where millions of young people are at today:

> Mr. McDowell,
> I wish someone would just love me (but not physically). I want someone to show me they care. I want to be loved, but I don't know how to accept it or give it.

If I were asked to list the contributing factors to our teenage sexual crisis, at the top of my list would be adolescent alienation brought on partly by parental inattentiveness. If you want to reduce the sexual pressures your child will undoubtedly face, develop a close relationship of mutual love and respect. Establishing sexual prohibitions and rules without a relationship often leads to rebellion. It causes a child to lose heart (Colossians 3:21). But rules within the context of a loving parent-child relationship generally lead to a positive response.

The thesis is: As parents provide the proper emotional, spiritual and psychological stability for their child in a loving relationship, closeness will increase, and the temptation to seek intimacy through sexual involvement will decrease.

What's in a Hug?

After a "Why Wait?" rally in Detroit, a girl about 14 years old came up to me with tears streaming down her face. She said, "Mr. McDowell, no one ever hugs me anymore. My dad doesn't hug me. My mom doesn't hug me—nobody."

Our study among Christian teenagers shows that 55 percent said they spent less than 15 minutes per week with their fathers! I know that as parents we have many demands on our time and that kids themselves are going in 20 different directions at once. But our kids are crying out for love and acceptance. If we don't give it to them, they may seek it elsewhere.

A 15-year-old girl wrote an essay on "What I Wish My Parents Knew About My Sexuality." Here is what she said:

> I had a rotten day at school, and all I wanted was a little bit of my parent's time—just a simple hug would do. But my parents both work, and by the time they get home, they are usually tired and just want to be left alone. So I went to see my boyfriend, and he talked to me about my problems, and I felt 100 percent better. Wow! I thought, from now on I'll go to him with my problems and forget about bothering my parents. One thing has led to another, and I've done things I would never have dreamed I'd do. Dad, Mom, I wish you would have been there when I needed you.

As parents, we don't have much control over the permissive attitudes of our secular society; we can't really control what our children do when they're alone on a date. But, we can control what *we* do. We can insulate our children from feeling alienated by letting them know they're accepted. We can show them our love through our words and actions—like hugs. Giving them our time sends a strong signal that they are important to us.

Information on sex, especially the reasons and benefits for waiting, is important. But the most important thing to your child is *you*. How you relate to your children—and they to you—will largely determine your ability to help them say no to sexual pressure.

It's not easy raising children in today's fast-paced society. I'm a busy parent, too. I've got places to go, audiences to speak to, books to write and TV programs to produce. At times I feel like my life is one giant rat race. A while back, Dottie said to me, "Honey, remember, there will always be another book to write and another TV special to do, but you won't always have our five-year-old girl to hug."

That thought has stuck with me. And since then, I have carried a letter with me from a 27-year-old woman who wrote an essay for our contest entitled "In Search of My Father's Love." Whenever I'm feeling pressured to be away from my family too much, I reread her moving essay. It never fails to bring tears to my eyes and a renewed commitment to be there for my four darling children. Read a small portion of it with me:

When I was only 14 years of age, I dated an 18-year-old boy. I really needed his love and if the conditions to keep that love were to have sex with him, I felt I had no choice.

I felt so guilty afterwards. I can remember sobbing in my bed at night, after I'd come home from being with my boyfriend. I wanted so much to have my virginity back, and yet, it was gone— forever. I began to feel so lonely inside, but there was no one I could turn to. Certainly not my father, who would really "hate" me if he ever knew what an awful thing I had done.

After two years, I broke up with my boyfriend, but soon had another, and went through the same cycle with him. And then with another.

Isn't that ironic? The very thing I searched for—unconditional love—was being offered to me conditionally . . . "If you love me, you'll let me."

I'm 27 now, and about six months ago I wrote in my journal to the Lord, these very words . . .

"I felt lonely tonight—intense loneliness. And I realized that what I was lonely for was a 'daddy,' to be able to call him up when I hurt and hear him say he understands and to listen to me. But, I never had that with my dad. And so I am lonely without that link to my past.

"There's a song by Steve and Annie Chapman that says, 'Daddy, you're the man in your little girl's dreams, you are the one she longs to please. There's a place in her heart that can only be filled with her daddy's love. But if you don't give her the love she desires, she'll try someone else, but they won't satisfy her . . . Don't send her away to another man's door. Nobody else can do what you do. She just needs her daddy's love.'"

Have you given your little girl her daddy's love? If you haven't, please do. Go to her and tell her that you love her. And that she is the most precious girl in the world to you. And what if you think it's too late? It's never too late. Even if she's 27, it wouldn't be too late.

31

DRUG-PROOF YOUR KIDS

Steve Arterburn and Jim Burns

I f I had it to do over, I would have looked for help earlier. We would have put together a plan to possibly prevent the heart-aches we've experienced from Tina's drug addiction. We just kept wishing it away, and it kept getting worse" (Tina's mom).

"When I was Reuben's age, I never heard of kids ditching school to take drugs and drink. Maybe I was naive, but I don't think it happened as often. Chemical abuse scares me to death, because I have no idea what to do" (Reuben's father).

If you're like us, many times you feel overwhelmed as a parent. You feel the battle is too difficult, the victories too few. You start to think you can't do anything to help your children make good deci-sions. Heredity or fate, you tell yourself, has already determined the outcome.

Take heart; don't give up. By your actions, you can help your children avoid a multitude of problems, including alcoholism and drug addiction. As parents, we can't prevent problems 100 percent of the time, but we can radically decrease the likelihood of drug use by our children.

The Parents' Role

Your example is the most important tool. Studies show that many factors influence teens' drug-use decisions, but parental attitudes and actions can influence them most. Ask yourself the following questions:

- Is your medicine cabinet full of mood-altering chemicals?
- Do you medicate yourself with prescription drugs or alcohol any time you feel distress or pain?
- Do you have a routine of needing an after-work drink or an after-dinner smoke?
- Do you hang onto prescription drugs—just in case—rather than throwing them out when the problem subsides?
- Do you lack respect for the law and ignore driving regulations?

If you find yourself answering yes to most of these questions, you need to make some changes. The key to being an effective prevention tool is being a *parent in process*. That means you don't claim to have all the answers. You're willing to admit mistakes to your children. By word and deed, you convey the idea that in your family everyone is growing, making mistakes, confessing errors, learning from the experience, and receiving encouragement to try again.

Often children make irrational decisions based on impulse. This is typical of a first drink. Under pressure, they succumb. If they've been brought up in an atmosphere of rigidity, they may feel trapped in the behavior.

Even though they want to stop, children who never see their parents admit mistakes tend to feel a person can't turn back from bad decisions. Show your children how to make good decisions. And when you make poor ones, be willing to admit them, learn from them, and go forward.

This is an area I (Jim) am working on with my family. My wife, Cathy, says I sometimes exude a "holier than thou" attitude, especially around the kids. Lately, when it's bedtime and we pray with our daughters, I've been discussing some of my struggles. I'm amazed how our prayer time has changed as a result. When I'm vulnerable, they're vulnerable. When I'm closed, they're closed.

Even in the most rebellious times, your children are begging for you to reach them. Listen and empathize with their problems. Offer solutions when possible and be a part of those solutions. Be sure they know you will always make time for them.

God's Standards Are Best

Unfortunately, the secularization of values has left many of today's youth without standards. God's standards, however, are still best. Too many young people picture God as the great killjoy in the sky, instead of their strongest ally who loves them unconditionally and desires the best for them.

In our experience, we have found that people who pursue a personal relationship with Jesus Christ have a better chance of staying clear of drugs and alcohol. Significant studies indicate that those children who are not merely church members but who practice their faith in tangible ways have less difficulty resisting drugs and alcohol.

The same studies reveal that kids whose parents—especially dads—have a visible, active spiritual life are less prone to drug and alcohol abuse. Thus, strong personal faith on the part of parents and kids is a type of prevention tool.

In the New Testament, the word for "sin," translated literally from the original Greek, does not mean "to break a rule." Sin means "to miss the mark." Sin occurs when a person doesn't measure up to his or her full potential. Isn't that the biggest danger for most of our kids who drink and use drugs?

In our society, people are afraid to moralize the drug problem, but that is exactly what's needed. The moral person is moving toward a higher mark. But many people don't even know what the mark is for their lives, much less that they've missed it.

When drug-free kids were asked why they chose to stay clean, many said it would not be pleasing to God. Others said they believed their body to be the temple of God and that to use chemicals would be dishonoring to Him.

It's rare to find God mentioned in secular discussions on how to prevent alcohol or other drug problems. That God is left out of *prevention* material is ironic, because mention of Him saturates the literature on *treatment*. The first three steps addicted persons must take in treatment are to admit they cannot handle the problem alone, acknowledge that God *can* handle it, and allow God to take control of their lives.

We don't know of any treatment program that doesn't use these principles. Doesn't it make sense that if God is integral to *recovery* from addiction, He should also be integral in the *prevention* of problems? The home and church are much better places for a child to be introduced to God than a drug treatment center.

Unconditional Love

Drug-proof kids are kids who are loved. They know that whether they've been good or bad, destructive or constructive, they are loved unconditionally.

By contrast, conditional love comes with strings attached. It implies that if you act a certain way or do certain things, love will be given (or withheld). There's always a sense that if children mess up too badly, the love will go away. When children feel the uncertainty of conditional love, they're challenged to see how bad they can be and still receive love. It's a way of determining their basic worth.

Rather than being motivated to greatness so as not to lose their parents' love, they're motivated toward delinquency, including alcohol and drugs. While bordering on the edge of rejection by parents, they seek acceptance in other places, often with peer groups.

You cannot win with children if they aren't guaranteed your love. Drugs and alcohol produce an instant gratification that some children in a love vacuum come to crave. Meet your child's needs for love and acceptance with great floods of unconditional love and devotion.

Behavior and Discipline

A few weeks ago, I (Jim) had a mother and son in my office. The problems were many, but one was that the son kept staying out past his curfew. His mother had threatened and screamed, but nothing had changed. I asked the 16-year-old boy, "Do you think your curfew is unfair?"

"Not really, except on special occasions when I want to stay out an hour longer," he replied.

"How about if your mom compromises and gives you 15 more minutes on certain weeknights and half an hour more on weekends?" I said. "She must always know where you are, and if you call, she'll give you a 10-minute grace period."

He smiled and said, "Sounds great to me."

I then asked, "What should the consequences be if you're late for curfew or don't let your mom know where you are?"

His suggestions were even more strict than his mother or I would have proposed, so I helped them modify the restrictions. But we had successfully involved him in establishing them. He knew the consequences; after all, they were his idea. My suggestion was that if, after six months, he proved he could be trusted, they should renegotiate the "contract" and give him more freedom. If he continued in his irresponsible behavior, however, his choice of less freedom would be the result.

Many parents tend to protect their kids from the consequences of behavior. Seeking love and acceptance themselves, or out of some other unresolved need, parents often rescue children when the best course would be to let them feel the pain that grows out of an irresponsible decision. Otherwise, children remain immature and problems flourish. A tough kind of love is hard to administer, but it is greatly needed if children are to be taught responsibility.

Contracts

Contracts governing children's behavior can be controversial. We don't advise them for every situation. However, when it comes to drugs, they work well. Contracting for appropriate behavior can also be good preparation for the adult world, where people frequently contract for jobs to be done and behavior levels to be met. When kids are 12 or 13, you can begin using a form similar to the one below:

Family Contract

In an effort to work well as a family and hold ourselves up as an example for other families, I agree to the following:

1. I will not use or experiment with drugs.
2. I will not drink alcohol in any form.
3. I will attend school unless I am sick or with the family.

If the contract is broken:

First time	Weekend restriction
Second time	Must stay away from participating with friends for two weeks
Third time	Family counseling

_____

Son or Daughter

_____

Father and Mother

The above contract is a rough example. You'll want to write out your own that relates to your specific needs. As children grow older, the contract should include the following: Never ride with someone who is intoxicated or using drugs; never date someone who uses alcohol or drugs; call to be picked up rather than ride with someone under the influence.

Besides insuring that children know their parents' expectations, contracts can help motivate kids to say no to negative pressure.

Friends of a Feather . . .

Another strong determinant for drug use is whether children have friends who use drugs. If your kids hang out with friends who use marijuana, your children probably do, too. Scripture tell us, "Do not be misled: 'Bad company corrupts good character'" (1 Corinthians 15:33). It happens every time.

Know your children's friends. Don't let your kids spend time with someone you don't know. A minimum requirement should be that your children's friends must come by the house before your children are allowed to go out with them.

Encourage your children to bring friends over; let your house be one of those places where kids *like* to come. Don't be so restrictive or intolerant that your children's friends feel uncomfortable in your home.

If your children have less than desirable friends, refusing access to them will produce anger and bitterness. But you have a responsibility to restrict access. Deciding when and where your child spends time with those friends is your prerogative, especially if you have conclusive evidence the friends are drug users or drinkers.

Even more important than restricting access to such friends is communicating your concerns to your children. Tell them why you're troubled by the decision to have these particular people as friends. A poor choice of friends should provide a teachable moment.

In Alcoholics Anonymous, it's common to hear people say they tried to solve their problems by moving to a new community, but it didn't work. However, it might be a more effective solution for kids. Sometimes a child becomes deeply involved in an unhealthy subculture at a particular school. All the child's friends may be drug users. Then the child is caught using or drunk, and the parents have to decide what to do to save the child.

In such a case, the best choice may be to remove the child from that subculture by moving the family. We know of a father who took his sons from Dallas to Nashville for this reason, and it really helped. Moving is not a cure-all or a quick-fix solution. But it can be a vital part of a plan to save a child.

A Great Opportunity

You have the opportunity and responsibility to shape your children's choices and behaviors. Your commitment to them can be your most valuable prevention tool against alcohol and other drugs. It teaches your kids to live up to that commitment through tough times.

Modeling behavior that goes beyond mediocrity isn't easy. It requires looking inward to find the areas that need improvement and the will to improve those areas. In the midst of trying new techniques for prevention, never forget that you are your most effective prevention tool.

Adapted from *Drug-Proof Your Kids,* © 1989 by Steve Arterburn and Jim Burns. Published by Focus on the Family.

32

THE FLOURISHING TEEN YEARS (for Child and Parent)

Jay Kesler

Who are those strange creatures inhabiting the rooms that once belonged to your cuddly little boy and your angelic little girl? Why are they always doing such odd things? Why don't they listen? What happened? How did they get this way and why?

To answer any of these questions, we must first realize that adolescents are caught in an in-between world as strange as the one Alice found in the looking glass. Trapped between childhood and adulthood, they belong to neither. But it is even more complicated than that. Though bored with childhood and embarrassed to be associated with it, teenagers are uncertain of the future. Thus they sometimes act like children, even as they try desperately to become adults.

When I speak to church groups, I often hear parents say, "I really dread the day my kids become teenagers." Or, "I can hardly wait to get through these teenage years." There's a lot of pain behind these words, and they're painful to hear.

Adolescence is not something to be dreaded or survived. My wife, Janie, and I have raised three children and are now enjoying six grandchildren. Yet we would both say that the teenage years were our most enjoyable years of child raising.

Don't spend a lot of time looking into the rearview mirror agonizing over things that can't be changed. Instead, concern yourself with learning to be a better parent *now*. Then the teenage years need not be dreaded or feared, but can be enjoyed as a wonderful adventure of growth for both you and your children.

A Model Teen

The description of Jesus' adolescent years is relatively brief. In fact, the span from the time He confronted the elders in the temple at age 12 until He was baptized by John in the Jordan River at age 30 is covered in one sentence: "And Jesus increased in wisdom and stature, and in favor with God and man" (Luke 2:52).

Scripture is given for our instruction and edification. Therefore, I'm convinced the heavenly Parent cited this biblical model to help us with our own children and to show His understanding of His creation. In it, He refers to the four major areas of our lives: the physical (stature), the mental (wisdom), and the social and spiritual (favor with God and man). We know that these areas are interrelated and that they must work together if we are to be whole persons. Most adolescents are confused about these major areas of life, and modern society only multiplies their confusion.

Changing Bodies

The physical changes in teens' bodies are new, often frightening, and tough to understand.

First of all, teenagers grow at an irregular rate, with girls maturing two to four times faster than boys, both emotionally and physically.

Internally boys feel certain urges and interests which they express clumsily by teasing the girls, hitting them, insulting them, or in some instances of immature bravado, talking dirty. All this seems childish and disgusting to the girls who are only interested in the ninth- and tenth-grade boys anyway.

The girls aren't secure either, of course. Like kittens who do a figure eight around your legs—leaning all the time—teenage girls need a lot of assurance. They need to lean even when they think they're standing on their own.

Adolescent girls spend hours in their rooms trying to imitate images they find in *Seventeen* magazine—images created by professional photographers and models. The teenager has only her K Mart styling brush and her Cover Girl make-up kit. Consequently, she derives as much frustration as satisfaction from the glossy ads and articles. The magazine girls look coordinated, confident and comfortable with themselves—everything teenage girls are not.

Today, the teenager who feels lacking in physical beauty or athletic prowess is not only insecure and fearful, but angry at their parents for not supplying them with the right genetic material or enough money to buy the right clothes. They may even be angry at God for having made them this way.

If you could listen in on kids talking to each other at camp or in locker rooms, you'd soon discover that many of their conversations somehow relate to sexual adjustment. Some of it has to do with the mystery and magic of these strange urges they feel; some is just bravado born of fear and a sense of inadequacy and ignorance.

Despite all the information about sex available today. I'm convinced that our young people understand it little better than we did when we were growing up. They don't know how their bodies work, and they believe the same myths and misinformation that have always been shared between adolescents.

Finding Independence

The second major crisis in a teenager's life centers around finding independence from the family unit. As our children grow older, we should begin loosening the screws—not tightening them. Our natural tendency is the latter, however, especially given the world in which we live. We are bombarded with data about adolescence; almost every magazine and daily newspaper carries some survey about the rate of teenage pregnancy, venereal disease, AIDS, alcohol, drugs, and teenage suicide.

These statistics are terrifying to parents, but we cannot let them frighten us into tightening the controls just when we should begin letting up. If we do, we create the kind of pressure that brings about explosions within the family.

Understandably, Christian parents seem to have difficulty loosening the screws. It is quite natural for parents to be fearful about the temptations and problems their children face in today's world. And this, coupled with our desire for them to follow Christ and live by His principles, adds even more pressure. As a result, Christian parents often panic and overreact—then the kids overreact.

One of the great advantages of being in a good church is having Christian friends who have children the same age as your own. As the children grow up together, they spend time in each others' homes, experiencing a type of independence—being away from home without Mom and Dad—in an atmosphere of relative safety.

This kind of support is one of the strongest arguments for choosing a church with a good youth group; one in which teens are nurtured in a loving atmosphere by responsible, concerned couples and young adults. Good youth workers do not drive wedges between parents and children. Instead, they help the young grow into independence while encouraging them to respect their own parents' love and good judgment.

Finding a Place

Concurrent with the need to be independent is the need to be accepted by one's peer group. Much of what young people do—and much of what frightens parents—is simply an attempt to fit into the current youth culture.

The need for acceptance is of major importance in the teen years. Most adults have matured enough to understand that there are certain times in life when one does not need the cheer of a crowd to do what's right. But when you're young, it's tough to comprehend this kind of lone stance.

In the larger scheme of things, the label on one's jacket or jeans is relatively unimportant. Brand X is often as good as the Brand A designer label. In actuality, appearance holds no deep or permanent significance for adolescents; they simply wear the uniform of the day to gain acceptance.

The Drawing Line

The fourth area young people struggle with is turning externally imposed standards into internal convictions. I call it "drawing the line." When children are small, we draw the line for them. We tell them what is right and wrong, and they obey or disobey, all the while observing whether we operate by those standards ourselves. They also observe kids whose parents have different values and backgrounds.

During adolescence, our children begin to draw this line for themselves. They experiment to find out what it's like to go beyond the line we have drawn for them. They test our values against the values of others.

Establishing the validity of parental patterns is part of growing up. When our children experiment, they are not necessarily rebelling against our values. Usually they are just trying to get all the facts—by trial and error—before they draw their line.

However, while adolescents are experimenting and examining their options, parents must cut them some slack and honor their personal search for values. Decisions made after this kind of testing are often much more valid than those beliefs assumed without question. And parents who allow their children to express themselves will see less rebellion than parents who are always defensive and condemnatory, trying to force their children into a mold.

One of the great principles of parenting comes from Newton's Law: *For each action there is an equal and opposite reaction.* If parents don't react strongly to everything their teenagers do, then teenagers won't act out contrary behavior with such enthusiasm.

You Want to Be *What?*

"Train up a child in the way he should go, and when he is old, he will not depart from it," says Proverbs 22:6. Until recently, this familiar verse has been interpreted to mean that parents are to make sure their young people are correctly trained in accordance with the will of God. That is good advice and something for parents to keep in mind.

But Charles Swindoll and others have suggested that in the original Hebrew the intent of this passage is: *Train up a child according to his or her bent.* The root word has to do with the bent of the tree. For instance, a willow tree that leans out over a pond toward the southern sun is bent in a certain way. If you try to force it to bend in another direction, you will break it.

I see as much wisdom in this interpretation as in the traditional one. Parents should try to raise their children according to Biblical patterns, correcting them and disciplining them so that they understand responsible and obedient behavior. On the other hand, children should be nurtured according to their own bent.

We need to be willing to acknowledge that our children are born with different temperaments and different personality types. Parents sometimes try to project their own dreams onto a child with dissimilar bents. Yet trying to mold a child into the patterns of the parent can be one of the most devastating of all rejections. Ultimately, the child feels that nothing he or she does, especially in the areas in which he or she excels, can ever please the parent.

I applaud parents who are willing to discover the bent of their children rather than seeing them as hunks of unsculptured granite to be chipped and chiseled into the forms they wanted for their own lives.

I was so saddened one day to hear a very successful doctor, a man I admired for his medical accomplishments and expertise, admit with tears and with some anger, "I hate what I'm doing. I've always felt God called me to be a missionary. But my dad was unwilling to let me do it because he had spent so much on my education. He said, 'No, you're going to have to make my expenditure worthwhile. The mission field is out of the question.'"

This doctor, at the height of what seemed to be a successful career, was regretting the loss of his great dream—a dream his father had overruled. Wise parents will turn their children over to God, invite His Holy Spirit to speak to them and then help them to achieve the goals He implants in them.

Made in God's Image

A lot of people think there's some kind of magic formula that will make kids turn out the way *you* want. That's a destructive cookie-cutter approach to parenting. And often, if you examine the cookie cutter closely, you'll see that it's the same shape as the person wielding it. Unfortunately, there is a lot of arrogance at the root of this attitude: Wouldn't the world be better if others were made in my shape?

In 1 Corinthians 12, Paul points out that God has given each of us different gifts. And as I see it, our God is big enough to have enough gifts to go around. Paul describes the members of Christ's Body as being fitly joined together: hands, arms, torso, neck, eyes, ears. One part, such as a hand, cannot say to another, a foot, "I don't need you." God gives His people special and differing gifts and abilities, and all are necessary.

God does not give bad gifts and good gifts; He simply gives different gifts. And when we can accept this in our children, we'll have come a long way toward understanding their uniqueness, and toward achieving family harmony.

Practice Saying the Words

To say to your child, "I'm proud of you. That was a good job. I'm so happy that you're my child," provides more positive reinforcement than almost anything you could ever do. Some parents say, "It's hard for me to do this. I always see the negative. I don't see the positive."

And I say to them, "Practice. Try mouthing the words. Blurt it out. Say it. Take a risk. You'll be glad you did." Even when a young person has tried and failed, a parent should take him aside and say, "I know how very much you wanted to do this, and I know how hard you tried. Even though you didn't win, I was very proud of you—of your composure, your sportsmanship, and the way you conducted yourself even in the midst of disappointment."

A young man once told me, "I can do the entire yard, trim all the bushes, trim around all the trees, do the best job possible, but when my dad pulls in the driveway, he doesn't see the yard. He just sees that one little clump of grass that I missed. He harps on that and never mentions all the other work I've done. It really discourages me and makes me feel like giving up. Why put in all that work if you're going to get chewed out anyway?"

What if that father had just once said, "Hey, great job." Or if it wasn't a "great" job, why not notice the boy's tenacity and industry? What if he had simply commented on how much time it must have taken the boy to do all that work and thanked him for it, or complimented the boy in the presence of a neighbor or a friend?

What would that have meant to the son? Probably a great deal.

My dad was part of a generation of men who found it difficult to openly express affection. I remember the first church meeting we attended where they asked people to hold hands and sing. Dad thought we were being asked to do something perverted! He had never held hands with a man in his life, and he couldn't do it and sing! He was a real man's man.

Dad hadn't missed a Notre Dame football game since 1921, and after every game I'd call him to go over it play by play. A few years ago—about three years before he died—at the end of our phone calls he started saying, "Jay, I love you." It had taken him years to be able to express his love for me that blatantly, and even though we had a wonderful relationship, those three words meant everything to me.

It's Only Halftime

The Bible is full of people—including parents—who faced hard challenges. Old Testament Jews lived in difficult times, among strange tribes with strange gods. Yet God told them to remain pure, to maintain their identity, to keep the truths He had given them, and to keep their Jewish identity before their young people.

They were instructed to share with their children about their relationship with God as they walked from place to place and as they sat at home. We, too, should always be conscious of our identity as God's people in the midst of a wicked and perverse generation.

The people of God have always lived in a world that is not a friend of grace. But I don't believe God would ask us to do something we can't do. What He asks is for us to raise our children to be sensitive to His Holy Spirit and to walk in His ways.

We dare not live like water coming down the side of a hill— seeking the path of least resistance. We must live with purpose and direction. We must understand who we are in contrast to the rest of the world. We must constantly stand guard—discussing, praying, talking, debating, forgiving, loving, waiting—using all the tools of grace as we lead our families.

Families are not destined to failure. They can succeed. In fact, to the glory of God, I see more families with purpose and direction succeeding today than in years past.

Don't count the score at halftime. Don't believe that your children are going to freeze where they are now. They will grow. The grace of God is working in their lives as it has in yours.

Parenting is one of God's great ideas, and parenting teenagers is the best part of it. Just remember, mind your instincts, parent with confidence, consult His Word, pray much; then believe God for the reward.

Excerpted from *Ten Mistakes Parents Make With Teenagers (And How To Avoid Them)*, © 1988 by Jay Kesler. Published by Wolgemuth and Hyatt, Publishers, Inc.

33

A PROMISE WITH A RING TO IT

Richard Durfield

With a flourish, the hostess seated my son, Jonathan, and me in El Encanto's main dining room, a nice restaurant in the foothills near our hometown. The expensive furnishings, subdued lighting and pricey menu told my 15-year-old that tonight was a special occasion.

Jonathan is the youngest of four children. As we scanned the large red menus, I mentally walked through what I wanted to say to him. He knew we were at El Encanto's for his "key talk," a time when we could discuss any questions he had about sexuality. Jonathan already knew the "facts of life"—my wife, Reneé, and I had raised him in a home where "no question is too dumb." We began telling him about sexual parts in his preschool days, Last year, Jonathan took a ninth-grade health class on human reproduction.

But this night would go beyond anatomy to talk about the special meaning of commitment and honor for a young man fast growing up. When the chilled jumbo shrimp appetizers arrived at our table, I quietly leaned over.

"Tonight is your night, Jonathan," I began. "This is a special time for you and Dad to talk about any sexual questions that might still be on your mind. Whatever might seem a little awkward at times, well, tonight is the right time to ask. Nothing is off limits tonight.

"If something's been bothering you about marriage or adolescence or whatever, it's okay to talk about it. As we eat through the course of the evening, I want you to just be thinking about any questions you might have."

Jonathan's all boy. He'd much rather ride his mountain bike in the hills than chase after girls. When we first sat down, he had seemed a little uncomfortable because I saw him looking around. But as we began talking, he relaxed a bit.

My son, who has never been on a date, wanted to know *for sure* what "the line" was. How far was *too far?* He had a good idea, but he wanted to hear it from me.

"A light kiss is about as far as you can go," I replied. "Sexual emotions are very strong, and if you're not careful, you'll do things you don't want to. So you need to avoid anything that leads you up to that."

For instance, I explained, certain types of kissing are going too far. Kissing a girl on the neck can lead to going much further.

The 'Key Talk' Beginnings

Jonathan has two older sisters and one brother: Kimberli, 23, Anna, 19, and Tim, 18. About 10 years ago, when Kimberli was entering adolescence, Reneé and I had an idea: have a private, personal and intimate time with the child to explain conception, the Biblical view of marriage and the sacredness of sexual purity. A time when a mom and daughter or a dad and son can candidly discuss the questions, fears and anxieties of adolescence. I called it a "key talk."

We also had another idea. At the time of the key talk, the parent presents a specially made "key" ring to the son or daughter. The ring, which symbolizes a commitment with God, is worn by the adolescent during the difficult teen and young adult years.

What is a key ring? The purpose of a key is to unlock a door, and the ring symbolizes the key to one's heart and virginity. The ring is a powerful reminder of the value and beauty of virginity, of the importance of reserving sex for marriage.

The ring also represents a covenant between the child and God. A covenant not only obligates us to God, but it obligates God to us.

As long as we honor a covenant, God will also honor it. Throughout history, God has blessed those who have remained faithful.

The son or daughter wears the key ring until he or she is married. Then the ring is taken off and presented to the new spouse on their wedding night—that sacred evening when a life of sexual experience begins.

Reneé had open and frank key talks with Kimberli and Anna. She described just about everything a child would want to know about sex. Because our daughters are attractive, intelligent and sought-after, they needed important reasons to remain virgins until their wedding nights.

The pressure of society and its "well, they're going to do it anyway" attitude pushes millions of teenagers into a world of promiscuity. Sadly, our daughters are members of a shrinking minority: less than 50 percent of women 18 and younger are virgins. And churched kids are having sex in nearly the same percentages as nonchurched kids.

Jonathan's Ring

As the main dishes were taken away, I told Jonathan it was time to make a commitment before the Lord. Yes, we lacked privacy, but I felt it added to the significance of what he was about to do.

I wanted Jonathan to pray—right there at the table—but I had to set things up a little bit. "Now this covenant is going to be something between you and God until you are married," I said. "We're going to include whoever your wife will be in this prayer. We're going to ask God that wherever she is and whoever she is, that He'll be with her also. We'll ask Him to help her to be chaste until the time you're married. I want you to ask God for His grace to keep this covenant pure, because even though you may have right intentions, sometimes things go wrong. I want you to pray and then Dad will pray."

Jonathan turned to me and took my hands. It surprised me that he would be so bold in a public restaurant, but I realized that was exactly what he needed in order to stand alone.

Jonathan bowed his head and prayed fervently. Then it was my turn. Before I prayed, I said "Jonathan, I have something for you." I took a custom-made 14K ring and slipped it on his finger. Bowing our heads, I asked the Lord to honor the covenant Jonathan was making and help him resist temptation in the coming years.

Then I read a letter from someone very special, someone who had befriended Jonathan when he was much younger. I didn't let him know who it was from:

Dear Jonathan,

Your dad told me that the two of you are about to have a very important talk. I've been invited to participate in the discussion by way of a letter. I was asked to say a few things about purity—sexual purity—though I don't suppose there's much I can tell you that you haven't heard before.

I'm sure your parents have taught you well. But I want to encourage you to act on what you already know. Believe me, it's worth it to save sex for marriage and keep yourself pure for the woman God wants you to spend your life with. The Lord designed it that way for good reasons. Plenty of people who disregarded His plan in that area will tell you how much they regret it.

You're going to need more of this kind of encouragement in the days to come. It's one thing to know what's right. Living by it is something else. Over the next few years, you'll probably face pressure to change or compromise your values—pressure from your friends, from advertising, television and movies, and a hundred other sources. You may even find yourself in situations where it could be easy to yield to sexual temptation.

One of the best ways of fighting back is learning to like yourself. If you feel good about you, you'll have the confidence to take a stand—even if you're the only one! Just remember who you are and what your parents have taught you. There's real strength in knowing that God loves you and has a purpose for your life!

But if you feel inferior to others, it will be that much easier to let them press you into their mold. Don't do it! The rest of your life is ahead of you, and it's worth fighting for. I hope this helps, Jonathan. I'm sure your dad will have more to say on this subject. You're a lucky guy to have parents who care about you so much! Take advantage of their wisdom and be encouraged by their love. God bless you!

Jonathan was amazed to learn the letter was signed by James Dobson, whom I met 12 years ago. In fact, my inspiration for the key talk came from Dr. Dobson. In his first book, *Dare to Discipline*, Dr.

Dobson described his intention to give his daughter, Danae, a small gold key that would represent the key to her heart.

A Parent's Influence

My key talk with Jonathan was one of the most memorable and moving experiences I've ever had. It seemed our hearts were bonded together.

Young people are romantics. They have a real need to identify their personal self-worth. Wholesome, Biblical thoughts instilled during their tender years open an avenue for parents to discuss sex with their children. The importance a parent places on the key talk will greatly influence the child's sexual behavior prior to marriage.

Key talks should happen when the child becomes interested in the opposite sex. That can be as young as 10 or as old as 17.

Obviously, the key ring is a powerful day-in-and-day-out reminder for the child. The more the child values his or her virginity, the more the key ring becomes a precious symbol of the commitment to God and the future spouse.

As I've shared the key ring idea with many families, I've learned that it's also a good idea for teens who have lost their virginity. Although they've jumped the gun, they can commit themselves to God to remain pure until their wedding day.

Teens who have fallen short can become virgins again in the sight of God. Once they're forgiven, it is as though they had never sinned. The Lord tells us in Isaiah 43:25 that "I, even I, am He who blots out and cancels your transgressions, for My own sake, and I will not remember your sins."

As Jonathan and I left El Encanto's that night, a couple sitting at a nearby table stopped us. They couldn't help but notice something special had happened, they said.

Something special *had* happened, and it was between Jonathan, his wife-to-be and the Lord.

PART SIX

FOCUS ON FAMILY ACTIVITIES

34

"I DON'T LIKE
SUNDAYS"

Karen Burton Mains

An insecure little character called Binkley in the nationally syndicated cartoon strip "Bloom County" by Burke Breathed represents the child in all of us who feels like he's the butt of all the world's humiliations.

One of the regular features is a cartoon panel with Binkley sitting up in bed facing his closet. "Pst, Binkley, over here," says a voice from out of sight. Then a horrible rhino-nosed monster sticks his face out of the closet and says, "On behalf of myself and the rest of your subconscious anxieties, we thought you should be given advance notice regarding our plan to jump out and grab you this evening."

"Thank you," says Binkley.

"Certainly," says the monster.

The last panel shows Binkley hunched beneath the blanket with a baseball bat in hand. The closet door is closed, and Binkley says, "A closet full of courteous anxieties is a dubious comfort."

It's terrible to be a child and have a closet full of anxieties.

It's even more terrible to be an adult with a closet full of anxieties; and I suspect that for many Christian adults, going to church on Sunday morning is like opening Binkley's door filled with monsters and Minotaurs, creatures and creepies, bugs and bears and bats and other pieces of personal whimsy.

Too Many Monsters

For many of us, something has gone wrong with Sunday morning. It's become filled with too many monsters: the late arrival panic monster, the waiting Minotaur of too many responsibilities, the creeping creature of inner-fraternal hostilities or resentments or hatred. This church closet is haunted with dull sermons and boring services. There is often a whole choir of voices singing the hymn, "You're not what you're supposed to be." Or how about the all-too-familiar anthem, "You'll never make it as a good Christian"?

One leaves church all too frequently Sunday after Sunday having peered into the closet full of anxieties, but never having truly exorcised the monsters who inhabit its dark territories. "Good," we think, "another Sunday behind us. Don't have to face that again for a whole week! Am I relieved!" And we leave, having no idea that we've just participated in a form of godliness without the power of godliness; that our Sunday attendance had been perfunctory, without meaning; an intellectual exercise in neutral without ever shifting into the high gear of heart and soul beating upward toward worship.

No wonder people stop going to church or their attendance becomes irregular. Any excuse, any excuse whatsoever—a slight cold, overdue homework, too much weekend paper work—becomes reason enough to stay away, and we sigh to ourselves and say, "I don't get anything out of it anyway."

What we need to undergo is an emotional and psychological closet-cleaning. We need to face into the dark of all those churchly anxieties, instead of just letting them lurk in the shadows, robbing us of our rightful Sunday enthusiasm. Like Binkley, we need to take baseball bat in hand and get rid of them.

For years, the big question in our home was: Why did our family equilibrium tilt precariously out of control between Saturday night and Sunday morning?

One child would be missing a crucial dress item that I had overlooked in the back of a closet. This precipitated a quick wash and dry, then ironing out the damp fabric on the ironing board. It seemed even the dog collaborated with confusion, invariably vomiting on the living room carpet.

There was never toothpaste in the right bathroom; there were the usual my-turn-first arguments—to use the blowdryer, to take a shower, ad infinitum. And about a half an hour before departure time for church, this overwhelming panic would begin to rise from the pit of my stomach, constrict my chest, and finally explode from my mouth.

"Let's get going! We're going to be late! Haven't you had your breakfast yet? Why do we have to go through this every Sunday? No, your shirt isn't ironed—I'm getting it; I'm getting it. I don't know where you left your Bible! Why does everybody think I'm responsible when they lose things? We're going to be late. Let's go. Come on! Come on! Out the door!"

I turned into Alice's white rabbit in the crazy wonderland of Sunday morning—"We're late; we're late, for a very important date"—and looking back, I suspect there were some members of my family who thought I turned into the Wicked Witch of the West every Lord's Day.

Actually, I was living out an unintentional lie, an unconscious untruth that develops due to many factors, one of which may be a family system in which we simply accept fiction for being fact. The vital lie I was creating stated: Sunday is the worst day of the week.

This was an untruth that hid itself in my heart, even through those years when a major effort of our pastoral ministry was to create new forms of meaningful contemporary worship. And this fiction hid itself in my heart, even though David and I had been working hard at creating a satisfactory form of Sunday family celebration.

Make Psychological Preparations

For years, we'd begun to get ready for Sunday morning on Saturday evening. We'd made physical preparations—clothes ready and lessons done and a peaceful house. We'd made spiritual preparations, time for prayer and time for meditation. But I still experienced the old, rising panic, the white rabbit sing-song, "We're late; we're late!", the gut-level churning, the Sunday morning anxiety attack.

I've since learned that Christians must make psychological preparations for Sunday morning as well as physical preparations if they're going to destroy the old, unintentional lie: Sunday is the worst day of the week.

David Seamond's book *Putting Away Childish Things* deals with the influence of the unhealed child of the past on the adult of the present. While reading this, the Holy Spirit brought to mind my barely controllable panic on Sunday mornings. I heard my husband's voice saying, "Why are you so upset? We have plenty of time." I thought of the kids complaining, "Mo-om, why are you in such a frit? I can make it by the time we need to leave." In prayer, I said, "Lord, show me why Sunday mornings are such a bad time for me."

A Very Full Day

Then I thought back to my childhood Sunday mornings, back to that house beneath its bending elms. Because Dad was the music minister in most of the churches we attended when I was a child, Sunday morning choir practices, the morning worship service, youth choir at four in the afternoon, and the evening service all fell into his capable hands; but these tasks also spelled a very full day.

Both my parents worked during the week, so Saturday was the day we attempted to complete all the household responsibilities that hadn't been finished. My parents' lives were crowded with people and family and students—my father giving private voice lessons in the living room on Saturday mornings and my mother making remarkable plans for her grand Sunday dinner. Consequently, Sunday mornings in my childhood home were also crammed with everything that didn't get done on Saturday to get us ready for Sunday morning.

Invariably, my brother or sister lost a shoe. I don't know why it was shoes particularly, but it always was. And keys were another thing that always seemed to disappear, necessitating a last-minute panicked hunt. With Mother in the kitchen putting her glorious Sunday cuisine together, a lot of the responsibility for herding siblings into clothes and sniffing out lost items fell to the oldest child. Guess who? You guessed right. Me.

The light dawned. My Sunday panic that was creating a fiction for me and my family that Sunday was the worst day of the week was nothing more than an old pattern, an unwelcome remnant from childhood. Even as an adult, I was acting out what every Sunday morning in my youthful life had been. In fact, the vital lie I'd been creating was threatening to become real. *Sunday morning was the worst day in our family life because I was making it the worst day!*

Some of the fictions in our lives don't burgeon from a deep emotional need. They simply come from old patterns we need to discard for newer and holier ones. We must learn to ask: Why am I behaving the way I'm behaving, and what does it remind me of?

My parents were wonderful people—but they did have a tendency to rush at life, and they needed to discover the calm presence of the real Christ on Sunday mornings. Many people have had childhood Sunday mornings like mine and must recognize that the old inward panic experienced Sunday after Sunday is an outworn habit.

I've discarded this childhood leftover by first of all anticipating that my habit is going to act up on Sunday mornings. I'm kind to the little child within still beginning to panic. I make warm noises—*now, now, you're going to be all right*. I mother, nurture, console my inner self—*you don't need to worry, everything's under control, take some deep breaths; I really am in charge and all is well*. Very infrequently, I might chide, *Oh, just grow up!* One of these self-parenting techniques invariably works like a charm.

Some of us come from backgrounds where a restrictive, narrow, confining legalism squeezed the life, the holy life, out of the Lord's Day.

Since a Sunday spirit, either negative or positive, can be caught, it behooves parents to be careful what kind of Sunday experience they are modeling. Some church-going lifestyles seem deliberately designed to spoil a child's inner emotional response to this special day. If we had intentionally decided to make the Lord's Day burdensome, we couldn't be doing a better job.

Do you rush and push and shout and become generally unpleasant on Sunday mornings? Do you complain about church? Are you sloppy in your attendance? Or are you over-conscientious about matters that are not really important? Are you compulsive about church attire, about Sunday good behavior? Do you always negate the pastor, the choir, the length of services and the usher crew?

Then don't be surprised if your children grow up to look at Sunday as the worst day of the week.

Spiritually Nuture Your Children

George Gallup Jr., the national pollster, warns that the youngest adults—those just growing out of their teenage years, some still living in their parents' Christian home—represent the least Christian segment of our population. If this is so, something has gone wrong in the Christian homes of our country and in the spiritual nurturing of our own children.

In an article entitled "There's Nothing Wrong with Hand-Me-Down Faith" (*Moody Monthly,* June 1976), Pastor Ray Stedman concentrates on a phrase from Deuteronomy 6: ". . . and you shall teach them diligently to your children." Then he writes to parents, "Notice that you shall teach. Like many licenses, this one should be stamped 'nontransferable.' The Sunday school and church cannot substitute for parents in teaching spiritual truth. Only parents have the time, the concern, and the relationship with their children to make it work. No one has as much influence on children as parents. Therefore, God holds parents responsible to teach their children how to love Him with all their hearts, and souls, and might."

Set the Emotional Tone

It is safe to conclude that if you are expecting Sunday school teachers to develop in your children a long-lasting regard for the whole Sunday experience, you are expecting too much from one hour a week. What happens in your home, the emotional tone you as a parent are establishing, your own inner attitude toward Sunday which is "caught" will be the strongest factor in determining whether your child one day abandons Sunday observance.

The late Dr. Donald Grey Barnhouse, for years the radio voice of "The Bible Study Hour," was once asked the question: "At what age can a child understand what it means to love God?" His response was: "You begin teaching a child about God 20 years before he's born."

He meant that the initial instruction about God grows out of the character of the parent. We cannot give to our children a spiritual life we ourselves do not possess.

A parent is the primary forceful model for developing a rich inner Sunday appreciation in his or her child. Therefore, it is imperative that we as parents come to terms with our own outworn childish Sunday attitudes so that we don't create a closet full of Sunday anxieties for our children.

Excerpted from *Making Sunday Special,* © 1987 by Karen Burton Mains. Published by Word Books. Used by permission.

35

MARRIED TO TELEVISION

Duncan and Priscilla Jaenicke

W e have a close friend in San Diego who, in a fit of frustration and rage, actually smashed the family TV to bits on the garage floor.

This usually mild-mannered father of three, a well-known Christian surgeon who values family life, simply *did* what many of us have *wanted* to do innumerable times. He must have asked himself, as he lugged the set toward the garage, just how great a loss would they suffer, anyway?

Apparently finding no great disaster in the offing, he gave that little collection of circuits and glass a heave, with apparently satisfying results.

Such a scenario begs the question that has plagued us for years as Christian parents: *How can we control TV's bad influence?* Must we toss the baby out with the bathwater, as our San Diego friend may have done?

Such concern is valid. Television has systematically invaded every area of our lives. Experts estimate that the average American child views a whopping 30,000–40,000 TV commercials per year.

245

This is easily accomplished, since the average American TV set drones on for more than seven mind-dulling hours per day!

Even the once TV-free classroom is being violated. Last spring, a satellite network named Channel One began beaming its 12-minute educational programs "free of charge" into participating class-rooms, replete with (you guessed it) teen-targeted commercials.

Perhaps the most alarming aspect of TV's assault on North American families lies in its ability to mold our children's values. In a recent issue of *Christian Retailing*, noted Christian educator V. Gilbert Beers warned, "Our children are being turned over to electronic parents [who give our kids] a new and different heritage by ridiculing our values.

"No parent would open his door to a bunch of strangers and say, 'Here are our kids, come on in, say anything you want!' Yet we are abdicating, to total strangers, the responsibility to teach our kids," said Beers.

An Insidious Addiction

Several years ago, bad TV habits forced our family to reevaluate the priority the boob tube had gained in our lives. Like many young Christian families, we thought we had the TV menace pretty much under control. *Au contraire*. It was a dark day when I (Duncan) ar-rived home after work and was unable to get as much as a "Hi, Dad" out of my kids. "Family Ties," it seems, was throwing cold water on *our* family ties!

Our two daughters, ages five and two at the time, had gradually crept into the habit (admittedly, their mother shares responsibility) of watching a considerable amount of late-afternoon TV. That's the time of day when Mom's energies are flagging, and the TV provides welcome relief.

A second warning came when Priscilla asked for prayer about her near-addiction to "Knots Landing," a soap opera-like saga simi-lar to that classic piece of TV trash, "Dallas."

Finally, our family was chain-viewing program after program fol-lowing dinner, since we found it difficult to "just say no" to the myr-iad of selections that followed our 7 p.m. favorite, "Jeopardy."

As Priscilla and I took stock of the situation, I felt that familiar rage toward the set that all parents must feel at one time or another. Yet this time it was tempered with a new twist.

"Priscilla, why don't we just get rid of this thing—for a month—and see how it feels?" I asked.

Many times in the past we had decided to junk the TV for the sake of our family; somehow we had managed to talk ourselves out of such a bold plan. We'd be depriving the kids, we thought, who would be considered weirdos by their friends. They would miss "Sesame Street"—or some other all-American staple. We wondered how our budget would manage without the cheap entertainment of the idiot box. So much for bravery and adherence to principle!

But going "cold turkey" for a predetermined period of time did hold a certain appeal. A month seemed long enough to break TV's stranglehold, yet not so long that we couldn't live with the deprivation. We agreed to sit down after four weeks and decide whether to continue the ban or to possibly reinstate the TV under clear and strict guidelines.

Both of us immediately knew—instinctively somehow, arising from gut feelings of family preservation—that the plan was worth trying. Like the recovering alcoholic determined to stay on the wagon, we decided to make a clean break, if only for a short time. We needed to show ourselves we weren't enslaved to TV, that the quality of family life we felt God had called us to was more important than continued TV devotion.

The next day, I wrapped the television up in a sheet and stored it high on a garage shelf. Our 30-day TV fast had begun.

Withdrawal Pains

Our most difficult moments came during the first week. Bethany and Grace, our two daughters, missed simply flipping on the tube when they had run out of ideas. Mom keenly felt the absence of her Wednesday-night soap opera escape, and even dear old Dad—in mid-season couch potato form—wondered how the Charger football game was going.

Invariably, we found ourselves walking over to where the TV used to be, only to stare into space! We were forced to find more profitable things to do with our discretionary time.

After a week of withdrawal pains, the rest of the month became more bearable. The children became more creative, and Mom and Dad began to realize that a TV-free life could actually be enjoyable.

Priscilla spent her evening hours—that precious chunk of every mother's day when the kids have gone to bed—exercising and developing her aerobic routines (which eventually allowed her to teach an aerobics class at our church, a first for her). I found myself with more time to read or to go to bed on time, which paid off in more alertness and energy at work.

After 30 days, a family pow-wow was called to evaluate our experience. We decided we liked our new environment so much that we'd keep the TV in the garage for at least another month.

After 93 days, our daughters—who take ballet and tap lessons—wanted to watch *The Nutcracker Suite* with Mikhail Baryshnikov. This was a turning point for us. We agreed to let the TV back in the house, but only under well-defined purposes and under clear guidelines. No longer would the TV dominate our lives.

Coming off our TV fast gave us the opportunity to formulate simple—yet firm—guidelines, ones we still follow today:

• No flipping on the TV "just to see what's on." Only a predetermined list of approved programs is allowed. That way there's no arguing or pleading with Mom and Dad. If it's on the list, okay. If not, forget it.

• The TV is viewed only in a less-than-comfortable, less-than-convenient room. As strange as it may seem, this was one of the key elements of our success. We chose to relocate the tube permanently in our garage, since cars can stay outside in the mild Southern California climate.

In colder regions, you could put the TV in a basement, spare bedroom or attic. If you live in an apartment, rearrange the living room so the TV isn't the most prominent piece of furniture. Just make sure TV viewing is less than optimum and—such heresy—a *bit uncomfortable*. Undisciplined TV habits flourish where creature comforts abound. Such an arrangement forced us to watch TV purposefully, not just view it "by accident" when it's conveniently located.

• We decided not to buy cable TV service. We wanted to avoid any extra motivation for turning on the TV based on the maxim "I'd better use it if I paid for it!" In our area, we receive a reasonable number of through-the-air stations, and the quality of reception is acceptable. Cutting out cable, however, may not be optional if you live in a rural area. But given its average yearly cost of $125–$250, we think eliminating cable from one's TV diet is the best route. For me, the 24-hour availability of the ESPN sports network would be a source of continual temptation.

• Although we have yet to purchase one, a VCR can help your family watch positive programming. Parents can tape worthy shows when the set isn't on, and then allow the kids to view them at appropriate times. Many parents rent or buy Christian videos for their children.

Results of the Experiment

After three years of curbing our TV appetite, the tube no longer holds much attraction for us. We're seeing positive results every day. For example, our children's attention span is longer and their creative drive far outstrips their playmates, many of whom live in TV-saturated homes.

Family communication has improved, especially in the early evenings. Instead of another round of "Wheel of Fortune," we act out Bible dramas before bedtime. Bethany loves to play Moses and storm down from Mt. Sinai to chew out the Israelites for worshiping the golden calf. Grace loves to play the angel who kept scaring Balaam's donkey. Naturally, they insist that Daddy play the donkey!

As parents, the new arrangement forces us to limit our use of the tube as a baby sitter. While we still acknowledge every parent's need for an occasional escape from the daily grind, we have developed more wholesome escapes—like taking a brisk walk or playing board games with the kids. We are freed up to focus on more worthy things.

Dealing Habits a Death Blow

We don't claim that our way is the only one that will work; many families use other methods. We know one family that issues half-hour coupons to their children each week, redeemable for approved programming. If the children refrain from using any coupons, their mother buys them back with real money.

Another great alternative is reading. Instead of an allowance, pay your children for each book they read. For instance, reward them one or two cents per page for books you approve of, and half a cent if they decide to reread an old favorite. The holiday season—when kids have a lot of free time on their hands—is a good time to introduce this incentive.

If you're like us, maintaining an enriching family environment is high on your priority list. Try a month without TV if bad habits are encroaching upon your family's quality of life. Then reassess the situation. Either reinstate the tube under new guidelines or banish it to the junk pile forever.

Our plan is a lot less messy than smashing your TV to bits, and possibly just as effective. Give it a shot—unless you *enjoy* sweeping up jumbled glass and electronic circuitry from your garage floor!

36

HOW TO PICK A VIDEO THAT WON'T SEND YOU BACK TO THE STORE SCREAMING

Ted Baehr with Bruce Grimes

S everal years ago, I walked into my local video store on Friday
night. My mission: find something suitable for family viewing. I
strode past several aisles to the children's section. My eyes caught
the video jacket for "The Golden Seal." It looked innocent enough: a
fair-haired young boy hugging a cute little seal. *Here's a good family
film*, I thought. I glanced at the credits, recognized a few of the
names, and checked it out.

I'm a Christian movie critic by profession, so to double-check, I looked up "The Golden Seal" in a comprehensive video catalog. Released in 1983, the movie had no rating. However, the synopsis sounded okay:

> "Delightful nature tale about the plight of a golden seal and how it affects the humans around it. Beautiful photography in a fable the entire family will enjoy."

Our family enjoyed the movie—for about five minutes. Shortly after the opening credits, obscenities and vulgarities filled our living room. Off went the video. I apologized to my children—and vowed never to get burned again.

When I returned the video, I asked to see the store owner. I chastised him for not placing a warning sticker on the jacket. A few weeks later, I noticed a little message on the box: "Contains bad language: probably a PG-13 rating."

Developing Discernment

Perhaps you have a similar horror story to tell. How can parents rent the right videos in the flurry of today's many offerings?

The first thing you should do is check the rating. "The Golden Seal" didn't have one. That was a red flag I ignored.

Unrated means unknown. You have no idea what you are getting. Obviously, the title didn't reveal much. On the other hand, if you rent "Stripped to Kill II," you can be pretty sure what you're getting.

In most states, videos do not have to display the Motion Picture Association of America (MPAA) rating. Although the MPAA system leaves much to be desired, it's better than nothing. The MPAA's G, PG, PG-13, and R ratings are mainly window dressing; they're Hollywood's way of making parents believe impressionable youth are being protected. Many people are not aware that these ratings are given by the movie industry itself, *not* by an independent body.

If the video is rated, you'll find it on the back side of the jacket box. "G" means the movie is suitable for all audiences. "PG" means parental guidance is suggested, but as I'll explain later, you'll want to avoid a lot of PG movies. The same goes for "PG-13," which often contain significant doses of sex and violence. "R" means restricted, with no one under 17 allowed into the theater without a parent or adult guardian. But the R rating is a joke: it's rarely enforced, especially by video store operators.

Keep in mind, too, that most video stores don't rent the video with the original box. Instead, they insert the videocassette in a clear plastic box. This presents a problem, especially if your children rent a movie and you want to know more about it before popping it in the VCR.

Like books, you really can't tell a video by its cover—or the brief synopsis written on the jacket. One must read between the lines to decide where the movie stands with respect to Christian values.

For instance, 99 percent of R movies are unacceptable to Christian audiences. But a few, like "The Killing Fields," are worthwhile movies. "Killing Fields" portrays the horror of communism taking over a country and systematically murdering men, women and children. The movie was given an R, even though there is practically no sex or obscene language in it.

Trying to pick a decent PG or PG-13 is also a difficult assignment. Driving past a theater marquee last summer, I noticed two PG-rated films: "Ghostbusters II" and "Honey, I Shrunk the Kids." With the PG imprimatur, parents would think both movies were acceptable for kids.

"Honey, I Shrunk the Kids" was good entertainment for the entire family. You didn't find any sex, violence, nudity, profanity or any other objectionable material. (One character did utter a mild expletive.) Although the film begins with family division, it ends with reconciliation. For the discerning viewer, the film is filled with principles from the Word of God. Most of all, it conveys a vital message: the importance of bringing families back together!

On the other hand, "Ghostbusters II" was a cesspool of child sacrifice, idolatry, profanity, obscenity, blasphemy, occultism and demonic activity. The film was evil. It presented the triumph of man through the use of occultic powers: the essence of the New Age movement and satanism.

But both of these movies were rated PG!

Ask the Right Questions

Even with an MPAA rating, discernment is crucial in choosing a videocassette. Movies are loaded with messages. Asking the right questions will help you look beneath the surface:

What is the premise of the movie?

What message does the film communicate? You can often find the premise on the jacket of the videotape. Remember—you have to read between the lines.

Does the premise agree—or conflict—with Biblical concepts? For example, "The Accidental Tourist" was a cute movie. Starring William Hurt, it was nominated for several Academy Awards. The premise of this popular film, however, was that adultery leads to happiness. This premise is abhorrent to God and aggravates the tremendous marital problems confronting us today.

A recent film, "Driving Miss Daisy," is a heartwarming story with a powerful premise: Dedication to Christian virtues can bring love and reconciliation into an alienated life.

Who is the hero?

What kind of role model is he or she? "Henry V" tells the story of a young Christian monarch who gives God all the credit for victory, but in "Lethal Weapon II," the hero is a totally despicable policeman who encourages his partner to take drug money. Later, he congratulates his partner when his daughter stars in a commercial for condoms.

Who is the villain?

All too often, the villain is a minister or person of faith, as was the case in "Poltergeist II" and "Fletch Lives." Hollywood delights in portraying moral people as nerds, prudes, kooks and psychopaths. "Criminal Law" depicts pro-lifers as cold-blooded killers. In "Shirley Valentine," the working husband is the villain, while his wife (the heroine) runs off with her feminist friend to have a series of adulterous affairs in Greece.

We know who the bad guys are in "Indiana Jones and the Last Crusade" when Indy delivers the immortal line, "Nazis, I hate those guys." As a matter of fact, the villain in this allegory is a bad guy—a greedy National Socialist who will stop at nothing to gain eternal life.

How is religion portrayed?

If you're looking for it, you'll notice how often believers are portrayed as evil, weak, insincere, obsequious, rotten and foolish.

"Born on the Fourth of July" portrays Christians and patriots as warmongers and fools. "Blaze" indicates that Christians are adulterers and strippers. In "Ministry and Vengeance," the minister is a vengeful killer. (What else? That's the title of the movie.)

How is the world portrayed?

Hollywood often distorts the way to look at the world. Many movies portray the world as full of wealth, sex and drugs. "Blaze" shows us a world where corrupt whoremongers are the good guys. In "Family Business," stealing is a legitimate profession. Sex and drugs are rewards for living the good life in Eddie Murphy's "Harlem Nights."

A good movie, "Prancer," shows a world with real problems. But the reality of God is central to the solution of the film.

How is love portrayed?

Love is at the heart of the gospel. Who can forget the godly mother in "Eleni" standing in front of a firing squad to save her children? "Driving Miss Daisy" shows that human friendship does not have to be coupled with the obligatory sexual relationship.

Yet most movies reduce love to one-night stands, tedious ordeals or homosexual liaisons. In "Skin Deep," John Ritter sleeps with one woman after another. In "Ruthless People," we're supposed to chuckle as the husband tries to murder his wife. "Desert Hearts" has a woman who is getting a divorce discover that lesbian love is better than heterosexual love. "The Kiss of the Spider Woman," a critic's favorite, lifts up homosexuality. Two recent movies, "The War of the Roses" and "She-Devil," suggest that marriage is war.

How is the family portrayed?

Unfortunately, the family is under attack—and has been for some time. You would think that "Parenthood" and "Uncle Buck" would be good family movies. They weren't. The children steal, swear and indulge in promiscuous sex. The parents lose all control. While played for laughs, the films lack any sense of moral perspective.

In three movies, "Distant Voice, Still Lives," "Shirley Valentine" and "Valentino Returns," the father is the root of the problem. "Down and Out in Beverly Hills" promotes free love. Steven Spielberg's "The Color Purple" attacks the basic building block of our society: the family.

When a couple are shown in bed, four out of five times they aren't married. Little wonder: 87 percent of the media elite feel adultery is okay. Films are a rationalization for their own conduct and an attempt to drag the rest of us down to their level of immorality.

We need more movies like "Dad," a deeply reflective film about three generations of fathers who are reconciled by learning to forgive one another.

Who's behind the camera?

Pay attention to the names on the credits. For example, George Lucas ("Star Wars") has a mission to proclaim an occult Force. Oliver Stone, who directed "Platoon" and "Born on the Fourth of July," hates America and loves communism. "I think America has to bleed," Stone said recently. "I think corpses have to pile up. I think American boys have to die again. Let the mothers weep and mourn."

Director Costa-Gravas is an avowed communist who designs his movies to attack what he abhors, such as Christianity ("Betrayed") and anti-communism ("Music Box").

You can be pretty sure that you won't agree with the premise of films starring the liberal Hollywood Establishment, such as Jane Fonda, Martin Sheen, Glenn Close, William Hurt, Holly Hunter and Tom Cruise.

On the flip side, Charlton Heston's clear stand for traditional values is reflected in the roles he plays. Heston recently starred in a remake of "Treasure Island," an excellent film released on cable TV. It should be in video stores soon. Barry Reardon, president of Warner Brothers Distribution, is a committed Christian who tries every year to release a few strong Christian films. Barry has been responsible for "Chariots of Fire," "The Mission," "Cry in the Dark," and the magnificent "Driving Miss Daisy."

Would you be embarrassed to sit through the movie with your parents, your children or Jesus?

When we are alone, we often deceive ourselves regarding the true nature of a movie; however, if we imagine that our parents, our children or the Lord are with us (which He is), then the movie's faults stand out clearly. If we ignore the faults in a movie we are watching, then we will slowly be conditioned to condone, if not accept, a non-Christian point of view.

Heading for the Video Store

Here are some more tips for renting a good video:

- Listen to word of mouth. What are your Christian friends saying? Perhaps your Bible study group could discuss suitable films and come up with a list.
- Consult resources that review movies from a Christian perspective. I'm the founder of *MovieGuide: A Biblical Guide to Movies and Entertainment,* a biweekly newsletter that reviews Hollywood's latest releases. I've also co-authored, with Bruce Grimes, two volumes of *The Christian Family Guide to Movies and Videos* (Wolgemuth & Hyatt). Each volume reviews hundreds of movies and provides helpful information on how to develop Biblical discernment.

  John Evans, a good friend of mine, has written *Recommended Movies on Video,* which contains brief reviews of more than 650 recommended videos. John also publishes *Preview Movie Morality Guide* twice a month.
- Know what you want to rent before you walk into the video store. If you are browsing, head for the "classics" or "musicals" sections. Movies made before 1963 stand a better chance of being good.
- Rent videos at a Christian bookstore. Although few Christian bookstores do rent videos, you're sure to find something good at those that do.
- Stay away from horror movies as well as teen "sexploitation" films.
- Don't be afraid to rent foreign films, even ones with subtitles. Lately, many foreign films have had the most penetrating Biblical messages. Not only are such films as "Babette's Feast," "Repentance" and "Manon of the Spring" entertaining, but they have the most to say to Christians.

A Closing Thought

Remember, the motion picture medium is not bad per se. Movies are tools for communication. Like any tool, they can be used for good or for evil. A hammer can be used to build a church or to crack a skull. Movies can uplift ("Trip to Bountiful") or degrade ("Emerald Forest" and "Cocoon").

Films are often viewed with suspicion by the church. It's true that too many movies are filled with nudity, profanity and immorality. They deserve our condemnation since we are called "to flee immorality" (1 Corinthians 6:18). On the other hand, Christians should support entertaining, uplifting movies (such as "The Hiding Place"), if only for the reason that our support will cause producers, who are primarily interested in making money, to make more wholesome movies.

Trying to ignore movies has proven to be counterproductive. Rather than bury our heads in the sand, Christians should be careful about which movies we support at the box office and in the video store. If Christians redirect their entertainment dollars away from immoral entertainment and toward moral movies, Hollywood will take notice. And we'll have more to pick from the next time we go into a video store.

37

CELEBRATING THE TIES THAT BIND

Kerry Klaassen Veale

It was the summer of 1945. As the yellow Oklahoma wheat fields rippled in the warm breeze, thousands of locusts whispered their monotonous chant. A 13-year-old girl walked briskly along the country road, kicking up little clouds of red dirt with each step. Sweat trickled down her face to her faded cotton dress, but she didn't notice. The young girl was returning from a revival in town, where she'd accepted Jesus Christ as her Savior. Knowing instinctively that life was somehow going to be different, she burst through the back door and told her mom the exciting news.

"You don't know what you're talking about" was her mother's angry response.

The young girl stumbled outside, crying. She ran to the chicken coop—at least the nesting hens would listen. She didn't know it yet, but for many years her parents, still rebellious from their own upbringing, would forbid her to visit her relatives—the ones who already shared her new faith.

This was just one of the many stories I heard at the Karber family reunion last summer, when more than 400 descendants of

259

David and Henrietta Karber gathered in Fairview, Oklahoma, to explore their common heritage.

I'm a Karber, too, although I'm five generations removed and living halfway across the country. At 29, I'm a writer for a large aerospace company in Southern California, where my husband, John, also works. My days are filled with computers, faxes and ringing telephones in the high-tech environment of the space business.

One evening about a year ago, my mother called from Oklahoma City. In no uncertain terms she told me it would be terrible to miss the upcoming Karber reunion. "Kerry, you weren't able to go to the first two reunions," she said. "Your grandparents aren't getting any younger, and it would mean *so much* to them if you could come."

Ever the dutiful child, I booked a flight (John took a pass) for points east. I was transported to a state—and lifestyle—far different than mine. As we motored along the highway from the airport, I saw the red dirt and rolling plains of my childhood days. Suddenly, everything seemed as it once was: the wide-open spaces, the wheat fields rolling to the gentle waves of wind, the sapphire, smog-free skies. My thoughts turned inward. I was home again.

Looking Back

I've always known a little bit about my family's background. Mom and Dad were born in western Oklahoma to parents who spoke *Plattdeutsche*—a peasant German dialect—in the home. Although our parents raised us in a different denomination, my ancestors were Mennonites who came to America to escape military service and religious persecution. As pacifists, Mennonites refuse to bear arms or take oaths.

My mother told me stories about how her father, David Reimer, was a conscientious objector during World War II. The other schoolchildren treated her cruelly, mocking her German heritage and my grandfather's decision not to enlist.

But that was about the extent of my family knowledge. Upon arrival in Fairview, we checked into the best motel this town of 3,370 had to offer. I climbed the stairs and sniffed suspiciously. The balcony afforded a wonderful view of, yes, a herd of cattle!

Pinching my nose, I slipped into my room and hastily turned on the air conditioner. *What other surprises were in store?*

Many, I'm happy to report. During a long weekend of round-the-clock activities, I watched a play that re-enacted the experiences of my great-great-grandparents, David and Henrietta Karber, the pioneers who left Eastern Europe in the early 1870s. They met in Kansas and were married in 1877. A few years later, with the help of other Mennonite immigrants, they built a new church and called it *Hoffnungsfeld*—Field of Hope.

I listened to the story of how Grandma Karber, as Henrietta was called, often prayed in her bedroom until midnight. She endured incredible hardships when her young family moved from Kansas to Oklahoma by covered wagon train. That first summer, the Karbers lived in a tent while David worked the land. Their first home had so little room that the chairs had to be placed on the table in order for people to walk by. They ate a steady diet of corn bread and prips (roasted barley coffee).

I met relatives I never knew I had—a flight attendant, a university vice-president, a lawyer, an accountant, a missionary, an elementary school principal, and *lots* of farmers.

Through it all, I discovered a sense of pride in *my* family. Their courage and determination over the years strengthened my values. I felt gratitude for the risks my ancestors took for religious freedom. It felt good to belong to a family that placed a strong faith in God.

Sharing the Past

At the reunion, family members hung quilts along the walls of the Mennonite Brethren Church auditorium, where most of the nightly activities were held. At one display, I fingered bright colors born out of an otherwise Spartan existence. These handmade quilts weaved family stories of hardship, sacrifice and triumph.

Placards identified each quilt, listing the date it was made and any unusual story behind it. One woman sewed a quilt from squares she collected on a recent European trip. My grandmother, Edna Reimer, won the prize for "Oldest Quilt."

I learned the most about my past from a slide show given by Richard Unruh, a distant cousin. The Unruh family had traveled to Europe on a family "roots" trip, visiting Poland, Czechoslovakia, Hungary and the Soviet Union. They strolled through towns where

David and Henrietta Karber lived and pored over old books containing births and deaths. They interviewed post office employees and local clergymen.

A Story from the Past

As Richard clicked through the slides, I heard about many Mennonite families, including Henrietta's, who left Poland due to military conscription. She and her family immigrated to America in 1874, eventually settling in Kansas.

David, just 21, was drafted into the Polish army in the late 1860s. As a Mennonite, he refused to serve. A Jew smuggled David across the border to Prussia (now East Germany). David traveled to Berlin, where he sought his long-lost brother, a successful businessman.

From Berlin, David decided to come to America. He traveled to Hamburg, where he boarded a ship for England. From Liverpool, he undertook the long, arduous trip across the Atlantic. It took 23 days to reach Ellis Island.

David found work toiling in the Ohio fields. In winter, he traveled north to Green Bay, Wisconsin, where he joined a logging camp. When David, who spoke little English at the time, sat down for his first meal at the camp, the lumberjacks began making fun of him. One fellow sitting next to David decided to fill his plate, whether he wanted more food or not. David picked up the plate and threw the food in the man's face.

The lumberjacks roared with laughter—but they never picked on David again. He was a tough man, but poor; he worked with bare hands because he couldn't afford gloves. Winters were so cold that his clothes froze stiff.

David eventually became a farmer in Kansas, where he met Henrietta. They married in 1877, thus laying the foundation for a family reunion 112 years later.

And now, memories of the Karber reunion are a tapestry in *my* past: Henry Martens in his red cap, working the biggest ice cream freezer I'd ever seen; Elda Martens standing over a hot stove teaching us how to make *verenika*, a dough-like ravioli filled with cottage cheese and onions, topped with gravy; Denver Klaassen, my dad, just as excited as the farm boy he once was, donning overalls to spend the day looking over farm equipment; Uncle Ben, at 95 the oldest member of the family, giving tours of the house where his sons were born; and the granite tombstone in the quiet country graveyard, where my great-great-grandparents are buried.

Planning Your Own Reunion

The richness of a family gathering is unique to each clan. Passing on a sense of heritage is something only you can do; no entertainment firm or video company can deliver it in a slick package to your doorstep. The event takes a lot of hard work—and you'll need a lot of lead time—but it's worth it. Here are a few pointers I learned from the Karber reunion:

• Start small. Family get-togethers don't have to number in the hundreds. Begin with a dozen or so relatives who live within a day's drive.

• Plan early. It takes at least four to six months to pull off a large reunion. Set up a committee to make the major decisions, such as location, theme and time of year. Typically, most family reunions are in the summer, when the days are long and most people take their vacations.

• Build a mailing list. Send out a mailer with the dates, lodging arrangements and cost of meals (so family members can begin planning and saving). Be sure to consider financial limitations. Ask for addresses of lost relatives.

For us, Fairview was an excellent location because many relatives lived within a three-hour drive. Lodging was inexpensive (my motel was $33 a night), and the Fairview-Mennonite Brethren Church rented its facilities at a reasonable cost.

• Find ways to celebrate your family's unique heritage. At Fairview, a bus took us to see family homes and farm areas, as well as the grave sites of David and Henrietta Karber. The Unruhs' slide show was a hit, as was their lengthy Karber history book, complete with pictures.

• Communicate time-honored values to the younger set. Menno Unruh, Richard's father, moderated a panel of representatives from each branch of the family. Each person drew out anecdotes from the past. At the same time, Menno wrote down values illustrated by their stories—love for God, loyalty to family, working hard—on a blackboard for everyone to see.

• Try to overcome geographic and generation barriers. To help people get acquainted, everyone was given a sheet of paper with blank boxes for each branch of the family. The object of the game was to get signatures for each of the boxes—a painless way to meet lots of family members.

Color-coded name badges with a different color for each branch of the family—there were nine—helped things run smoothly. In addition, placards used for the quilt display and signs at the graveyard were color-coded.

• Showcase the talents of as many people as possible. Family members enjoyed dressing up in period costumes and performing a play on how the Karbers took a wagon train to Oklahoma before settling on their homestead.

For a talent show, each family was allowed two entries. We clapped our hands for everything from a children's rhythm band to a male chorus to a guitar duet.

• Provide activities of interest to everyone. The antique car parade, narrated over a loudspeaker, showed off prized vehicles owned by family members. I saw one of Fairview's first fire trucks, as well as a steam-powered tractor. What a din!

Children were kept entertained by playing horseshoes, exploring the doll and antique toy room, riding a small train, and taking old-fashioned hayrides.

At the ethnic cooking demonstration, I learned how to cook *kielka*, a German dish made up of small pieces of boiled dough and a creamy gravy. "Our parents used what they could produce—flour, eggs, milk, cream—and bartered for sugar and salt," explained Elda Martens.

Each family was given a table in the family history room, where young and old alike browsed through old wedding albums. I fingered an old baby cradle and read a yellowed list of babies delivered by midwife Amelia Karber nearly 100 years ago. Some of those babies—now grandparents—grew misty-eyed reading the old list.

• Involve as many people as you can. From day one, volunteers were needed. Family members were asked to sign up for at least one task, be it kitchen duty, serving food or organizing games for the kids.

• Communicate clearly to avoid mishaps. The reunion ran smoothly as the windmill above the Major County Historical Site in downtown Fairview. Why? Because we had good communication, much of it in writing. Upon arrival, each family member was handed a detailed registration packet containing information on all of the weekend events. All of us knew *exactly* when and where we should be.

• Keep a record of all your arrangements for the *next* reunion. After your first get-together, you'll have so much fun that you'll probably want to do a reunion every few years.

• Create memories that will live past the reunion. On Sunday morning, the Karber family choir sang the "Doxology" *a cappella* at the church service. One of the Karber descendants, Rev. Linden Unruh, delivered a moving sermon. After church, we ate Sunday dinner in the fellowship hall, where each table centerpiece held a bunch of brightly colored balloons.

Following the meal, we all went outside. Standing in the balmy Oklahoma breeze, we released our balloons. As the multi-hued balloons soared into the heavens, we softly sang, "God Be with You Till We Meet Again." Many of us wept.

> *The 13-year-old girl grew in the Lord. On Sundays, she could walk down the dirt lane to the main road to catch a ride to church. On the days when her ride didn't come, she waited, waited and then walked home alone.*
>
> *When she was 18, she left home to attend a Christian college. The encouragement of her Christian cousins buoyed her during difficult times, as she tried to support herself and go to school at the same time. At college, her life changed again. She met a fine young Christian man, Eldred Kunkel, and they married. The young couple settled in San Jose, California, where Eldred became a successful building contractor.*

That young woman, Evelyn Kunkel, is now 57, and she's my mother's first cousin. Evelyn told me that story as we drove to the reunion. Although her walk along that country road happened nearly 45 years ago, the emotion in her voice told me she was walking that same road again. I was there right next to her—a partner in the family heritage that is not just a record of our common past but a gift for the future.

38

FAMILIES AT HOME

Dean and Grace Merrill

Who's in charge of the family? Young couples sometimes fantasize about egalitarian home life, where sweet reason prevails and all decisions are reached by consensus. Then children arrive!

It doesn't take long to discover that kids are occasionally lacking in calm objectivity (ditto for parents) and, therefore, not all decisions will be greeted with smiles and applause. We finally came to the time when we decided there was too much ambivalence among the troops about where the buck stopped.

Tuesday evenings—from the time Dad arrives home from work until the kids go to bed—are "Home Together Nights" in our house. On a particular Home Together Night, we passed out various colors of construction paper to each family member and said, "Draw and cut out a full-length picture of yourself." That was fun enough.

Then we produced string, a punch, and a coat hanger. "Now we're going to put our cut-outs together into a mobile," we announced.

"Who goes on top? Who's in charge of the whole family?" Answer: God. We rummaged for a piece of gold wrapping paper, cut it

267

into an oval, cut out construction paper letters G-O-D, pasted them on, and pasted the oval to the coat hanger.

Next we strung the figure of Dad under God, followed by Mom. This reflected our understanding of Scripture's teaching about family structure and responsibility. (We realize some couples would read the same Scripture and choose to place themselves parallel.)

Next came a horizontal straw suspended from both Dad and Mom like a trapeze, from which hung the three figures of the kids. If we'd had our dog Frisky at the time, she would have come last.

We hung the completed mobile from the curtain rod beside the kitchen table, admired each other's self-portraits, but also studied the relationships it illustrated.

> *Do kids tell parents what to do?*
> *No.*
> *Do parents tell God what to do?*
> *No.*
> *Do kids tell each other what to do?*
> *No.*
> *Do parents tell kids what to do?*
> *Yes.*
> *Does God tell parents what to do?*
> *Yes.*
> *How does God tell kids what to do?*
> *Mainly through parents.*
> *What will happen when you finish school and move out on your own?*
> *You'll move up and be in the middle, so a string will run directly from God to you. The middle rank will be removed.*
> *And then what will happen if you marry and have children?*
> *You'll have a straw of your own, with others for whom you'll be responsible.*

"We want you to know," we said, "that it's an awesome thing for us to be directed by God for your lives. We don't take it lightly. We really aren't smart enough to raise you alone. We need His direction, and we try to pass it on to you as best we can.

"We also look forward to the day when you take your place in the same level as we are now."

In previous generations, this kind of activity probably wouldn't have been needed. As Haim Ginott says in one of his books, "Whatever grandfather did was done with authority; whatever we do is done with hesitation. Even when in error, grandfather acted with certainty. Even when in the right, we act with doubt."

Sometimes we are too flexible and accommodating for our own good. While we should not be tyrants, neither should we be jelly-fish. A clear statement of how the household runs—along with a glimpse of the future—is sometimes helpful.

A Time to Celebrate

Other Home Together Nights are set aside as "Honor Nights," for celebrating the specialness of an individual family member. In a world of giants, it is sometimes hard for dwarfs to think highly of themselves. And we grown-up giants are often too busy, too self-impressed, to remember what it was like as one of the little people.

The writer who has taught us most about remembering this is Wayne Rickerson. Throughout his books on family life, he is con-stantly calling parents to affirm, stroke and elevate the fragile per-sonalities of children. Psychological terms such as self-worth, self-esteem, self-acceptance, and a good self-image may come to sound effete after a while, but they describe a very real need in the life of every God-made boy and girl.

Cockiness? No. Boastfulness? No. But good, comfortable feel-ings of value—yes. That's why the Gaithers wrote the children's song "I Am a Promise." We must help our offspring believe that every week.

How? By searching with them for their particular field for excel-ling, be it a sport, an instrument, or something else. By guarding against an overload of correction in any one day, mixing in plenty of "I still like you" messages and actions. By taking time to listen atten-tively. As someone with a great measure of wisdom has said, "Love is giving a person your undivided attention." Do we love our chil-dren?

Rickerson talks in his book *Getting Your Family Together* about the Honor Night concept, and at our house, we're great believers in its value. One child is selected for special limelight throughout this evening—which isn't his birthday or anything else, just a selected time each year when the family zeroes in and says, "We think you're great!"

Let's say it's Rhonda Night. When she was younger, she got to select the main course of the meal. Now she not only chooses it, but also goes shopping with Mom for the necessary groceries and then prepares the food.

The table centerpiece is a display of her favorite things: Cabbage Patch doll, flute, her copy of *Charlotte's Web*, a piece of beloved jewelry. Once we sit down to eat, a homemade star with glitter is pinned on her. She beams.

After the meal, she sits on a chair in the middle of the room for a "press conference." The rest of the family take turns asking things such as "What is your favorite book/color/hobby?" We actually learn some things we didn't know.

We may bring out her baby remembrance book and read some significant parts. We may discuss how her name was chosen and what it means, or tell about her birth—the miracle of her survival in spite of being born six weeks early and having severe breathing distress the first couple of days.

We may show slides from the first year of her life. For each of the three children, we have shown slides of their dedication at church and played the tape recording of the pastor's prayer and comments. We share our spiritual commitment, made that day, to raise them in a godly home. They love hearing these things over and over.

We may make a "compliment flower" for Rhonda, with her name in the center and four construction paper petals, on which each of us writes a word such as "loving" or "enthusiastic" or "talented" before gluing the pieces together. The flower is then taped to her bedroom wall, where it stays for weeks, sending out its encouragement.

(For Nathan, the art was switched to a basketball court with compliments written on basketballs headed for the hoop.)

We may choose a special verse of Scripture that expresses our feelings about this child (2 Corinthians 7:16, for example) and turn it into a puzzle by writing one word on the bottom of each nut cup or a piece of paper under each placemat. Once the meal is over, the children try to assemble the verse in proper order. By that time, they've virtually memorized it.

A Special Time

Grace once planned our "Circle Time" (10 minutes or so when we gather in a circle for devotions) around Psalm 139:13–18, where

David praises God for the wonder of being created in his mother's womb. "God planned and shaped you inside of me, before you were ever born," Grace said, "and each day is a little more of his plan for your life." Then came a special prayer of thanks for Rhonda, and requests for guidance in the future.

More recently, we've asked the child to select a favorite Bible story, read it to us, and lead a discussion based on questions he or she has written. Too much for a grade schooler to attempt? Not really, especially when the pattern of a Circle Time is well established.

The finale of the evening is for the child of honor to choose a game for everyone to play.

This has become an annual event for each of the three children over the years, and it never seems to wear out.

Beyond these special occasions, there are scores of ways to keep building up our children, boosting their morale:

- Draw names out of a bowl and write complimentary poems about each other.
- Have each person write the letters of his first name vertically on a piece of paper. Then turn the papers over, shuffle them, and pass them out again. Each person writes something positive about the person whose name appears. Example:

  Tall
  Really plays violin well
  Is bouncy!
  Clever in creative writing
  Is a Christian
  Artistic

  Or you can circulate the papers round-robin style, adding a positive note to the next line of each paper as it comes your way.
- Make a compliment chart and pass it around collecting entries. (This kind of activity works best while some other project is underway.) Dad fills in a short compliment in each box on the top row except his own, then passes the chart on to Nathan, and so forth. When you're finished, post it on the refrigerator. It's guaranteed to dispel a week of miscellaneous blues.
- During dinner: Say something nice to the person on your

right, not about them, but to them—for example, "I like the way you draw."

It's this kind of reinforcement that makes a Home Together Night sparkle. It's the reason we don't allow interruptions, telephone calls and all the rest. The message both spoken and unspoken is "You are special. You are valuable. You are a treasure."

The Bible and the Zoo

Why do children love the zoo so much? Because they're in love with life—all forms (even reptiles!). Children the world over are fascinated with the luxuriant variety of created beings.

While major zoos usually require a day-long excursion, many areas have smaller wildlife preserves, animal shelters, park district rehabilitation centers where injured animals or birds are nursed back to health, and children's farms that are just the right size for a Home Together Night trip.

Town families often have farming friends who would be glad to show visitors around the feed lot and let them explore the haymow along with the kittens.

Christian parents have a special addition to make to these outings: the news that the Lord God made all these wonderful colors and diversity, and He cares about the many needs of animals. He shows how much He knows about zoology in his major pronouncement to downcast Job (starting with chapters 38 and 39, and running all the way through chapter 41).

Such reading enhances a child's wonder at such a creative, awesome God. It connects real, tangible surroundings with their Source.

PART SEVEN

FOCUS ON EDUCATION

39

TWELVE TIPS TO HELP YOUR CHILD SUCCEED IN SCHOOL

Robert W. Smith

On the first day of school, Jimmy (one of my fifth-grade students) approached me. "My mom says I lose TV for a whole week every time you call home to complain about my behavior or my work. I guess the party's over," he said with a sigh as he strolled disconsolately out to recess.

That mother, if she follows through on her promise, has just issued herself the cheapest insurance policy in the world against a year of wasted energy and failure.

As a teacher, I have found that parents who stay involved in the learning process of their children create a climate of success which serves as a springboard for future achievement. Here are some other tips I have learned from 17 years in the classroom:

Start Right Off

Let your child know right from the beginning that his success in school is very important to you and that you expect him to reach his fullest potential. The time to begin is the first day of school. Follow through and make sure he forms his work habits correctly.

Regular Homework Periods

Every child needs a routine. Designate a specified time slot each night when he is expected to be doing homework. This means peace and quiet—not with the television blaring or the stereo belching for the latest rock hit. The period will depend on the age of the child, but it should run, on the average, 30 to 60 minutes each night.

Meet the Teacher

Soon after the school year begins, it is important to meet the teacher. Attend a "Back-to-School" event or simply drop by the classroom. Ask about the homework policy. Don't discover with the first "F" notice that your child—who said he never had homework—wasn't completing his assignments.

At the same time, tell the teacher any special concerns or problems your child may have. I didn't learn until March one year that one of my students was supposed to wear glasses for reading. It's amazing how "bright" children become when they can see the page.

Don't Become a Pawn

Children can become remarkably adept at maneuvering parents and teachers against one another. If you have a question or complaint, call the teacher. Don't use your child as a sounding board for your frustrations. A good deal of misunderstanding between home and school is created, intentionally or not, by the child.

And don't think that you are bothering a teacher by calling. Parental concerns are a major part of any teacher's job description.

Value and Praise Work

"Why didn't you take your folder of papers home?" I asked one student. "Your mother wants to see them."

"She just glances at the top one and tosses them into the trash," the girl responded.

There is no quicker way to discourage a child from putting forth his best effort than this mother's approach.

You should praise the papers and projects your children do, even if they seem childish or poor. They aren't supposed to be perfect; they are learning experiences. Put the best paper on the refrigerator or a bulletin board. What you value, your child will value, too.

Build Responsibility

The child with a sloppy desk at school generally has a pigpen for a bedroom. The one who doesn't get his work done on time usually doesn't show any responsibility at home, either.

Be careful not to say, "That's just the way Johnny is." Create a system of rewards and punishments for keeping a bedroom in order. Give the child certain cleaning duties at home, even if he doesn't do them as well as you can at first. The allowance system should always be based on chores being completed. Nobody should be paid for just breathing.

Control the Television Set

Every expert on child development in this country acknowledges that children watch *far* too much television. It is not only the amount of time, but the inferior and inappropriate nature of the programming that is destructive to their creative processes and their sense of reality.

Parents must monitor the quality of the programs their children watch and limit time spent in front of the tube. Shows developed for adult entertainment are never appropriate for children. An hour of this passive activity an evening seems plenty. Better yet, turn the TV off during the week.

High Expectations

Expect your child to achieve his or her very best. Doing work correctly *and neatly* is a value that will serve him well in school and later in the work place. Children should aim to garner the best grades they can achieve. Don't accept less just because it's a passing grade.

Be Realistic

Assess your child's ability with blunt honesty and without being embarrassed as if you were somehow responsible. Some children are going to be better in academic areas than others. Some will struggle their entire school careers simply to pass.

Parents set themselves up for disappointment if they hold aspirations for having a doctor in the family when their son's interests are directed more towards resuscitating car engines. Be mindful that your child's life is not yours. Be proud of his skills, in whatever area they exist.

Encourage Outside Interests

Every child needs activities beyond school. Whatever a child's interests are—piano lessons, ballet, soccer, scuba diving or stamp collecting—encourage him to pursue and channel his energies in this direction also.

A child should develop a sense of identity beyond school, especially in the junior and senior high school years. This is true for the students who struggle in school as well as for children with excellent marks.

Every child needs to see himself and be perceived by others as having some special skill or talent. This attribute pays off in self-esteem and peer-respect.

Working for Money

Having a job or chores to do is an important part of the growing-up process, even for grade schoolers. A child with a job simply feels better about himself.

Mowing a neighbor's lawn, walking an elderly person's dog or washing the family car are several ways for him to learn some important on-the-job skills. Babysitting is also an excellent way to learn responsibility.

A child who earns his own money will use greater discretion in spending it than he will about spending yours. Trite but true: Boys and girls need to learn to recognize the value of a dollar and relate money to effort expended. After-school jobs can teach them this value.

Communicate

A child needs to share the problems and joys of the day through small talk. Often, he will use his parents as a springboard to test his ideas or as a safety net for posing questions.

Sometimes these questions are expressed as outrageous opinions. The child may really be seeking affirmation that you truly care about him or that your values are what you say they are. He may simply be trying to determine what he really thinks.

In any case, be calm and talk. Care enough to describe what you think. Listen to your child, even if you're bored or outraged. You really need to worry more when children won't speak than when they do. The dinner table, without the ubiquitous television set, is a good time for this sharing to take place.

Remember, no parent ever feels successful all the time. But you can limit your frustrations and profoundly influence your child's school success by involving yourself fully in all areas of his life. So, start right now by building a climate of success in your home.

40

QUESTIONS PARENTS ASK ABOUT SCHOOLS

Cliff Schimmels, Ph.D.

Though we don't go to school with our children, our concerns do. While some children love school and breeze through, others have a more difficult time. For a small minority, school is one of the most exquisite forms of punishment the world has ever invented.

As parents, we are caught in the middle. We want more than anything in the world for our children to get something worthwhile from school. We also want to see them enjoy it.

We often get the idea, however, that we are somehow outside observers, trying to catch a glimpse into that mysterious monastery set on a hill that swallows up our children each morning and spits them back to us each afternoon. How can we make school profitable for our children?

In the course of a year, I visit more than 200 classrooms in more than 75 schools. During the past five years, I have worked as a teacher in 20 schools. Thus, my opinions are based on personal observations.

What follows are some of the most prominent questions I hear parents asking:

How early should a child learn to read?

Everybody has an opinion on this—which is all right—except no one agrees with anyone else. What's a parent to think? One expert says start at age two. Another says start at eight. Which one do you listen to?

I am not sure I have the right answer, but I do have an observation.

Teach your child to read when he *wants* to read. If you watch your child, he will tell you when he is ready. In fact, a lot of children teach themselves to read before any adult even knows about it; then one day they surprise the world by revealing their accomplishment.

Most parents are usually embarrassed at this point. They celebrate the achievement, but they feel a bit guilty the child learned something on his own without having to be taught by the parent. Aren't children wonderful? If your child shows signs of wanting to read at three or four or five, don't be afraid to encourage him. You can do several fun things to get him started. You can make name tags for items around the house, such as a stove or table, so he can easily pick up the written symbol for that item. (Remember that reading is the process of interpreting symbolic language.)

Help your child learn to recognize the sounds of language. Help him discover the sound in a specific word. Then you can introduce him to hand-drawn flash cards with those sounds on them. With that foundation, he learns that reading is the process of putting sounds to letters.

Our son has been going to first grade for six weeks, and he hates it. He cries every morning. What could be his problem?

I assume that this is his first all-day school experience. If he hasn't gone to an all-day kindergarten or an all-day preschool, he is making a tremendous adjustment to an entirely new experience.

No matter what the age, moving from the home to the school is a major transition in a youngster's life. Let's look at some of these adjustments.

Social adjustment. School is about friendships. It is almost impossible to function in school without some friendships. You need a friend to line up with you in the bathroom line. You need a friend to share your eating spot at lunch. You need a friend to help you study. You need a friend to lend you a pencil when yours wears out.

Establishing all those friendships is an exhausting enterprise, even for gregarious children, because there is a risk involved. You send out your feelers, and if no one picks up on them, you stand there with your emotions all exposed.

Let's see if I can make this into a general principle—ANY CHILD WHO DOESN'T HAVE A FRIEND IN THE CLASSROOM WILL HATE SCHOOL. Well, it may be a little harsh, but I'm willing to live with it.

Adjustment to the regimen. Learning to go to school is learning to live with having someone in control of your body, mind and soul from 9 a.m. to 3 p.m. The teacher really expects you to sit still, read when she tells you to, walk straight to the bathroom rather than looking at all the neat stuff in the hall, get a drink when she tells you to, and keep from looking out the window even when a man is mowing the grass.

Adjustment to authority. When a child is at home, the only people who boss him around are those who love him. When you go to school, everybody tells you what to do—the bus driver, the teacher, the lunchroom monitor, the school secretary and the principal.

Adjustment to the ever-present threat of failure. Failure is as rampant in school as success is. You can fail in many different ways. You can misspell a word everyone else knows. You can color outside the lines. You can read too slowly. You can drop your books during quiet time. You can go to the bathroom in your pants. In other words, if you aren't careful, you can make a complete fool of yourself. You always have to be on your guard, and that not only wears you out, but it makes life miserable as well.

Help your child establish a friendship with someone in the class, even if you have to invite someone over every afternoon for a week. At this point, you need to be diligent and frequently express your love for your son or daugher. Pick him up and hold him. Hug him when he isn't expecting it.

We've never had any trouble with school until this year. Our daughter is in the fourth grade, and her teacher is terrible. The class is in constant chaos. How damaging could this year be for these children?

It depends on the individual student. Some students are so sensitive that a year like this one could have repercussions for a long time, not only in what they lost in subject matter, but also in just being able to relate to a teacher.

On the other hand, some students just adapt, accept what is, and go on about their business.

How are *you* responding to this? If you are panicking and fretting, you will surely pass part of this on to your child. If you are cool and accepting, your child will have a better chance of learning to adapt to an unfortunate situation. In fact, if you are particularly skillful, you might even turn this situation into a learning experience.

Obviously, you'll have to make sure this is a true report. Go to the school and get the evidence for yourself. If the teacher *is* doing a poor job, you need to consider a few things that could go wrong with a teacher.

1. The teacher has trouble handling her own authority. When this happens, one of two things occurs. Either she is so inconsistent and disorganized that the classroom is in a state of chaos; or she comes down so hard on students that she controls through sheer fear. Either way, the students don't get much work done.

2. The teacher is lazy, tired and burned-out. Some teachers simply spend so much energy that it finally catches up with them. They don't care anymore. They quit preparing lessons, or at least they don't prepare thoroughly enough. They don't read and grade the students' papers. Students soon catch on to a teacher like this. They not only quit working, but they begin to play around in class.

Now you are in a better position to help. Let's explore some steps you can take:

1. Help your daughter understand what is happening to her. Help with her lessons. Supplement, if you have to. And while you're doing that, help her understand that not all human beings she meets in life will be pleasant people.

2. Go see the teacher. If at all possible, see her under friendly terms. Try to find out what might be bothering her. You may find that she has some personal or family matter making her life miserable. Offer to help. And help your daughter understand.

3. See the principal. Again, go in a non-threatening but straightforward way. If the class is total chaos, the principal probably already agrees with you but may not be able to admit it to you. State your displeasure. Give specific examples if you can. If the principal has a course of action, give that new plan time to work. Offer your support, but at the same time make sure the principal knows the problem.

Our sixth-grade son tells us he's going to take typing. Isn't that a bit early?

With so many children beginning to use computers at early ages, some as early as kindergarten, when is the appropriate time to teach students the correct activities of a keyboard?

Some experts tell us a child can properly finger a computer keyboard as soon as he's old enough to finger a piano. Others say youngsters can't be effective until high school.

I'm not sure with whom I agree, but I do have a couple of observations: (1) I've seen sixth-graders master the fingering process, so they *can* do it; (2) Every student must take typing sometime. Let me restate that. Every student growing up in the last quarter of the 20th century *must* learn to master the keyboard. It should be criminal to let students out of high school without this skill, but we are doing it.

When our son was in the elementary school just around the corner, we knew all his friends. But now that he is in junior high across town, we don't know any of them. Are we normal in feeling we have lost control?

Yes, not only normal but justified. But you don't really have to despair—not yet, at least. If you work this right, you might be able to turn it into a positive educational experience, both for you and your son.

You will need to get to know his new friends. Of course, you may never know them as well as you knew the playmates from the neighborhood, but you can at least get an idea of what they look like and what they wear.

Encourage your son to invite his friends over. This means that you have to have the kind of home where young adolescents feel welcome. This may mean a few home improvements, such as a basketball hoop out by the driveway or even a new stereo set in the living room, but these could be sound investments.

If he still seems reticent, you may give him permission to have a party—with adult supervision, of course. Thus, you will at least get a glimpse of the new friends when they come through the door.

If your attempts to get the new friends over to the house fail, volunteer to drive him around. Now, I know that is a big commitment, but the extra time is worth the effort. For some reason I don't fully understand, young people tend to loosen up a bit when they are riding in the backseat of an automobile.

If your son is involved in any kind of extracurricular activities, become a supporter. This accomplishes two goals. You get to see his friends in action because in all probability his friends come not from his classes, but from his activities. Even more importantly, being there to support your son will make your relationship stronger.

Our sophomore daughter is taking geometry this year. She started the year working hard and doing well. She worked on homework almost every night. She studied hard for the tests, and she had a strong B average. But just after Christmas, she missed three days of school with chicken pox. Since then she hasn't even tried. Now she's failing the class. What happened? Could missing three days of class make all that difference?

What an excellent question! Students and teachers everywhere will thank you for asking it. The answer is an emphatic *yes*. Yes, missing three days of a class like geometry could make all the difference in the world.

The reason is rather simple when you think about it. Geometry—and other classes—build concept on concept. Every day the teacher sets out to present a new concept to the class. In fact, the good teacher will write one new concept on the board so the whole class will understand the objective for the day.

But the teacher often covers three other concepts before he gets to the main one. If a student misses any one of those preliminary concepts, he won't be able to get the main one. When a student is absent, a good teacher will be deliberate in showing the student the main concept, but even the best of teachers forget about all those other concepts en route.

How do we know which concept is missing? We don't get far asking a general question such as "What don't you understand?" If your daughter knew what she didn't understand, she could probably find it somewhere and learn it on her own. At this point, however, she doesn't understand *any* of it. She needs to go through a series of specific questions until she and her teacher can identify the missing concept. I know this sounds like tedious work, but I don't know of a shortcut.

Is it possible for my child to get a value-free education in the public schools?

No. How's that for a short but frightening answer? Let's face it: There is no such thing as a value-free education; there never was and never can be. Education, by its very definition, is an enterprise in preparing people for a future. To do this, someone has to guess what that future holds and what is the best way to prepare for it. Those guesses constitute values. We can't escape it.

Let's look at some of the ways human values are consciously or unconsciously incorporated into the school process. For starters, just the structure of the school day teaches certain values, such as the importance of being on time, the importance of following instructions, and the importance of the mind. Students really don't have any options. If they go to school, they are going to learn that we Americans believe in being on time. That is the way the program operates.

Teachers make hundreds of value judgments every day. They decide which piece of material gets three days of emphasis and which piece gets only one day. They decide what they'll explain and what they won't explain. They decide what is a good piece of work and deserves an A. Conversely, they decide what *isn't* a good piece of work and gets a D.

I don't want to frighten anybody, but a lot of what we adults value is what we learned from some teacher whose name we probably don't even remember. No, there simply is not something called a value-free education.

Aren't extracurricular activities just frills that weaken the educations of our young people?

No, I don't think so. Still, I do hear those cries for emphasis on the basics, and I agree. We must be diligent in teaching young people the skills of reading, writing, organizing, calculating and using their minds. This is what school is all about.

Yet, at the same time, extracurricular activities can—and should—contribute to that mission, at least in a couple of ways. For one thing, the student who takes an active role in extracurricular activities is usually more excited about life, about school, and about learning. Because of this excitement, he is more highly motivated to apply himself to the sometimes difficult task of learning the basics.

One thing that we have learned from recent research is that the more students enjoy coming to school, the more they learn. That point is so obvious that we probably knew it long before the research proved it to us.

Besides, extracurricular activities carry some significant lessons. Notice how many corporate executives were active in a variety of extracurricular activities. Notice how many military leaders were high school athletes. These activities provide young people a practical arena in which to develop such skills as leadership, commitment to a group project, dedication, and personal discipline. I am prepared to argue that these lessons are just as important as the lessons of reading, writing and calculating.

For these reasons, I think extracurricular activities are valuable. I would hope that we have enough variety—sports, music, speech, yearbook, etc.—that every student has an opportunity to participate. Providing a broad base of extracurricular programs within the school structure is one of the strengths of American education.

Do Christian students really have much influence in the public schools?

Yes, yes, a thousand times yes! Christian students have an impact on other students, on teachers, and even in the community at large.

There may be a few laws restricting what Christians can say in a public place such as a school, but there is no law keeping a Christian from being a Christian; from thinking as a Christian; from looking at other people through the eyes of a Lord of love; and from keeping a lifestyle that is not conformed to this world, but is transformed by spiritual commitment to a righteous God.

Some Christian students witness by doing quality work. Frequently, teachers will comment that students from "church" families are easier to teach. What they are saying is the solid family unit that has God at the center makes a difference in the lives of young people.

Let me give another example. Roger and Sue were a perfect match in high school. Sue was a cheerleader, straight-A student and homecoming queen. Roger was president of a couple of school organizations and captain of the football team. It seemed obvious to everyone that the two should be dating.

But there was one small glitch. Sue was a Christian and Roger wasn't. Finally, when Roger got up the nerve and asked Sue out, she agreed only on the condition that Roger would attend church with her each Sunday night. Since Sue was one of the prettier girls in school, Roger decided the price was not too high. He agreed. Shortly after they began dating, Roger responded to the message of the Gospel and became a believer.

The two dated through high school, but when they went away to different colleges, the romance faded into just another high school memory.

Today, Roger is a successful minister, pastoring a large church in the Midwest—an effective servant of God who was first introduced to Christ because a high school girl was not afraid to stand on her convictions.

Adapted from *Parents' Most-Asked Questions about Kids and Schools,* © 1989 by SP Publications. Published by Victor Books. Used by permission.

41

HOW GOOD IS YOUR CHILD'S SCHOOL?

Robert W. Smith

What did you do in school today?"
"Nothing."

Unfortunately, parents, this may be true. Choosing a school is perhaps the most important decision you'll have to make between the time your child is six and 12. Whether your youngster is already in school, will be changing schools or entering for the first time this coming fall, you will want to know just how well that school is going to deliver its product: a solid education.

So how do you judge a school's quality and performance? Of course, you might consult with neighbors, friends, and other parents. But only you can decide what is best for your child. To do this properly, you will have to check out the school for yourself.

The first step is to call the school you are considering and make an appointment to visit the building and sit in on some classrooms.

If the school refuses, something's wrong. No school with any faith in its program is going to deny you an opportunity to observe it in operation. A public school in today's scrutinizing environment should welcome your visit. If the school is not cooperative, contact a school board member, explain your desires, and you will invariably find that the next time you call the principal, he or she will be extremely anxious to accommodate you. Any quality private school will likewise be anxious to have you view its program.

What to Look For

When you talk to the principal, ask him to describe the school's program. Encourage him to keep talking by being an attentive listener. Ask leading questions: How long have the teachers been there? Are they planning to return next year? Does the principal honor parental requests for a specific teacher?

Most smart principals do. Not that many are going to bother; but if parents make a request, they are basically committing themselves to work in tandem with that teacher. It's usually a good deal for all involved, especially the child.

Classroom Visits

Sit in on one or more classrooms for at least a morning or afternoon. Watch the movement of the children. Is it controlled and purposeful? Are the children on task? That is, are they reading, writing, working on a project, or doing some other appropriate activity? Are the children able to do the assignments? Do the children seem bored or enthusiastic? Enthusiasm is contagious. Kids get it from their teachers.

Curriculum

Does every pupil have the same assignment, or is the work tailored to fit the needs of the special learner—for example, the gifted child or the child with learning difficulties? Are the expectations challenging to all students? Are the activities imaginative and creative, or are they fill-in-the-blanks workbook activities? A little of this busy work goes a long way.

Look for assignments that involve "real" writing—letters, stories, reports, essays. Kids don't learn to work from textbooks or workbooks. They have to do it. Look for evidence of real, hands-on science experiments. Reading about science is reading, not science. Science is doing.

Reading also means doing. Almost every school has some textbook program. But what counts is how much time and encouragement the children have to read library books and literature. Students from third grade on should have a daily program primarily based on reading and discussing children's literature. Some of the best writing done in the last 20 years has been for children.

Homework

Every good school has a policy emphasizing routine homework assignments. These might be drill or practice materials designed to reinforce basic skills. Children in the primary grades should receive at least a half hour of homework nightly. Upper grade students (grades four–six) should spend at least an hour on homework.

Reading should be a part of this assignment. Also, by encouraging your child to read for enjoyment at bedtime, you will help build a habit that can last a lifetime.

Class Environment

Take a good look at the classroom. Is it bright, cheerful and interesting to look at? Are the bulletin boards vibrant, or scuffed and worn with age? Are animals or other science activities visible? Are reading materials available? A classroom without a wide assortment of books on hand is sterile.

Class Size

How large is the class? Some schools—both public and private—try to make ends meet by shoehorning more children into each class. No matter how bright or well-behaved the children are, they need individual attention, and it's sometimes difficult to get in a class with more than 30 pupils.

Parent aides are no substitute for smaller class size. It's nice to have an aide in the classroom, but don't be fooled by the adult/child ratio. You want to know the teacher/pupil average.

Are the children the primary responsibility of one teacher, or are they shunted from teacher to teacher on a "tracking" system? Grade school children are too young to become numbers.

The Teacher

All other things being equal, your child's success in school for a year is going to depend on one person: the teacher. She (or he) has to be effective. Most of all, she must care enough to do the job with imagination and commitment. A burned-out teacher just putting in time is not likely to give the kind of energy and enthusiasm necessary to ensure learning.

Organization is crucial. Learning does not occur in an uproar or in gaping hunks of idle time. The materials need to be right at hand, and the teacher should move from one lesson to another with smooth transition.

Laughter and learning travel together. The joy of learning should be evident in a classroom, and the teacher is the fountain of that joy.

The Principal

The principal needs to be available to parents, teachers and students. He or she should be highly visible during the school day—in classrooms, in the cafeteria at lunch time, in the corridors—talking with students and offering correction and encouragement as needed. A principal locked away in his office is out of touch with his school.

School Site

The school grounds are important. Does the area appear safe? Are buildings well-maintained or is graffiti scrawled all over the walls? No area is immune from the scourge of graffiti, but it can be contained by promptly removing it.

Is there enough room on the school yard? Children need plenty of space to play games and sturdy equipment such as swings, bars and ball courts. Is there enough play equipment for the school population?

Bathrooms

Check the bathrooms. It sounds ridiculous, but many schools are lax about sanitation. The bathrooms should be clean, properly ventilated, safe to use, and equipped with soap and hand towels.

Apart from the sense of cleanliness itself, poor hygienic facilities mean that your children will be exposed to more illnesses and miss more school.

Recess

Watch the kids at recess and listen to their chatter. A sensitive and alert observer can quickly sense their attitudes. Notice if they are properly supervised with at least one adult on duty. Misbehaving children should be promptly corrected.

At a good school, most students will be involved in some sort of physical activity during recess. Too many children hanging around, moping about, or disturbing others indicates problems.

Values

Values are the adhesives which hold our society together and ultimately make life meaningful. As parents you want the values you have instilled at home to be reinforced at school. These values ought not to conflict with the mores of the school or your children's peer groups.

Parent Involvement

Many parents work and can't help at school, but good schools are still able to recruit committed parents and retired people to help as aides, volunteers and PTA helpers. See how many parents are involved at the school, what they are doing, and how you could help.

Overall Assessment

Your final judgment of your child's school is based on all of these criteria along with your own special needs.

Schools will be better in some areas than others, of course, and you should decide to work on improving those weaker areas by bringing your concerns to the teachers, the principal, or if necessary, the district authorities. A good school is going to welcome input and make every effort to correct weaknesses.

By taking these steps and doing some homework, you can send your child off to school with some confidence that school days will be "learning" days.

❦ INSIGHT ❦

Criteria for a Good School

- Committed teachers.
- Easy access to the principal.
- Children are on task doing meaningful work.
- High expectations for all students.
- Routine daily homework assignments.
- Values are fostered.
- Clean rooms.
- Good play areas.
- Bathrooms are clean, safe and properly stocked.

42

MAKING THE GRADE

Sara L. Smith

I waken fully alert, as I do only when I haven't slept well the night before. Ominous dread hangs over me like a hungry vulture. I cannot choke down my breakfast. My fingers are cold as ice, yet my body is damp with perspiration. I know my apprehension will last for hours, until the fateful time when my worst fears will be confirmed or denied.

It's report card day.

My own report card days are over, thank goodness. But I have four school-age children, one of whom has academic problems, and I still feel trepidation when report cards arrive every January and June. Now that parents and educators are calling for a return to high academic standards, now that social promotion is a thing of the past, and now that colleges are tightening admission requirements, report card day is more important than ever.

Like all parents, I want my children to get good grades. But many times, report cards are magnified far out of proportion to their real significance. School grades should never be looked on as a measure of a child's worth. Too many children fear their parents won't love them if they don't get good grades. And, too many conscientious parents give their children just that impression.

Once, our principal gave a sad account of a kindergartner who was afraid to get on the scales to be weighed. She was terrified she would fail.

I vowed not to make this mistake with my children, and I found myself searching the Scriptures for guidance. How can I encourage my children to strive for excellence without burdening them with guilt and fear?

Prepare. *"Train up a child in the way he should go"* (Proverbs 22:6). Before a child ever starts school, he should be learning self-discipline. He needs to be shown that gratification is not always instant. A thirst for knowledge is a priceless gift. Reading to him, taking him to the zoo, the museum or on nature walks show him that there is a whole world out there to explore.

Don't compare. *"Judge not"* (Matthew 7:1). When my daughter brings home a "C," it's a warning signal that something is wrong. When my oldest son brings home a "C," it's cause for celebration. I try to keep individual discussion of grades private, and I've told my children that their grades are a matter between themselves, their teachers and their parents, not their friends and their siblings. We all have our strengths and weaknesses.

Beware, *". . . lest any man should boast"* (Eph. 2:9). It's easy to get caught up in grades, to treat them as an end in themselves. Too much emphasis on grades may discourage a child from taking an advanced or difficult course. I don't think a child should ever be paid for a good report card. A hug and a quiet "I'm proud of you" is all the reward he needs. Bribery encourages the idea that everything has its price. It can also tempt a child to cheat, and it may ultimately backfire in open rebellion.

Be fair. *"Provoke not your children to wrath"* (Ephesians 6:4). In how many homes does a poor report card bring ugly recriminations: "How do you expect to get into college with these grades?" "What is the matter with you?" "I'm so ashamed of you I could die!" Such attacks will only foster resentment.

Instead, the child should be given a chance to explain. Perhaps he didn't understand the material. Perhaps there was a personality conflict with the teacher. Perhaps the child suffers from an impairment such as dyslexia or needs glasses and hasn't been able to see the blackboard.

Sometimes parents decide that penalties and restrictions need to be imposed. But the child always holds trump in the report-card game. "You can take away all my privileges, but you can't take away my 'F' in algebra," a rebellious teen may respond.

Report cards should not turn school work into a no-win contest of wills. This is not to say a child who doesn't try to do well in school should never be rebuked. Scripture tells us that children need to be corrected—but not to assuage their parents' egos.

Learn to care. *"Blessed are the merciful . . . the pure in heart . . . the peacemakers"* (Matthew 5:7–9). There was a boy in my high school class who received a nearly perfect score on his college boards, but he had no friends. His life could hardly be termed successful, let alone abundant.

Such qualities as kindness and compassion ultimately matter more than scholastic honors.

When we go back to basics, we shouldn't forget the most basic need of all is love. Christian parents need to emphasize the fruits of the Spirit over the way the world keeps score.

A member of my church gave a testimony that shows how love and acceptance can encourage a child to "reach for the mark." He had received notice that his daughter had been placed on academic probation at college, and he was bitterly disappointed in her. It had been a financial hardship to send her to school. He planned to give her a furious tongue-lashing and withdraw her from college.

But when the girl arrived home, the angry words would not come. Instead, he put his arms around his daughter and assured her of his love. Tearfully, the girl confessed to a semester of partying and asked for another chance. She went on to graduate with honors.

Our Heavenly Father loves us even when we fail Him. No one can meet His standards. Yet, if we trust in Him for salvation, we won't flunk out of heaven. Our children learn spiritual truths from our example. Good grades must be earned, but our love for our children, like God's love for us, should be an unconditional gift.

43

HOW TO IMPROVE THE PARENT-TEACHER CONNECTION

Cheri Fuller

O pen house. As I raced to my son's next class, the heel of my shoe turned, and I slipped on the slick hall floor. A man walking by grabbed me just before I hit the ground.

"Are you all right?" he asked.

"No," I answered, "but I'll be okay."

We only had five minutes between bells to find classes, and this was a big high school. My foot hurt, and I knew I was going to be late.

Hurried, I slid into the seat closest to the door in my son's history class, just in time to hear the teacher say, "I like to teach ninth-graders, but I'm certainly glad they have to go home to you!" Teenagers, she explained, are a handful. Oh, how I knew that—or at least was beginning to find out. But this time, I was on the other side of the desk, sitting in one of the small wooden chairs my son sat in every day.

Open houses, usually held early in the school year, are one way to meet your child's teacher(s) and to start becoming involved with his or her school. Recent research reveals a strong correlation between parental involvement in school and student achievement. Parents and teachers are partners in education, and if we are going to work for the best interests of our children, we need to know our partners.

At open house, parents may see a sampling of their children's work. At all levels, each teacher gives a presentation, explaining the curriculum and what the students are learning in the class. Often, he or she will explain the grading scale, homework requirements and goals for the school year. Parents get a sense of the teacher's expectations. But most teachers don't have time to discuss individual students at open house; instead, it's a get-acquainted time.

I have heard teachers say to parents, "Don't believe everything you hear about me, and I won't believe everything I hear about you!" Effective communication between home and school is vital to avoid misunderstandings—or to clear them up when they occur. Despite our best efforts to make our educational system effective, the truth is that schools are imperfect institutions run by imperfect people working with imperfect students. Mistakes will be made by all parties involved. But together we can work to identify and solve problems before they affect our children's progress.

You may be thinking, *But my child is doing above-average work.* Even if your child is doing well in school, it helps for you to get to know his teacher and keep the lines of communication open for future needs. You want to know that your child is being challenged, not just sliding by. You can gain important insights into your child's development and how he interacts with peers. You will learn ways to encourage your child's special skills and to provide needed support at home. The teacher needs your interest and support because education is a team effort, and you are a vital part of the team.

The Parent-Teacher Conference

Another means of establishing communication between home and school is the parent-teacher conference. Schools generally set aside a certain day for these conferences, but if there is a legitimate need, you can request a meeting with your child's teacher at any time during the year. Here are some guidelines to help make it a productive time of working together:

1. If possible, both parents should attend the conference. With both parents present, you can get a more balanced picture of the child and his school situation.

2. Be aware that nervousness or anxiety may surface because you are meeting with someone you don't know who teaches your child every day and is "in charge." Realize that these feelings are normal.

"Butterflies raced in my stomach before the conference with Jennifer's teachers," said Carolyn. "I was so nervous I couldn't think of what I wanted to say. I was afraid that the teacher was going to tell me Jennifer had a reading problem or talked too much or something. I didn't know *what* she was going to say, and I didn't know if I really wanted to hear it."

For some people, the educational setting and jargon is intimidating. If your own school days were painful, old memories may rise and cause you to become defensive. Be patient with yourself and know that some anxiety is normal. The better you get to know the teacher, the less awkward the conferences will be.

3. Be on time and prepared by having talked with your child in advance, asking how things are going at school, what he likes best and if he has any problems.

4. Most teachers work very hard and need encouragement. Express thanks for the teacher's efforts in working with your child, for some interesting project the class has done or for some class activity your child particularly enjoyed.

5. Bring a list of questions you may have or subjects you would like to discuss. Here are some good questions to ask at a conference:

- How is my child doing in class?
- Is he consistent about turning in class work or homework?
- Does he use time well? What are his work habits like?
- Does he pay attention? How is his behavior in class?
- How well does he get along with other children?
- Does he have friends? Does he seem to be happy?
- What can be done at home to reinforce or support what you are doing here at school?

- Are there any learning activities you can suggest to be done at home?

6. Remember, a conference is a time for both parent and teacher to talk *and* listen. Be tactful but honest. Let the teacher know about any health problems or handicaps, any recent crisis or change at home that may affect your child's learning. In addition, you can share your goals for your child. You can gain valuable insight into the child's development by listening carefully as the teacher describes how he functions in class and how he is progressing both academically and socially.

7. If there is a problem that you know about, don't wait until it becomes severe before you call the teacher to schedule a conference. If you are concerned about something, write a note or call to request a parent-teacher conference. Then, when you and the teacher meet together, try to determine the cause of the problem. Often it will stem from a single situation in one class that is negatively affecting the child's whole school experience. It may be that he is disorganized or just behind in math. You may see one side of the puzzle and the teacher the other.

Begin by sharing with the teacher what is happening at home, describing what feedback you are getting from the student. Then ask, "What is happening with my child here at school? What do you see?" By putting your views together with those of the teacher, you will likely get a more complete picture of the situation.

Working together, parent and teacher can identify the problem and discover ways to help the child. Be careful not to blame the teacher; avoid an adversary relationship. As one teacher said, "Some parents see a parent-teacher conference as a meeting of opposing forces." Don't approach your child's teacher in a negative frame of mind. Instead, let your attitude be, *What can we do together to further the best interest of this child?*

8. Follow up on the conference. The teacher may suggest some home-learning activities she believes will strengthen the child's skills. Try your best to follow through on these suggestions and then get back with the teacher to share the results. Show interest in school work, not just at report card and conference time, but throughout the school year. Encourage your child to respect the teacher and cooperate with her, to be quiet and attentive in class,

and to communicate with the teacher when a problem arises or when he needs help.

You can be a partner in your child's education by finding some school-related activity you enjoy participating in or helping with. Some parents like to organize school carnivals, while others prefer to help out in the computer room or library.

Even working mothers and fathers can find time to become involved. The Durham County school system in North Carolina reports one of the highest percentages of working mothers in the United States. Yet the school system recruits 200 volunteers a year under a PTA Partnership Program.

The Yarmouth (Maine) elementary schools have over 150 parent volunteers who work with children in the computer lab, type their stories and transform them into books in the publishing center, work in the library, teach crafts at the annual Colonial Crafts Day and serve in many other areas of school life.

Other school systems are discovering ingenious ways for parents to become partners with the school. Here are some ways you can get involved in your child's education:

- Help with field trips; make materials for the classroom or assist in class.
- Help with class parties.
- Provide one-on-one tutoring for students with learning disabilities.
- Go to school one day and have lunch with your child in the cafeteria. (Check with the school office first; most schools welcome a parent guest for lunch, if previously scheduled.)
- Join and participate in the local PTA, which affords other opportunities for involvement: raising funds for needed equipment, helping in the library, supervising in the cafeteria and taking part in many other supportive activities.
- Attend school sports events, awards assemblies and fine arts presentations such as musical programs, stage productions and art shows.

Classroom Observation

One of the best means of parent-teacher contact is visiting the classroom to observe how your child is being taught. You never know what is going on in the classroom or what method the teacher employs until you sit quietly in the back of her room and watch the proceedings.

"This first-hand observation shows parents how the teacher teaches and gives parents ideas on what they can do at home," say researchers in *What Works: Research About Teaching and Learning,* published by the United States Department of Education.

One year my husband and I became concerned about persistent reports of poor discipline, general chaos and teacher tardiness in our son's junior high school classes. So my husband called the principal, and in a diplomatic way asked if he could spend an afternoon at school. He was graciously allowed to do so. First he had lunch with our son, then he went through the rest of the school day with him. Although my husband had to take time off from work, it was a valuable and insightful afternoon.

Often the only time we visit our child's classroom is to drop off cookies for the Valentine's Day party. I have heard parents say, "Johnny would just die of embarrassment if I came up to his school." Actually, Johnny may not mind at all. Even if he does mind, it would be better for him to be a little embarrassed now than for his parents to discover at the end of the school year that there had been a big problem that could have been solved with a little personal attention.

Here are some guidelines for effective classroom observation:

1. Notify the principal ahead of time that you would like to observe the class. Explain that you would like to get a clearer picture of what is expected of your child and to better help him at home. I have never known of a parent being denied permission to observe his child in class.

2. Before arriving in the classroom, check to make sure the principal has notified the teacher of your visit.

3. Arrive on time, at the beginning of class rather than right in the middle, so you don't disrupt instruction.

4. If you would like, ask for a copy of the main textbooks so you can follow along with the class.

5. Sit in the back of the room and be very quiet.

6. From the schedule on the board (if there is one), note *how* the teacher and students spend their time. Also try to determine the teacher's particular learning style.

Here are some clues:

A *visual teacher* puts up lots of colorful bulletin boards and displays (even in upper grades) and uses a variety of visual teaching materials such as written instruction and handouts. She may even use an overhead projector. Usually she does not provide a great deal of oral explanation and may quickly grow weary of answering oral questions. (All this is great if your child is a visual learner.)

An *auditory teacher* usually keeps a little plainer classroom, one that is functional but attractive. She provides lots of verbal explanation and welcomes discussion. There is more talking about the lesson, reasons for activities and questions. The students may be allowed to study together or participate in small-group discussions. The auditory teacher usually gives instructions for class assignments or homework orally, rather than in written form. (That's fine as long as your child is also auditory; otherwise, he may not get all the directions and may fail to follow through on his work.)

A *kinesthetic teacher* will usually place an emphasis on hands-on learning activities—more doing and personal involvement on everyone's part. Rather than having all the chairs arranged in the traditional back-to-front order, all facing the teacher's desk, she may prefer an open classroom, with several circular "learning centers" scattered about the room. She allows for more physical movement than other teachers, relies on demonstrations rather than explanations, and assigns projects and posters for reinforcement of her student's learning. It is a real treat for a kinesthetic child to have a kinesthetic teacher! (It may not, however, be the ideal learning environment for the visual or auditory learner.)

Being aware of the learning-teaching style of your child's teacher is valuable. Although teachers are being encouraged to allow for varied learning styles in their classrooms, sometimes your child will have a teacher whose teaching style is just the opposite of his own way of receiving and understanding information.

If your child is a kinesthetic learner and his teacher uses primarily visual and auditory strategies, it can be a prime source of frustration for the child, perhaps resulting in a low level of achievement. By classroom observation, you can note any gaps in learning style and better determine what you can do to help fill those gaps at home.

Perhaps you can even suggest some methods of study and classroom coping strategies which will help your child adapt. He needs to adjust to a variety of teaching styles, and you can give him the tools to do so.

7. When you leave, don't forget to thank the teacher, saying something positive to her before you go.

One mother found that a good time to observe her child's classroom for a short period was when she came to the school to give a birthday party or attend a PTA committee meeting. She would go a little early and watch the teacher and students interact, observing how her child related to the other students in the class.

You will get a much better and more realistic grasp of your child's school experience by actually visiting his class while it is in session. So much of what we know of school is hearsay; sometimes we need a first-hand view.

Support, encourage and pray for the teachers, administrators and students of your child's school. Remember that many problems can be prevented by keeping in touch. With good communication between his parent and his teacher, aided by your active interest and cooperation, school will be a much more positive experience for your child.

44

DISCOVERING YOUR CHILD'S LEARNING STYLE

Cheri Fuller

One night recently our fourth grader, Alison, had 30 irregular verb forms to memorize in the present, past and past perfect tenses—that's 90 words! She had been sick one day and missed the class explanation, so at first the task looked overwhelming.

Nevertheless, I went over the list orally with her. I've learned that Alison needs to hear and verbalize information in order to understand and remember it. I helped her record on tape each verb and its forms, which she enjoyed thoroughly. We played the tape over several times, and she recited along with it. Then I gave her an oral practice test and circled the missed verbs. She studied the ones that gave her trouble, saying them aloud. The whole process took half an hour.

The next morning, Alison used her recording to practice the verbs during breakfast. At school, she received a 95 on her test—and a jolt of confidence.

This a good example of finding a "learning style" that works for your child. As a teacher, I've often looked out at my students and thought what a difference it would make in their learning if their parents actively helped. For most children, school could become a more positive, successful experience.

Whether your youngster is in a private, public or home school, *you* are his most important teacher. William Bennet, former U.S. Secretary of Education, said, "Parents are their children's first and most influential teachers. What parents do to help their children learn is more important to academic success than how well-off the family is."

Unfortunately, many parents don't know how to help their children learn. A good way to start is by understanding and then utilizing your child's learning style.

What Is Learning Style?

Just as your child has a distinct temperament, personality and spiritual motivation, he also has a particular way of learning. There are 21 different factors that make up learning style. Perhaps your child learns best alone or when studying with peers. Maybe he needs a structured setting with an adult. Some kids learn best in a quiet room, others with background noise; some learn in logical steps while others see the whole picture.

The senses through which each child absorbs and retains new information are the *auditory, visual* and *kinesthetic*. Some children, like Alison, are auditory learners. They learn best by hearing and verbalizing new information. Others need to see and retain a mental picture; they are visual learners. Kinesthetic learners need to touch and use movement to process new concepts. They learn by doing.

Let's look at three children with three distinct styles of learning and some ways to maximize their learning at home.

Meghan, an Auditory Learner

Meghan talked early and constantly, with a wide and colorful vocabulary. Her clear speech sounded like a little adult as she related riddles and creative stories to her family. She is a bright, sociable child, but she often has difficulty with spelling and math.

Meghan spells everything phonetically, so her words are often written incorrectly. She also has trouble remembering multiplication tables, which slows her during arithmetic tests. And Meghan is easily distracted in class. She verbalizes everything and needs to hear information and then say it in order to learn it.

Meghan should use her mind's ear to "sub-vocalize" when she's reading, studying spelling words or doing math problems. By saying to herself what she needs to learn, difficult information will be recalled.

A tape recorder is the auditory learner's best friend and will boost Meghan's comprehension. Tape-recorded addition, subtraction and multiplication facts can help the auditory learner gain speed in doing math. She can use flash cards with the tape recorder or summarize a chapter on tape and play it back for review. When studying spelling at home, the auditory learner should say a word aloud and write it several times.

Because auditory learners are distracted by background noise while studying, they need to study in a quiet room.

Brian, a Visual Learner

Brian relies more on seeing things and visualizing them. As a baby, Brian could be quieted by the sight of his mother's face or by the movement of his crib mobile. As a toddler, Brian learned colors quickly. When traveling in a car, he looked attentively at passing billboards, often noticing some detail that his parents missed. Brian loves to draw and has a great imagination. But he cannot listen for long periods without beginning to doodle, squirm or daydream.

A strong phonics-based reading program at Brian's kindergarten has been difficult for him. He is already behind in reading. Since he learns best by seeing and retaining a mental picture, he can learn to make his own flash cards for vocabulary and spelling words (with the word in bright marker on one side and his illustration of it on the other side). This can be done for math, too.

The visual learner is easily hooked by television, so TV time should be limited and parents should provide plenty of interesting and accessible books and magazines.

The visual student is also distracted by a disorderly study area, and works best on an organized, neat table or desk. He will enjoy working alone and taking responsibility for assignments, but should also do oral drills before tests.

Visual memory can be improved by organizing a simple memory

game using a variety of interesting objects. Place the objects on a tray and cover them. Then take the cover away and let each person view the objects for 30–45 seconds before covering them again. Whoever can list the most objects is the winner.

Josh, a Kinesthetic Learner

Josh was a wiggly baby. As a toddler, he was in perpetual motion. He explored things by pulling and taking them apart. He was also an athletic prodigy. At age four Josh delighted his family with his ability to ride a bicycle without training wheels. Today, he excels in a local gymnastics class and is the star player on his soccer team.

Because of his constant squirming and short attention span, however, Josh has not been a teacher's favorite. Learning to read has been a frustrating experience, and all academic subjects are hard for Josh.

A kinesthetic child like Josh needs a multi-sensory phonics reading and math program using plastic or sandpaper letters and numbers to emphasize touch in learning. At home, one of his best tools will be a large chalkboard. When learning new spelling words, Josh can write them in large letters and then erase them. Or, he can practice writing spelling words on large sheets of colored construction paper, first with a marker, then a pencil, then a bright crayon.

The kinesthetic learner often lacks good listening skills. Using games and activities at home will improve his auditory memory. Listening to taped stories and books is valuable, and read-aloud books with plenty of action will hold their appeal.

Josh, Brian and Meghan show a bent for learning in different ways, but we must be aware of some cautions. Being a visual, auditory or kinesthetic learner does not mean a child cannot learn in any other mode. About 30 percent of children have no specific learning style.

Moreover, as a child grows, learning styles can shift, blend or develop. Infants through kindergarten children are very kinesthetic; most children develop visual skills by grade two, and auditory skills strengthen by grade six.

Develop your own ideas for your children's homework and study time. As you understand how they learn, you can be more supportive when they need help. With these secrets to school success, both you and your children will find joy in learning, and you will help prepare them for the special purpose God has for each of their lives!

❦ INSIGHT ❦

What Is Your Child's Learning Style?

To determine a young child's learning style, imagine you are reading aloud from a book with a repeated refrain like "and the rabbit went hop, hop, hop" or "There once was a boy with a little toy drum; with a rat-a-tat-tat and a rum-y-tum-tum." Does your child:

- Come up close, perhaps insisting on being on your lap, to see the pictures? This is a sign of a visual learner.
- Mimic the words of the refrain or interrupt to talk about the story? This is a sign of an auditory learner.
- Move around and do what the refrain says—hop and jump? This is the sign of a kinesthetic learner.

45

DISCOVERING THE CLASSICS

C. Joanne Sloan

R ead the first two chapters," the teacher explains as she passes
out copies of Cikens' *Great Expectations*. "Be prepared for class
discussion and a quiz tomorrow.

Patrick, a bright high school sophomore, opens his book. After
staring at the first page for a while, he turns to the girl behind him.

"This books looks boring," he whispers. "Are you going to read
it?"

"No," answers Leigh. "I bought *Cliff Notes*. The chapter sum-
maries tell you everything you need to know."

"Do you think the bookstore has any more?"

"Yes, but you better hurry. Everyone in the class will be wanting
them."

As a former high school teacher, I've found that many young
people—even students in college preparatory classes—are turned off
by the classics. Unfortunately, they never allowed themselves the
privilege of discovering great literature.

Parents can have a significant influence on their children's reading habits. Here are some suggestions for helping youngsters develop a love for the classics.

Encourage your children to read the Bible.

Patrick Henry said it well: "The Bible is worth all other books which have ever been printed." The Bible has been called a complete library because it contains adventure stories, romances, history, law, philosophy and poetry. In the early days of our country, the Bible was the only book available, and readers immersed themselves in its pages. Many of our nation's leaders read the Bible regularly, including John Quincy Adams, the sixth president, who made it a practice to read the Bible cover to cover every year.

What a contrast to our modern society! Today, many children recognize Mr. T and Captain Kirk, but don't know who Abraham, Moses and Paul were. You can help your children set up a schedule for reading the Bible each day. If you don't believe they're ready to tackle the entire Bible, suggest they read the books that contain familiar stories, such as Genesis, Exodus, Ruth, Samuel and one of the gospels. From a literary standpoint, it is important for your children to become familiar with the Bible because many great works of literature contain Biblical allusions.

Set an example by what you read.

If you only read romance novels, you're not exposing your youngsters to quality reading. If you feel inadequate about choosing classics for yourself or suggesting them for your children, consult resource guides such as Clifton Fadiman's *Lifetime Reading Plan* or Mortimer J. Adler's *Great Books*. English teachers and librarians usually recommend lists of classics grouped according to age levels. You might also peruse the classics section of a bookstore or library. Students bored with assigned reading of classics at school may have a different perspective if they see their parents reading classics at home for recreation and enjoyment. If children grow up in a home where parents normally turn to books, chances are they will learn to like reading.

Build your own home library.

You can start a library with very little expense. Look for books at used bookstores, garage sales and community events. Our family anticipates our public library's semi-annual book sale, where hardbacks go for 50 cents and paperbacks cost a quarter. Give books for Christmas and birthday gifts. Begin by giving your young children

such classics as Beatrix Potter's *The Tale of Peter Rabbit* or Robert Mc-
Closkey's *Make Way for Ducklings.* Your children will begin to perceive books as special possessions at an early age. Keep books in
convenient places in your home. We have books in every room of
our house—even the kitchen. Give your children a place to store
their own books.

Share classics you enjoyed when you were young.

Read favorite classics aloud to your children when they are small. As
they get older, talk about books that influenced you while growing
up.

A few years ago, I suggested to my daughter that she read *Jane
Eyre* and *Wuthering Heights,* two of my favorite British classics. This
was during a time in her life when she was spending all of her allowance on teen romances. She reluctantly agreed to read the two novels. Now, three years later, she has read more than 100 classics.

When suggesting books to your children, be enthusiastic. Don't
say, "Get *Tom Sawyer* from the library and read it." Look through the
book first with your child and point out some of the interesting aspects. Get your children talking about books and provide a climate
for discussion.

Help your children cultivate their own interests.

If your 13-year-old son enjoys adventure stories, suggest that he
read Defoe's *Robinson Crusoe* or Wyss' *The Swiss Family Robinson.* If
your 15-year-old daughter is fascinated with mysteries, suggest that
she read du Maurier's *Rebecca,* a story of romance and mystery set in
an English country estate. After you have discovered books that interest your children, give them similar ones as gifts.

Keep in mind that your children may never enjoy the books you
cherish. My daughter doesn't like Twain's *Huckleberry Finn* as much
as I do, but we do share a love of Remarque's *All Quiet on the Western
Front* and Buck's *The Good Earth.* Because my daughter has been interested in the classics for a few years, she now has her favorite
authors—F. Scott Fitzgerald, Edna Ferber and Ernest Hemingway.

Sometimes movie and television adaptations of classics stimulate
interest in them. Books such as Stevenson's *Kidnapped,* Dickens' *Tale
of Two Cities,* and Dumas' *The Three Musketeers* have been vividly
brought to the screen. After watching Humphrey Bogart and

Katherine Hepburn in "The African Queen," my daughter read the C. S. Forrester novel on which the movie was based.

If you have a reluctant reader, a good abridgment of a classic may be the answer. My 12-year-old son has been introduced to classics such as Melville's *Moby Dick* and Scott's *Ivanhoe* by reading the condensed editions.

Books can also be "heard" these days on cassette tape. Bookstores have classics such as *Alice's Adventures in Wonderland* and *Treasure Island* readily available on cassette. You can also check them out at some public libraries. Because many children enjoy listening to tapes, this may be one way to expose them to the classics. Tapes can also help to improve listening skills.

Children are often not mature enough to understand a book's theme or symbolism; therefore, it's important to help them choose books that are right for their age. For example, Golding's *Lord of the Flies,* which has a number of young boys in it, has a complex theme that only older teens would comprehend. Your 16-year-old girl might enjoy Hawthorne's *The Scarlet Letter,* but your 12-year-old daughter might prefer Alcott's *Little Women.*

Don't force your children to read the classics.

The most important thing you can do is to provide a climate that is conducive to reading good literature. Mark Twain may have had children in mind when he said, "A classic is something that everybody wants to have read and nobody wants to read." A young person who is made to read a book and dislikes every page of it will probably associate reading classics with boring and unpleasant activities.

Classics can play an important role in helping children reach maturity. Literature confronts young people with basic eternal problems of human beings and helps them better understand themselves and their world. Youngsters can find role models in the heroes and heroines of fiction. Good books can soften loneliness, eliminate boredom and enrich a child's life.

As a parent who values the classics, you must use your intelligence, time and imagination to encourage your child to read. Who knows? Soon the tables may be reversed, and your son or daughter may say to you (as my daughter said to me), "Mom, you mean you haven't read *Pride and Prejudice?* I thought everyone had read it. Let me tell you about it, and maybe you'll want to read it . . ."

46

TEACHING YOUR CHILDREN THE VALUE OF MONEY

Larry Burkett

It's the responsibility of parents to teach their children God's principles, and that includes principles of managing money.

When armed with God's truth, our children will be able to detect the lies that society throws at them, lies such as, "Go ahead and do it, you owe it to yourself"; "You need to stretch yourself financially if you're ever to be a success"; and "Interest is a good tax shelter."

How old should my child be before I begin training him to handle money?

The younger the better. In the very early ages (one to six), teach your children through fair but consistent financial discipline around the home. Have some jobs the children do without pay, such as cleaning their rooms and picking up their toys.

As they grow, establish some elective jobs they can do for pay. This might include cleaning the garage, washing cars and mowing lawns (yours as well as neighbors, when they can handle that responsibility), cleaning the bathrooms, vacuuming, etc. This teaches both the value of money and the ethics of doing a job well. The earlier you begin to do this, the better off your children will be.

Two principles should guide as you begin to teach your children about finances. First, whatever you do, be fair. Don't overpay, but don't underpay.

Second, be consistent. If you have announced that you won't pay until a job is done to your satisfaction, then stick to it. If you have promised to pay on completion, pay promptly. Don't promise what you can't or won't do.

One way to teach young children the value of money is to help them establish a goal. This can be as simple as earning 50 cents to buy ice cream or to save enough to buy a coloring book or a record.

Associating work with reward is an important concept. As Proverbs 16:26 says, "A worker's appetite works for him . . ."

Should a child have an allowance?

Proverbs 3:12 says, "For whom the Lord loves He corrects, even as a father the son in whom he delights." Don't teach your children to expect allowances, teach them to work and earn money. The term "allowance" implies something is given rather than earned. If God doesn't provide us with an allowance, and He doesn't, then we probably should not provide allowances to our children.

If you have a child who demonstrates discipline in handling money and you want to give him a gift from time to time, there's nothing wrong with that. Just be certain that you're establishing long-term values in your children that will guide them when they are adults.

At what age should children open savings accounts?

Encourage your children to do this at the earliest possible age. But help them understand that a bank is not a place where they put money and never see it again. It's a place where money is saved for future use. Young children especially should be encouraged to save for short-term projects, such as a trip, a toy or a tricycle. This lets them associate saving with a reward. I encourage you to add to or match their money. This "bonus" may be the key to start them saving regularly.

Saving money is a short-term sacrifice to achieve a long-term goal. As children get older, help them to begin saving for longer-term goals: clothing, an automobile, and eventually, college. Saving money is good discipline. As Proverbs 21:20 says, "The wise man saves for the future, but the foolish man spends whatever he gets."

How can a parent teach children the value of money if the other parent spends it foolishly and spoils them continually with gifts? Won't the children learn to imitate the parent who is the least disciplined?

Sometimes children will imitate the least-disciplined parent because children are enthralled with spending, particularly when they are younger. Many times, however, children migrate toward the disciplined parent, because that person represents security. A permissive parent or grandparent could lose the children's respect if he or she gives too freely.

You and your spouse should sit down together and discuss this, clearly and objectively, from God's Word. Help your spouse understand that love doesn't mean giving children all they desire. Scripture says that a person whom God loves, He disciplines, and the same is true of parents. A parent who really loves a child will establish boundaries for giving, not to restrict the child's freedom, but to teach the concept of stewardship.

As my teenagers grow toward independence, they will be deluged with offers of credit cards. I'm concerned that they will get trapped by easy credit. What can I do now to prevent that?

You can teach your older children how to handle credit cards by letting them use the cards while they are still home. I know many people will be shocked to read this and say, "Do you mean Larry Burkett recommends that children have credit cards?" I sure do. I don't think there's anything inherently wrong with credit cards. It's the way they're used that creates problems.

If you allow your children, 16 or older, to have credit cards, establish firm rules and enforce them. First, don't let them use their cards for anything that is not in their budget. (So they must have a budget before a credit card.) Second, they must pay off the charges every month, no matter what. Third, the first time they can't pay off their credit cards in one month, you will destroy the cards, and they will not be allowed to have new ones.

If these rules are explained in advance and then enforced, your children are unlikely to have credit card problems as adults. Proverbs 22:6 says, "Train up a child in the way he should go, even when he is old he will not depart from it." Establish fair rules, enforce them consistently, and be firm.

Do you think it's a good idea for children to work their way through college, or to pay at least part of their own college costs?

Since all children are different, the same advice can't apply to everyone. But in principle, I believe children should work, not only while they are in college, but also in high school, at least during the summers. Many students go to college only because their parents are footing the bill. If these students had to work to pay tuition, most would probably drop out, and many should.

I worked my way through college, and I don't regret the experience at all. I found that I appreciated my education, and I was still keeping up with other students. On graduating, I had many job opportunities, simply because of my work experience.

Each family must decide what's best for them. Once husband and wife decide together, share the decision with your children. Give them plenty of time to financially prepare for their college education.

We have grown children living at home who refuse to take our advice. One can't hold down a job. He refuses to contribute to the family financially. I believe that, as a parent, I have the responsibility to ask him to leave, but my wife can't stand to do that. What should we do?

Weakness is not a substitute for love. As Dr. James Dobson says in one of his books, *Love Must Be Tough,* tough love means that you do what is right, not what is easy. If you really love that child, then make the decision that's best long-term for him or her, even though it may not be easy for either of you. "Correct your son, and he will give you comfort; he will also delight your soul" (Proverbs 29:17).

Allowing a child to be slothful, disobedient and disrespectful is not going to help him or her in the long run. Take upon yourself the role that God has often taken with His own people. He would exile them for a period of time to help them understand their responsibilities.

I once counseled a woman whose daughter was a nurse. She lived at home but refused to help in any way and spent her money frivolously. In an effort to help discipline her daughter, the mother asked her to pay for room and board. She refused, saying, "You don't need the money. I'm not going to help you. This is as much my house as it is yours."

The mother asked her daughter to leave. When the daughter refused, the mother had some friends from church help her pack up the daughter's things and move her out.

For almost a year, the daughter was alienated from her mother, although the mother wrote regularly and told her how much she loved the daughter and that she was welcome to come back anytime she was willing to conform to the rules of her mother's home.

The daughter got married and ended up in great marital difficulty because she adopted the same attitude toward her husband. She refused to share the money she earned or help maintain the house. She wanted to live the life of a single while she was married.

When her husband left and filed for divorce, she "woke up" and went to her mother for help. Her mother began to counsel her, and she was finally wise enough to listen. As a result, she is now a happily-married mother of three.

Let me assure you that she is raising her children in a disciplined fashion, so that they will not repeat her mistakes. Love must be tough, and God says that those whom He loves, He disciplines.

Excerpted from *Answers to Your Family's Financial Questions,* © 1987 by Larry Burkett. Published by Focus on the Family.

PART EIGHT

FOCUS ON DIFFICULT FAMILY PROBLEMS

47

"I CAN'T RAISE KIDS ALONE"

Bobbie Reed

I'll never forget the day I say in the counselor's reception room, waiting my turn to pour out my hurts and anger at having to cope with an impending divorce, all because my husband no longer wanted to be married. I struggled to hold myself together, but tears kept leaking out. The pain was so great I didn't think I could bear it.

All of a sudden the realization hit me with the shock of a physical blow. After the divorce I would be a single parent! I couldn't do it! My sons were only four and six. What did I know about raising sons alone? I had never been a little boy!

I panicked. How was I going to support all three of us on my meager salary? How was I going to teach them all they had to know? Was I wise enough to cope? Countless questions blurred in my head. I was sure I couldn't do it.

But I did.

The next 10 years as a single-again mother were full of laughter and tears, highs and lows, fun and fears. Sometimes all of these occurred in just one day. Many times I felt I was on an emotional roller coaster ride full of unexpected turns and twists.

Like the time Mike (age 10) won a diving award and I was so

proud I felt like Mother of the Year. Then the next day he was suspended from school for misbehavior, and I felt as if I were a total failure!

There were tough times financially when making ends meet took extraordinary effort and long hours of overtime. There were tough times emotionally when we found ourselves at the family counselor's office, struggling to hold together as a family. There were nights when I paced the floor both angry and scared because my 15-year-old had broken his curfew. There were hours when I sat up late devising new ways to challenge the boys to do better in school or in real-life situations.

There was joy: special holidays; close, cuddly times, just the boys and me; unexpected moments of honesty and shared feelings; flashes of maturity, hinting of what the boys were becoming.

I know that I could never have survived some of our experiences with my sanity intact had I not had the Lord's help. My parents brought me up with a strong, unshakable faith in God and His miraculous power. I learned as I grew into adulthood that God loved me enough not only to send His Son to save me, but also to care about my daily walk, struggles and triumphs. I can't count the number of times I've cried out to God for help and wisdom, claiming James 1:5 as my personal promise: "If any of you lacks wisdom, let him ask of God."

The best you can do is teach, train, set a good example, provide role models and then turn your sons over to God. After all, they are His children, too, and He cares about how they grow up. So you must learn to trust in His power, not only when yours begins to wane, but also when you are feeling strong.

You can make it! You can do it! And you can even enjoy it!

There are many different responses to being a single parent. No one feels the same way all the time. Often we experience several conflicting emotions at the same time. But there are four basic responses to single motherhood.

Type One: "I Can't Do Anything!"

I found that I felt this way whenever I had tried my best and everything seemed to be going wrong. When I tried to put together a bike for Christmas (why don't they come assembled?) and the pedal screw got stripped because I twisted it the wrong way, I felt stupid and inclined to quit. When the budget wouldn't stretch far enough to cover things the boys really wanted, I felt inadequate. But these times became fewer and farther between as I gained confidence that I was doing the best I knew how and that most of the time I did OK.

A mother experiencing this response may feel helpless, discouraged and depressed; she may give up easily, appear dependent or weak; not enjoy family times; sleep a lot; be non-assertive; not have a strong supportive group of friends; blame others; or have very few house rules for the children.

The basic beliefs behind this feeling may be:

- I am not a capable person.
- I have been abandoned, so I am worthless.
- Life is unfair, so why try?
- I cannot cope.
- I am a failure.
- I have no control over my life.

When the mother is feeling this way, her children tend to respond accordingly. They experience a loss of self-esteem and display their inadequacies; they have little self-control; they learn to be manipulative and play on the guilt of the mother. They become experts at taking advantage of the parent.

Type Two: "I'll Do It or Die!"

Most of the time during my early years as a single mom, this was my basic approach. I was convinced that I had to do it all. Who else was there to do it? I got up early to pack lunches, clean house, do chores and catch my breath.

As soon as the boys were old enough to get off to school by themselves, I would go in early to work overtime for extra money and to keep my evenings free to be with them. Of course, I left everything ready for their breakfasts, little love notes and many other special touches. But that took planning and energy—energy I began to run out of as I met myself coming and going. Sure, I was home in the evenings, but I was often too tired to be much company. Finally, I began to set realistic expectations for myself and for the boys, so our lives could settle into a more livable routine.

Some women respond to the challenge of single parenting by

showing their determination to conquer any obstacle. They are compelled to work, work, work, and feel guilty if they sit down to relax.

These moms tend to be assertive and perhaps a bit aggressive, particularly if their schedules are interrupted. They set absolute rules for their children, and when the children fail to follow the rules or live up to their pace, these moms may become critical and angry.

Women who behave as described usually believe the following:

- I must be a good parent.
- I can/must do everything by myself.
- I dare not fail.
- I must maintain control of everyone and everything.
- No one must suspect I sometimes get scared or feel like giving up.
- If even one thing goes wrong, it is a disaster.

Children typically respond to this do-it-or-die approach by letting their mothers do all the work. They learn that if they procrastinate long enough, do the job poorly or too slowly, Mom will step in and quickly handle the task herself. Also, the children sometimes feel pushed, rushed, resentful, rebellious or insecure because "Super Mom" is a hard act to follow.

Type Three: "I'm Surviving!"

We all fall into this approach from time to time. I found that my writing deadlines always seemed to coincide with the boys' extra activities—ones they needed my help on or to be driven to. Of course, that's also when the refrigerator quit, the plumbing clogged or the car wouldn't start. The worst months were September through December. Getting the boys back to school, handling birthdays, Thanksgiving and Christmas just about depleted the budget and my energies and patience. Every New Year's I resolved to take it easy next year. But the following fall things would be very nearly the same!

Single moms in the survival mode may feel overwhelmed sometimes and OK at other times. They may appear courageous or frazzled, or both. But they have learned to acknowledge their inabilities to meet everyone's expectations all the time, so they try to meet the needs they can. They find that "no" is frequently their first answer, but too often they can be talked into a "yes." They change the house rules too frequently, based on the situations, their feelings and their energy levels. Sometimes they encourage and affirm the children, but sometimes they yell at them or criticize and blame them.

A survival-oriented parent is often operating on these beliefs:

- I think there's hope, if I can just hang in there.
- I just take one day at a time, because I can't face any more than that!
- Just when I think that things are on an even keel, I can expect them to fall apart.
- Things will settle down someday, I hope.
- Surely one day I will be repaid for surviving and have peace and quiet and the whole house to myself.

The children will probably respond by testing Mom's limits frequently to see what the rules are today, taking advantage of her rough days to get their own way, and being confused about what is acceptable and what isn't. On the up side, they will also learn flexibility!

Type Four: "I'm Doing OK!"

This last approach to being a single mom is the one that makes the most sense but is not always the easiest to adopt. I had to constantly check myself to ensure that I was looking at parenting in the appropriate light.

First, I reminded myself that children are a gift from God (Psalm 127:3) and that they are people, not my possessions. I made a list of ways I was attempting to train up my sons in the ways they should go, per Proverbs 22:6. When I felt inadequate, I checked my list. If I was doing everything on the list and I couldn't think of anything else to do, then I reassured myself that I was doing my best.

Next, I made a list of the ways God has promised to help children without fathers and women without husbands. I found so many promises that I cannot list them all here.

The third thing I learned to do was compare my feelings and experiences with friends who were in a similar situation to mine. Their feedback helped me maintain a proper perspective of the daily ups and downs of parenting alone.

The single mom with a positive self-image and a high level of self-esteem will probably feel good about her parenting role and will accept the fact that there will be times when things are out of control. She has learned when to say no to the demands of others, to be fairly assertive and to prioritize expectations and goals. She makes time for herself, in addition to family times, and accepts the limitations of her time, energy and abilities. She is reasonably even-tempered (with some highs and lows), has fairly consistent family rules and usually encourages and affirms her children.

The I'm-Doing-OK Mom believes:

- Nobody's perfect.
- I'm doing the best I know how.
- This too shall pass.
- In the final analysis, the children will make their own choices.
- I am an important person, as well as a parent.

Her children tend to respond by growing toward maturity (at their own rates, of course), accepting themselves and testing the limits whenever possible. And she knows that some of them will grow up and succeed in life, while others may not.

Life is a series of peak-and-valley experiences. The good times don't last forever, but neither do the bad. As long as we remember that one setback doesn't mean we have lost everything, we can keep on keeping on. The struggles and the wear and tear are worth it when every so often, just when you need it most, your son or daughter gives you a quick hug and says, "You're the best mom in the whole world!"

Excerpted from *Single Mothers Raising Sons*, © 1988 by Bobbie Reed, Ph.D. Published by Oliver-Nelson Books. Used by permission.

48

WHEN YOU'RE MOM NO. 2

Carol Daniels Boley

You're not my REAL mom! You can't tell me what to do!" 12-
year-old Kelly shouted. The door slammed as the words
pierced her stepmother's heart.

Such screams echo in thousands of American homes everyday,
including—more and more often—Christian homes, splintering relationships and shattering dreams of blissful family life.

One in every six children in this country lives in a reconstituted
or "blended" family. If the trend continues to the year 2000, families
with stepchildren will outnumber families raising their own children. As in nearly all families, the bulk of the childrearing falls upon
the stepmother.

"If anybody had told me it would be this difficult, I never would
have gotten into it," Kelly's stepmother said with a sigh.

While not all relationships include such stormy scenes, the role
of stepmother is draining and demanding. As one Christian stepmother said, "Being a stepmom is harder than biological parenting,
and the delights are fewer."

So how does a Christian stepmother cope?

When I first joined the ranks of stepmothers six years ago (I married a widower with a five-year-old daughter), nothing had prepared me for the daily realities of being a stepmother.

I learned in a hurry. Like Nehemiah of the Old Testament, I "consulted with myself," searched Scripture, interviewed pastors and family counselors, and compared experiences with dozens of others raising their spouse's child. Here are some practical guidelines that apply the grace of Jesus Christ to the hard work of stepparenting:

Keep a close, open relationship with your spouse.

While it's true that marriage and children arrive at the same time for a blended family, the marriage is still the primary relationship and therefore must be nurtured. The failure rate for second—and third—marriages tops the divorce rate for first marriages. Often, the strain of raising children is too much for a remarried couple.

"It was the children—not my husband—that I wanted to divorce," one Christian stepmom told me. "They continually drove a wedge between us at home and nearly destroyed our marriage and each other."

Seek counseling, if necessary, to build skills in communicating feelings. Clarify and deal with issues before they become full-blown problems. Make decisions together.

Lower your expectations.

Dreams of "one big happy family" often set up stepmothers for a big downfall, resulting in bitterness, jealousy and guilt. It takes from two to five years for a stepfamily to begin to emerge. Be patient.

Start out by trying to establish a friendship based on trust. As respect for you grows, your authority will become an earned privilege, rather than an instant right, as it is in biological parenting.

Agree on a plan of discipline.

Alone with your mate, develop a plan, then present a united front to the children. At least initially, the major part of discipline should be administered by the natural parent, who must clarify to the children that the stepparent possesses authority to discipline in his or her absence.

In the case of divorce, children suffer greatly by bouncing between households where standards of behavior differ. When coparenting with the "ex," try hard to maintain consistency and avoid an emotional tug-of-war.

Discipline in a blended family includes combatting an almost universal phenomenon: the "Poor Little Thing" syndrome. This occurs when children are not held accountable for their behavior in an attempt to "make up" for the painful realities of life. As one Christian stepmom relates: "At a large family gathering soon after our marriage, my husband was criticized by a relative for landing a well-deserved slap on the hand of his misbehaving child. That same relative later told me it seemed harsh—even cruel—to discipline a child who had 'been through so much.'"

If left unchecked, such an attitude guarantees the creation of a spoiled brat.

Accept your children and the reality of your situation.

A difficult aspect of stepparenting is accepting a child's looks, personality, habits, manners, behavior, style of dress, speech, choice of friends and feelings—all of which you had nothing to do with.

You might not even like these children, who may resent and reject you. But you have accepted some degree of responsibility for their care.

"When I first dealt with unacceptable behavior in my stepchild, I caught myself thinking, 'If I had reared him from birth, I wouldn't have allowed this in the first place,'" one stepmom recalled. "But I discovered only resentment and a 'poor me' attitude result from that kind of thinking."

Another stepmom advised, "Don't expect to 'live happily ever after.' No family does. Time spent wishing you were in a 'normal' situation, or that your family were like the Brady Bunch, is wasted."

Let an attitude of love—not merely feelings—direct your behavior.

"I thought I should be able to love my husband's children just because they were his children," one Christian stepmom told me. "It relieved me of so much guilt to realize it wasn't my feelings so much as my actions and attitudes toward them that mattered."

An intense feeling of love for stepchildren may never come. That's okay. Keeping a child's best interest at heart and acting in loving ways represents the best of parenting.

View your role of stepmother as a ministry.

Motherhood in any dimension can be the purest form of discipleship—nurturing and guiding a young life in your own home.

Jesus said, "Whoever receives one such child in my name receives me" (Matthew 18:5). When loving is hard, treat the child as though Jesus Himself stood before you. Imagine Christ asking you to love this child for Him.

"I'll do this for you, Lord" has gotten many a stepmother over a rough spot. It also helps to find something to admire in each child daily. Tell him or her about it, too.

"Some days I was reduced to commending my stepson for his color choice in clothing," one stepmom said with a smile, "but I always found something positive to say."

Practice forgiveness.

You will have to learn to forgive your stepchildren, your husband, the other influential adults in your blended family, any interfering in-laws, those who gossip about and criticize you, yourself, and—in short—everybody.

Yet forgiveness does not keep you from stopping continued disruption of your family. Confrontation may be necessary.

"At one point we were forced to tell my husband's parents that we could not allow them to continue to armchair-quarterback our parenting," one stepmom stated.

Stage such a confrontation with love and respect, acknowledging the contributions made to the child's life up to this point, but insisting that the future relationship will be determined by their fitting into *your* family.

Realize that all the responsibility for the success of your blended family does not rest on you alone. Every problem your stepchild faces does not stem from the fact that he is a stepchild. "Don't take all the credit; don't take all the blame," a wise mother once said.

Sometimes, no matter how hard you try, a relationship between a stepmom and a child will go sour. Be assured that you gave it your best effort before God and leave the results to Him.

Take time for yourself.

Your life involves more than your role as a stepmom. The pressing needs of a blended family can sap you physically, emotionally and spiritually. Refresh yourself in time alone with God, with special friends and with a hobby or sport you enjoy.

To increase self-esteem and broaden perspectives, take a class, read all the books by a favorite author, volunteer at a hospital or start a stamp collection. Choose a relaxing activity that will reduce stress in your life. Balance is your goal.

Seek support.

Pastors and counselors agree: "It's a tough ball game; it's going to be hard. Expect a struggle."

You will need support, someone in whom you can confide, someone who will listen non-judgmentally and accept you unconditionally. Stepparenting can be a lonely job.

A support group will help fulfill Paul's admonition in Galatians 6:2 to bear one another's burdens. "I have an ongoing support group of four women that hold me accountable and love me through the tough times," one stepmom confided.

Build a strong relationship with God and other believers.

Saturate yourself in Bible study and prayer. Ask God to fill in the gaps for you. He alone understands all your feelings, triumphs and defeats. He alone guides you over those rocky spots. And He alone keeps your secrets.

Involvement with other believers helps in a practical way. If you're part of a loving Christian community, helping to meet the needs of others, it will be more natural to take responsibility for the nurturing and care of children other than your own.

One stepmom quoted her favorite Scripture: "And it came to pass . . ." not stay! Time passes, children grow up, circumstances change.

My husband asked me the other day if, knowing what I know now, I would do it all over again. I know some people, like Kelly's stepmom, who would not.

I thought about it just long enough to scare him, then answered with great certainty, "Oh, yes!"

Then a flood of memories hit me: some of the questions about my stepdaughter's early childhood that I couldn't answer; the close scrutiny of our relationship by curious, sometimes judgmental observers; and the odd sensation of being both bride and instant mother. But I have also learned that life in a blended family can be just the instrument God uses to make you a "real" mom, in every sense of the word.

49

"A FATHER TO THE FATHERLESS"

Terri S. Speicher

I stared mutely at my friend, a numbing fog seeping into my brain. I struggled with the words she had just announced.

"Paul is dead," she repeated. "Something happened while he was waterskiing. He died instantly when the boat ran over him."

Sue's voice was dull, zombie-like from the terrible knowledge she had harbored for the last half-hour. My husband, Paul, was gone. Dead. I had just talked to him on the phone a couple of hours ago at five o'clock. After a day-long business retreat at Lake Tawakoni, an hour northeast of Dallas, Paul said he was going to stay and water-ski before coming home.

He will never come home again, I thought. My mind raced—16 years of marriage, three precious sons, a future without him—before my brain shut off with the blessed anesthesia of shock.

First things first, I told myself. I called each of my three children downstairs one at a time to tell them, my oldest first and then the next. They sat in the living room and cried. I didn't—until later. I felt out of my body, observing myself and everyone else from a corner, somewhere near the ceiling.

Then the phone rang. Sue took it. The Sunday school committee

339

was meeting to choose officers for the coming year. Even though we had lived in Texas for only two years, they wanted to nominate Paul to be president of the class. Soon after Sue told them the news, the house began to fill with shocked and tearful friends.

The phone calls started pouring in, too. I had calls to make to my family in North Carolina and Paul's in Florida. Arrangements for the memorial service—date, time, what type of casket, who would conduct it—passed by in a blur.

That night as I lay in bed, the hymns and Scriptures I had learned as a young girl ran through my mind like a self-winding tape. In spite of my shock, their meaning was crystal clear. Later on, the agonizing pain of grief settled in for its necessary stay. I've never been so grateful to know the Lord as I was then.

'He Giveth and Taketh Away'

It's been six years since Paul died in the chilly waters of Lake Tawakoni. My belief in God's sovereign hand on our lives and His perfect love was the only answer to the "whys," especially after I learned I was pregnant a scant two weeks after Paul's death. I was left to raise a fourth child who would never feel a father's touch, never ride a tall man's shoulders in a crowd, never see a godly man lead his family and love his wife.

Yet my pregnancy was an answer to a long-standing prayer for a fourth child. The Lord was saying to me, "I've taken Paul from you for reasons you may not understand, but I've also given you a "yes" to this prayer. I give and I take away."

With God as my foundation, peace pervaded every area of my life except in the frightening arena of single parenting. I had four sons ranging from infancy to early teens. A long road stretched ahead of me, a young widow at age 39.

"Okay, Lord, how does this work?" I muttered one day. I knew in the Psalms that He describes Himself as a father of the fatherless, as a defender of the widowed and orphaned.

"Religion that God our Father accepts as pure and faultless is this: to look after orphans and widows in their distress and to keep oneself from being polluted by the world," James 1:27 told me. In the Old Testament, the command to care for the fatherless—or judgments for failing to keep that command—are mentioned nearly 40 times. The Hebrew word for *fatherless* indicates that these children were actually called orphans, even with a surviving mother. In the Hebrew culture, a widow was totally dependent on her family and society for economic support.

Today, women have rights to property, access to the job market and greater social mobility. Yet rarely is the young widow left with the financial resources to remain a stay-at-home mom. She must re-enter the work force and learn to juggle the demands of home and work. Similarly, many divorced and single moms must raise children in a fatherless environment. We all struggle with filling that enormous void.

Where Do We Look for Help?

I have experienced God's promise to provide fathering in expected and unexpected places:

Family. The first responsibility falls to the men in the family—uncles and grandfathers.

Shortly after Paul died, my children urgently wanted to know what would happen to them if I should die. They were assured to learn that Paul and I had named my sister and her husband as guardians.

Since Paul's death, we've gone out of our way to spend time with our scattered grandfathers and uncles. We either invite their families to visit, or we make the long trips to their homes on the East and West Coasts.

The men in the family are "available." Uncle Dick takes on all youthful challenges to his title as "Scrabble King" during our annual Thanksgiving reunion. One Uncle Bob rules the basketball court; the other Uncle Bob takes my boys individually on family ski vacations. Paul's dad gives loving guidance and encouragement during his visits and frequent telephone conversations.

My dad prays for the boys daily, a practice he began when they were born. I rely on the wisdom and experience of these grandfathers and uncles when I call to get a man's perspective on a boy's problem. Yet distance prevents our families from the consistent hands-on fathering my boys need. The Lord revealed other sources to me:

Church. Our family in Christ has met our needs in tremendous ways. Youth pastors, Sunday school teachers and Christian camp counselors have all emerged to meet special needs.

The day following Paul's death, two volunteer youth workers took the day off from their regular jobs to be with the boys. They listened to their pain and helped them get ready for the memorial service. Friends from the church have since taken the boys to Cowboy games or to see the Mavericks play. They've even dropped by for a quick game of Ping-Pong or backyard basketball.

The director of our junior high ministry became the overnight baby sitter of choice for the older boys, allowing me an occasional weekend out of town. Precious to me was the time and attention one church elder showered on Jeff and Drew when he personally guided them through a special class for church membership.

Neighbors and friends. Another dear couple provided the answer to a burning question I put before the Lord. Where would Will, my baby, observe the love, respect and gentleness of a happily married couple?

Jim and Susan Rice, who live across the street, offered to look after Will while I participated in the older boys' school and athletic events, did my volunteer work, or escaped for an evening out with friends. The Rices' beautiful marriage has been the model that Will would not be able to see at home.

Another time, Gregg failed to come in one night well beyond his usually respected curfew. I began calling the homes of his friends with rising panic. On the third call, Todd's dad told me his son was safely in bed. D. A., Todd's father, took time to pray over the phone with me. Then he got up, dressed and went searching. It seems Gregg had conked out on the floor of a friend's house. Everyone fell asleep watching a late movie.

Several fathers of my boys' friends, as Little League and basketball coaches, have taught them more than pickoff plays and pick-and-rolls; they have taught them about life. Drew has become an avid hunter and outdoorsman because two dads invited him on hunting trips to East Texas with their sons. Another dad shares Gregg's love of baseball card collecting.

Shortly after Will started preschool a couple of years ago, they announced a "Father's Night." When his older brothers couldn't make it, I called the only father I knew with a child in the class, but he was going out of town. I cried and kept Will home that night. But the next year, before I even asked, another dad called and invited Will to go with him and his son.

Schoolteachers and coaches. Male teachers and coaches have perhaps the best opportunity to father the fatherless. What a high calling! Male teachers can serve as exhorters, disciplinarians, encouragers and role models.

Coaches have the delicate job of spurring their charges to do the best they can while not applying too much pressure to win. Believe me, fatherless children watch a coach's every move.

I've seen the players on Jeff's varsity basketball team respond to quiet instruction from their coach, in contrast to the yelling sometimes heard from the other bench. Drew's baseball coach always finds something to praise in each player whether they win or lose. Jeff's baseball coach talks frankly about the dangers of alcohol and drug abuse.

Employers and mentors. When a teenager takes that first part-time job, a father seems more necessary than ever. Fatherless children don't hear their dad talk about the highs and lows of work, how they relate to supervisors and employees or the importance of a good attitude. Employers can teach the fatherless a proper work ethic and reinforce the values Mom is instilling at home: punctuality, good manners and tenacity.

My older boys are starting to think about what careers they want to pursue. Mentors come in many forms. One attorney friend has given my debate-loving Drew a chance to observe his litigation practice. This will help Drew decide whether he wants to pursue a law career.

Our sports director at church has found openings for all three older boys to coach, referee or keep score in youth basketball leagues. Gregg is considering the youth and recreation ministry because he has served as a day-camp counselor in the summers.

Law enforcement. Jeff's always struggled to get up in the morning. It's a mad rush to get him off to school. Several times, all the parking places were taken when he arrived for classes, so Jeff occasionally parked the car in a two-hour zone.

I had no idea Jeff was accumulating parking tickets until the day the police came and towed the car away. He received a good shock when the car wasn't there after school. Jeff learned an important lesson—and paid a hefty fine out of his lawn-mowing money to retrieve the car from the impound yard.

When I called the police officer to thank him for holding my son accountable to the law, there was dead silence on the phone. After a moment of astonishment, he was grateful. Fathering the fatherless means holding boys accountable.

The mother. No, I haven't forgotten myself. But I hate camping, and I have a tough time balancing the checkbook. Mothering the fatherless is a unique, difficult calling, but I can learn, adapt and trust in God to fill in the gaps.

The business news has become part of my regular morning reading. Gregg was surprised to discover recently that I could converse with him about one of his college economics courses.

Reading the sports section is a must. Perhaps I don't digest all the box scores and league standings, but my growing knowledge of sports paid off not long ago. One of the boys asked me to critique his moves from the low post to the basket—and I actually knew what to say!

Of course, I pray for energy, wisdom and strength each day. I pray for trustworthy men to fill the fathering needs I cannot. I continue to read the Word of God, learning from the model of a perfect Father dealing with his imperfect children. Then I can rest confident that He will father my children with a love beyond any imaginable.

I had an interesting time with Will the other day. He was watching TV news when President Bush appeared on the screen. "Is George Washington alive and George Bush dead?" he asked.

I told him George Washington was dead and George Bush was alive.

"Oh," he replied thoughtfully. "Then it's George Washington and my dad who are good friends."

My boys have the security of knowing where their dad is, but the challenges of growing up without him continue. They have experienced love in rich and creative ways. My prayer is that they will allow God to be the father they had to relinquish.

By the way, my two older sons are now well over six feet tall. Will gets all the rides he wants on big, tall shoulders.

50

MARRIED, NO CHILDREN

Becky Foster Still

A unt Becky, why aren't you a mommy?"

The frank question, posed so innocently by my curious five-year-old niece at a family gathering last year, sent an instant, familiar stab of pain straight to my heart. Looking down at the little girl's expectant face, I inwardly prayed that my reply would close the subject: "God just hasn't blessed your Uncle Mike and me with any little ones yet, sweetheart."

At that time, more than two years had passed since my husband and I first started "trying" for a pregnancy. I should have been used to questions like my young niece's—but I wasn't. And not only children, but well-meaning friends and family members sometimes offered comments or questions that stung: "So when can we expect a great-grandchild?" "Loosen up! You two just need to *relax*, and it will happen." "Has Mike switched to boxer shorts yet?"

The ability to have children is something most of us take for granted as we grow up, marry and make plans to start a family. One couple out of every six, however, discover that a fertility problem means childbearing is not so easy for them.

A couple is generally said to be "infertile" when they have tried unsuccessfully to conceive for one year or longer. The term should never be confused with "sterility," which is a permanent condition. Many infertile couples eventually do bear children, with medical help or just with time; others do not, and decide to adopt or live without children in the family.

Infertility is an increasingly common problem today, largely because many are waiting to have children later in life. Conditions that impair infertility are most often hereditary in origin—but can arise, or worsen, with age.

The cause of fertility impairment is equally likely to lie with *either* husband or wife. Many times, as in my marriage, a combination of factors in both partners affects the ability to bear children. And for some childless couples, a medical explanation is never determined with certainty.

Endless Frustration

Infertility is a private subject, one that few of us are comfortable talking about. Yet the anxiety the infertile couple feels is very real, and the "under-wraps" nature of the problem often serves to compound their pain. Those who desire children have no tangible loss to mourn; there are few socially acceptable ways for them to vent their emotions of sorrow and frustration. And their fertile friends— parents who might be absorbed themselves in the challenges of child raising—sometimes find it hard to fully empathize.

The frustrations of infertility can indeed seem endless. Not only are many of the medical procedures expensive, but frequent trips to the doctor's office are time-consuming and stressful. For my husband and me, every visit was a scheduled reminder of our "problem." Many doctors who treat infertility are obstetrician/ gynecologists who also deliver babies; I can recall many a miserable moment spent in waiting rooms filled with glowing pregnant women.

In the darkest hours, it seems to the infertile husband and wife that God is not being fair. It was hard for me to hear about a "surprise pregnancy" from friends who had already been blessed with several children. *Why them, Lord, and not us?* Childless couples usually feel strongly that they would be good parents—yet we all see the media saturated with accounts of child abuse and abortion. *Don't we deserve a pregnancy more than they do, Lord?*

Those who truly desire a child will usually do whatever they can to improve their chances: taking the wife's temperature every morning, discussing intimate details with their doctor, scheduling sex on the calendar and abstaining when ordered. Sometimes it seems as if a medical team has been invited into the bedroom. At first, Mike and I joked about the "prescription" we were given that detailed when and how we were supposed to be intimate with each other. It didn't take long, though, for the humor to wear off.

Such a loss of spontaneity and privacy inevitably causes strain between husband and wife. And other concerns surface, too. When an actual medical condition is found, the "responsible" partner often experiences guilt—and the other spouse might destructively cast blame. Or the husband and wife may not agree on the extent to which medical treatment should be pursued. A friend of mine, for example, would like to consider surgery that could potentially correct their problem, but her husband prefers to "let nature take its course."

Mike and I were fortunate: The infertility experience bonded us closer together. For many others, though, the ordeal can create tension and conflict that gnaw away at the relationship.

The Goal of Motherhood

Although there are exceptions, women tend to face a greater emotional struggle with infertility than do men. Many women, especially those raised in Christian homes, develop a sense of identity that is closely linked with motherhood. Little girls look forward to someday bearing and nurturing their own children, and those dreams are strongly reinforced up through adulthood. Even if she becomes committed to a career, a woman will still hold motherhood as a deeply cherished part of her plans.

Little boys, by contrast, don't give a lot of thought to fatherhood as they grow up. For the Christian man, being a parent is important—and for many it does become their primary goal—but a man is just as likely to also find identity in his occupation or other interests.

Women, too, encounter reminders of their childless state more frequently than their husbands do. Traditional women's magazines target mothers with a house full of toddlers or teenagers. Other people usually see the wife as the one who is responsible for "family" matters. Outsiders almost always ask me, not Mike, whether we have any children in our family.

And in social situations among married women, conversation often turns to family, children, babies and pregnancies. A woman I used to work with, expecting her second child, took to confiding in me daily about her insatiable cravings and ever-expanding waistline. Secretly I wished she would feel as free to discuss these details with Frank, our friendly co-worker across the hall, instead of me!

Because infertility can threaten a woman's firmly ingrained hopes, dreams and very self-image, women often feel the pain of infertility quite deeply—more than even their husbands recognize. It is extremely common for the infertile woman to be envious or even resentful of others who are blessed with easy fertility. For those who are struggling, it can be tough to act overjoyed at the news of another friend's pregnancy! And the Christian woman, in particular, may have trouble accepting such negative emotions in herself—so often she will bottle them up, leading to *more* stress.

The mini-"baby boom" that is now sweeping our continent can rub salt in the wound, too. Babies and pregnant women are everywhere—in the mall, on the bus, at work—and you can be sure that the infertile woman notices every one of them. Most, as they come to terms with their infertility, eventually become less sensitive to such things. But for some women, unfortunately, the longing to have children of their own develops into an obsession, dominating their thoughts constantly.

As my husband and I have worked through our own fertility struggles, we have discovered how significant a role friends and family can play by providing us with needed emotional support. Infertility being such a delicate subject, though, many don't know what to say to the childless couple they care about. Having listened to other infertile husbands and wives share the same feelings, frustrations and experiences that we have confronted, I now understand that there *are* things others can do to help their friends weather the infertility process.

Be informed.
- With more and more couples facing infertility today, you may not realize how many of the people you know are encountering the problem. Don't joke about the subject—your comments might hit a sour note for someone listening to you.

- Infertility affects *couples*, not individuals. Don't think in terms of the problem being either partner's "fault."
- Remember that infertility is not a lifelong condition for many. According to Dr. Joe S. McIlhaney Jr., a noted Christian infertility specialist in Austin, Texas, at least 50 percent of those who seek infertility treatment will eventually conceive—and, because of improving medical techniques, this success rate is increasing.
- Causes are most often hereditary in nature. Such conditions as sexually transmitted disease or prior abortion can lead to infertility, but in the vast majority of cases, a couple did nothing "wrong" to bring about their problem.
- Recognize that your childless friends might be under financial stress. Many assume that since these couples don't have children, their bank accounts must be healthy. Fertility treatments, however, can be very expensive—corrective surgery, for example, can total $8,000 or more—and health insurance does not necessarily cover all the costs.
- Be aware of the expenses and stresses involved in adoption, too. Today, a couple can expect to pay anywhere from $2,000 to $20,000 for an adoption, and it is common to wait at least two years for a baby.

Be sensitive at holiday times and other special occasions.

- Know that Mother's Day can be one of the hardest days of the year for the woman who wants to be a mother but isn't. Going to church can be rough, because this Sunday service tends to focus attention on the institution of motherhood, honoring the mothers in the congregation. Make it a point to spend some extra time with a childless friend on Mother's Day—even if it's just to call her up, or pull her aside at church and chat for a bit.
- Other holidays, too, center on children—Christmas and Easter, for example—and can be difficult for the infertile couple. Growing up, many of us fantasized about how we would celebrate holidays with our children and carry on family traditions. But for those who still have no young ones in the home, holiday times can seem hollow, with festivities bringing painful reminders of their frustration.

    Holiday family gatherings also provide the perfect scenario for curious relatives to ask insensitive questions. Aunt Mabel doesn't hesitate to ask what the baby hold-up is—and to offer unsolicited advice. In large family gatherings, too, joyful announcements of other pregnancies and new babies are common. Be sensitive to your childless sister's feelings at these times, and understand if, on occasion, she and her husband decide not to attend the family get-together.

- Baby showers can be especially tough. The infertile woman finds herself in a room full of women, many already mothers, watching a hugely pregnant friend open cute baby gifts. If she declines to attend a shower you're organizing, be understanding and don't take it personally.

Be a good listener.

- Don't offer advice unless it's asked for. If a couple is trying to have a child, they are almost certainly well aware already of the steps that can be taken to improve fertility.
- Tread lightly when it comes to discussing a friend's infertility. Take your cues from him or her. Broach the subject only if your friend has already told you she has a fertility problem, and only if she seems to want to talk about it. Offer to be there for her, to pray with her if she wants to, but don't push. She may feel like opening up more with you at a later time.

Don't assume that men don't hurt.

- Women may *generally* have a harder time with infertility, but every individual is different. Men can hurt deeply, too. For many men, infertility represents a threat to their sense of masculinity. Be sensitive to the husband—and remember that this is by no means a "woman's problem" only.

Treat the infertile friend just as you would any good friend.

- Don't pity your infertile friend, be overly solicitous or treat him differently from any other friend. Your friend may have already come to terms with this condition in his life; infertility is a process during which feelings and levels of acceptance evolve. And individuals cope differently—having a biological child, for some, is *not* a major goal in life. Just try to know your friend well.

Above all, remember the wisdom of Proverbs 17:17: "A friend loves at all times." Be a good friend . . . and a sensitive one. Know that infertility can cause great emotional strain, and that many conceal their stress well.

If you suspect a friend is struggling with this problem, think of the little things you can do. When you sense your friend's mood is low, call on the telephone for a chat. Or send a note that just says "Hi." Pray for your friend. Show the infertile couple your Christian love—with actions more than with words!

51

WHEN DEATH CAME BEFORE BIRTH . . .

Dale Hanson Bourke

C an we snuggle for a minute, Mommy?" my four-year-old asked as I put him to bed. "We can try," I said, maneuvering my enormous stomach into the bottom bunk.

The bed creaked in protest as I eased in next to my son. Chase moved over, placed his ear against my stomach and listened for a moment.

"They're talking in there, Mommy," he said with a twinkle in his eye. And then, turning toward my tummy, he said, "Time to go to sleep, twins." He kissed my stomach twice, moved over next to me and gave me a hug.

I hugged him back, grateful that he was taking my pregnancy so well. I was determined to maintain as many of our routines as possible so that he wouldn't feel displaced or jealous. But I knew that the addition of two siblings would inevitably change many things for our firstborn. It was the aspect of my double pregnancy that most concerned me. How would I ever find time to give Chase the attention he needed while attending to the myriad needs of two new-borns?

Chase said his prayers while I listened. "Bless Mommy and Daddy and the twins, too," he murmured. I marvelled at the ability of my son to accept two unseen babies. I still had to remind myself periodically that I was about to become a mother to two more children.

Later, I lay in bed, unable to sleep as I felt the kicking and stretching of four tiny legs and arms.

My life had always been so carefully planned and controlled. Even this pregnancy had been scheduled to give Chase enough time to feel secure, but not too much time so that he would have little in common with a sibling. I had the feeling that God was smiling at me as I held on to my illusion of control.

I thought back to the earliest days of my pregnancy. When a friend asked Chase whether he wanted a little brother or a sister, he replied confidently, "I want a brother *and* a sister." And then he added, "And a dog!" My husband Tom and I laughed at that, but tried to explain to him that he would have a brother *or* a sister—and that a dog was out of the question.

The Miracle of Creation

A month later, when an ultrasound test revealed not one but two babies in my already enormous tummy, Tom and I were in shock. All the talks about family planning seemed so laughable. We'd never even considered the possibility of twins. And yet, when we saw two little babies on the screen, we both fell in love with them. We were awed by the miracle of their creation and humbled by our own inability to determine our lives.

When we told Chase that we would, in fact, be bringing home two babies, he looked at us and said, "I know. A brother and a sister." We tried to explain that only God knew that, but his mind was already made up.

As the months passed and further tests were conducted, the doctor told us that the twins appeared to be a boy and a girl. We were thrilled and a little sheepish as we told Chase that he had been right all along. He acted as if it was the most apparent fact and seemed to wonder why it had taken us so long to come around.

While Tom and I went through all of the worries and plans that accompanied the news that our family was growing by leaps and bounds, Chase calmly accepted the fact and began placing outgrown clothes and toys in two little piles in his bedroom.

Tom and I, on the other hand, were busy replanning our life. A station wagon replaced the little Honda. We began calculating diaper usage logarithmically. We'd lay in bed at night discussing everything from the trivial (Should we dress them alike?) to the important (Will Chase feel left out as the twins grow up together?).

I read books on sibling rivalry and tried to include Chase in my pregnancy as much as possible. He loved to come to the doctor's office with me and watch the ultrasound screen as the babies moved and stretched. The nurse even gave him a Polaroid picture in which the baby girl appeared to be waving. It was captioned, "Hi, Chase!" and he showed it to all of his friends.

We were thankful that Chase continued to accept the pregnancy so well, even when I became so large that I couldn't get down on the floor and play with him, or kneel next to his bed while he said his prayers. And we were even more grateful for my good health throughout the pregnancy, and the apparent lack of complications I had been warned could be common.

By the time I reached my eighth month, we breathed a sigh of relief. The greatest concern was early labor and the delivery of babies too small to survive. But ours were thriving, my doctor assured us, and were large enough now to be delivered with some confidence. Chase began to pray, "Help our twins to be born soon," to which I added an enthusiastic, "Amen!"

The Impending Birth

On a hot August day I drove to the doctor's office feeling lighthearted, despite an additional 40 pounds. The initial shock had worn off, and I had begun to apply all of my organizational skills to the impending birth. I mentally went down my checklist, knowing that the babies could be on their way at any time and I needed to be ready.

What I wasn't prepared for was what happened in the next hour. I had visited the doctor's office so often that it felt like home. I joked with the nurses and then went through my usual procedures. But today was anything but normal. The nurse frowned as she searched my stomach for the tiny heartbeats.

The baby boy's was there as usual, strong and regular. But when she placed the monitor on the other side of my stomach there was only silence.

"Wake up," I coaxed, urging my baby to move, thinking that she was in an unusual position and the monitor couldn't detect her heartbeat.

Another nurse came in. She too, searched, and then, with tears in her eyes, said "I have to go talk to the doctor."

I lay alone in the room for a long time begging God to let the equipment be faulty or the nurses be confused. I prayed for a miracle. And then finally, as reality hit me, I prayed for protection for the other tiny life within me.

The next few hours were filled with tests, discussions with doctors and dozens of questions. Then the news: the baby girl had died.

My husband was in a meeting and couldn't be reached. When it was finally time to go home, I left the doctor's office and drove for a long time, unable to face the nursery with two of everything, and my son, for whom I would have to find the words to explain the loss.

How could I make sense of something that made no sense to me? How could I explain that we had been given two very special gifts and now one had been taken back before we could even know her?

When my husband came home, we cried together, feeling the loss of a baby we had never even suspected was there a few months before. Then we did our best to pull ourselves together before facing our son.

As the three of us sat on the bed in our room, we told Chase, "Remember when we told you that Mommy was bringing home two babies? Well, something happened and now we're only bringing home one."

Feeling the Loss

Immediately Chase's face grew concerned, "Why? What happened?" he asked.

"One of the babies died," I said gently. Chase began to cry.

"Was it my brother or my sister?"

"It was your sister," I said, beginning to cry myself, realizing that

I had been mentally painting a family portrait in which Chase stood with his arm around his little sister.

We spent a great deal of time crying, hugging and trying to understand how we could lose this precious little life so suddenly. After awhile Chase looked at me and said, "Mommy, can we have a baby sister next time?"

I hugged him and said, "We'll see, Chase."

Three weeks later I brought home a healthy, energetic little brother for Chase. Tyler's presence helped ease the pain for all of us, and I prayed that Chase would be able to forget about his little sister just as easily as he had changed his prayer at night from "Bless the twins" to "Bless my little brother."

Once again I had underestimated my son. Tyler was three months old when Chase came over to me one day, hugged me and said, "I wish my little sister hadn't died."

I hugged him back tightly, sad to realize that he thought of her, perhaps as often as I did. We talked for awhile about the same questions I still asked. Then Chase said, "Should we give her a name, Mommy?"

His question surprised me. Tom and I had talked about it, but for some reason, had never settled on a name. It seemed strange to name a baby we hadn't known. And perhaps we were afraid of one more painful reminder of our loss.

"What would you like to name her?" I asked Chase. "Joanna," he answered without hesitation. "I think we should name her Joanna."

I don't know where he'd heard the name or what caused him to feel so strongly about it. But it seemed fitting that our son, who had believed in her existence before we had, would be the one to name her and give her a special place in our family.

God has used Joanna's short life to teach us many things about faith. She would always be real to us, even though we had never held her. And, as I kissed my firstborn son and held him tightly, I realized once again that God had made me a parent, not so I could teach, but so I could learn.

Excerpted from *Everyday Miracles*, © 1989 by Dale Hanson Bourke. Word Books. Used by permission.

52

REACHING OUT TO SINGLE PARENT FAMILIES—A FOCUS PANEL

Panelists:

Don: Financial manager with a Christian ministry; married for 34 years, divorced for four years; two children.

Nanci: Resource specialist working with learning handicapped children; divorced for eight years; four children.

Mike: Wildlife photographer and exotic bird breeder; married for 13 years, single parent for three years; two sons.

Marie: College psychology teacher; single parent for five years; one son.

FOCUS: **What do single parents need most from the church?**

Don: Acceptance. At our church, there are activities and programs designed specifically for single parents and their children. The desire is for the married couples to accept the single parent and include them in things where the church may not have a single parents program.

Nanci: Married couples need to be consistent toward the single parent. Invite them to sit with you at Sunday church service. One gentleman came up to me one day at church and said, "If you ever have trouble with the washer, or the refrigerator goes out, call me." That meant a lot to me. There also needs to be a real awareness and acceptance of single parents. Coming to church as a new single parent can really provide a sense of protection and encouragement. But, it can also create pain. You walk in and are vividly reminded as you see a husband and wife together with their children. You need to feel like people accept you and love you for who you are.

Marie: For single moms, more male Sunday school teachers are needed as role models for their children. There is one male teacher who talks to my son between Sunday school classes and has befriended him. I just can't say how much that male role model has helped. Also, after church can be difficult—Sunday just seems like a family afternoon. It's almost like, where do I go now? Also, churches need to coordinate small group Bible studies for single parents as well as child care during that time.

Mike: You need Christians who listen and say, "We're sorry and we accept you!" The church needs to reach out and accept single parents by establishing single parent fellowship groups—separate from singles groups. The ministry needs of single parents are different than for those who have never been married and don't have kids.

FOCUS: It's been said that children really are the silent victims of divorce and often suffer the most. What is the effect on children and how can others reach out to them?

Nanci: My youngest was 12 at the time that his dad left. I had a son in law school, a son in college, and a daughter in college. I found that the pain was equally intense at each level.

Marie: I remember right after the divorce—my son was three years old. I was wondering what pain it was going to inflict on him. One day he said, "We're not a family. We don't have a mom and a dad. We just have a mom." And I remember sobbing with my head in my hands, saying I cannot be a single parent. I thought, what am I saying to my son? He got on his tip-toes and put a Kids Praise album on the stereo. One of the songs was "In His Time." I just sobbed, and he patted me and said, "You're a nice mom. You'll be OK." What was hard for me to take was that *he* was parenting *me*. I was saddened and devastated that I was putting the burden on him. We've both come a long way in five years. I thank the Lord for going through the valley with me—I thank Him for the lessons I've learned. And, today I think my son would say that we are indeed a Christian family—a small one, but a family nonetheless.

Mike: When my wife made the decision to leave me, I told her I wanted joint physical custody because I believe kids need to have both a mom and a dad. When the court awarded me joint custody, I made a commitment for my boys to have as stable an environment as possible. The first year of the divorce my oldest son was very unhappy. You couldn't tell him to do things. Now, three years later, he is incredibly good. He cleans up his room; he talks to me like an adult. Where are the struggles? I believe they have subsided because we went through so many at the beginning. Seven months ago I quit my job—I made a choice to stay at home. I now work out of my house and have made a commitment to always take my boys to school and to always be there to pick them up. I'm a stay-at-home single parent. I love being with them, though it's not easy.

FOCUS: **What practical things can the church or others do to help children in single parent homes?**

Mike: More Christian couples need to reach out to the children in single parent families. How are my kids going to have an example of a Christian man and wife when they are adults? They need to see Christian couples interacting. Also, because the majority of single parents are women, there need to be strong Christian male role models for both boys and girls. Masculine is not macho. Masculine entails gentle, self-sufficient guidance.

FOCUS: **So not only do the children in the single parent home need to see how a man interacts with his wife, but they also need to see the man as a leader, as a father image.**

Marie: My neighbor does that all the time. He and his wife will have my son over for dinner. I'm very concerned about him having masculine role models. His uncle taught him how to swing a baseball bat and how to use tools. Recently, we had our yard landscaped by a young Christian man. He was from a divorced home, and he really befriended my son. I was thinking how perfectly the Lord provides—the young man didn't even realize how much he was impacting my son.

Don: An extended family can play a significant role. An aunt or uncle, grandparents, cousins—they can really help meet that need.

Nanci: We also have to be concerned that children have the opportunity to share their emotional turmoil and to have an outlet. I was blessed with mature, caring friends. But who would my youngest son share with? I don't care if he says he hates me; I want him to have someone to walk and talk with—to get his anger out.

FOCUS: As far as meeting the needs of the single parent, what can friends do to help?

Marie: God really used my friends. The Lord has brought families into our life that have accepted us as a family. They've given the gift of friendship and companionship.

Nanci: One of the marvelous things one couple did was to go and cheer for my son in his soccer games. That meant so much to him— even to this day he will mention that they came and cheered for him when Dad wasn't there. Single parents also need friends that will hold them accountable. They can share your tears and your emotions, but they can also say, "Wait a minute, that smacks of self-pity."

Don: Time can be a terrible enemy at first; you need to be doing things. Friends can help get you involved in activities—skiing, jogging, clubs, etc.

Mike: A good friend listens. In the early stages after a divorce, you're not rational. You're angry. You're tired. In the beginning you really need a good listener—a shoulder to pour it out on. At first, you go to work, and you literally can't function. When I was going through court, my friends noticed me and supported me. Friends are vital around the holidays. The first Christmas after my divorce was probably the worst experience of my life. At holidays, friends need to literally push into your life. They need to invite. "Hey, do you have somewhere to go? We've got three chairs for you and your boys. We'd love to have you." What they did is they let me have the choice; they invited. It was wonderful.

FOCUS: What are some of the myths about single parenting?

Marie: One myth is that you can't be a single parent family and be an intact family. In fact, you can. The custodial parent needs to say, "We are a family." People from the church and your friends need to reinforce that as they accept you as a family.

Nanci: One myth that I had to get over was believing that being divorced and being a single parent was equivalent to being a lesser person. For two years I would not check "divorced" on any form. I would just leave it blank. I couldn't deal with it. Finally, I stood in front of the mirror one day and I said, "You're divorced. You're a divorced woman!" I did that until I was finally exhausted. Then I could move on.

FOCUS: How can friends spiritually minister to single parents?

Marie: At the beginning, many days it was difficult for me to pray. It was so nice to have a close friend of the same sex—I call her a soul mate—to pray with. We meet for prayer every Thursday, and that is such a gift. Another vital ministering role for the friend is to help keep the parent accountable. For the five years since my divorce I have lived a celibate life—I know that is what the Lord wants from me. And I've actually asked my friend to keep me accountable. People need to encourage single parents to walk close to the Lord.

Mike: Close relationships need to be same-sex friendships. If you look at most successful, enduring relationships, they are like-sex. This applies right after a divorce, during the early stages when you are devastated and more sexually vulnerable.

Marie: For most recently-divorced single parents, the first year is the crisis time. They say that it takes a year to recover for every five years of marriage; but the first year or two are extremely critical. Friends need to encourage them to get involved in a church where there is a single parent fellowship; a place where other brothers and sisters in Christ are present and can offer support and encouragement.

Nanci: Plant seeds of confidence. Pick out something that the single parent does well. Pick up on that—they need to hear that praise . . . something that they do well with their kids, or with the church . . . some way to let them know they are making a contribution. Then they will begin to open up because they feel that they are genuinely appreciated and accepted.

Don: I think a good approach is to ask the hurting person, with absolute and total sincerity, "How are you doing? How is it *today?*" And then you get, "Oh, just fine." "No, I want to know, how is it really?" Because the first answer that's going to come back is the superficial one we all walk into. When you are in this process, the best therapy is to be able to tell someone how you are feeling—how angry you are or whatever. But the person is not going to tell the truth on the first question unless you have built trust over a period of time. You may have to push a little bit.

FOCUS: What other things can friends do to spiritually minister to or support a single parent?

Nanci: Make yourself available. If you have a close friend or someone in the church who has been divorced, if you are willing to invest some time with them—that says more than a million words.

Marie: The helping friend also needs to strike a balance. You may think to yourself, "Am I going to be talking all night to this person—am I going to have my time usurped?" You must be willing to say, "You know, right now, I can't talk. I have an appointment, but I will call you at 8 o'clock." Don't leave them hanging. That way, the single parent doesn't feel that the friend is trying to get rid of them.

FOCUS: What is your greatest need as a single parent family?

Mike: Time. Without a spouse, the work that both of you could do in an hour now takes two or three. The demand on your physical energy is doubled, and the demand on you mentally is tripled. You need someone to help you replace that lost time. You need a friend who will help you restore order in your life and who will offer to help out around the house once in a while. A well-ordered life equals time.

Nanci: For me, the greatest need at first was to make sure that my children were going to make it through without being scarred. My older sons said they would never marry because if their dad could leave me, they worried that they would do the same thing. They had a hard time putting confidence in themselves as potential husbands and fathers. But by God's grace, they grew through that. For the single parent whose children grow and move out, the greatest need is to be needed.

FOCUS: How can the church give you that sense of being needed?

Nanci: I think by taking you seriously. When I came to my current church, I felt like I was taken seriously. I felt that if they wanted me to be on a committee, they truly wanted me for what I had to offer— it wasn't out of pity.

Marie: Emotional needs. We said it before, but being listened to is crucial. Right now, one of my needs would be for adult conversation. Although I have a precious son, and we have a lot of wonderful moments, he's entering a stage where peers are very important. Sometimes a loneliness will set in when he says, "Bye, Mom. I've gotta go!" But that's exactly what healthy development is all about. So then here I am out on the patio, eating dinner and thinking how I would love to have some adult conversation. Another need relates to what Mike was saying—that overwhelming emotional and mental feeling of not having enough time. I tell you, you really appreciate anything a former husband did for you. Maybe married couples reading this can say, "Hey, maybe I don't have it so bad." When I'm feeling overwhelmed, I just have to slow down and let go and fit some leisure time in. Otherwise, I burn out and feel guilty because I think I'm not being a caring, loving Christian parent.

FOCUS: What is the greatest blessing of being a single parent?

Nanci: There's no question—you are forced to grow closer to the Lord. You learn that God is really a loving Father and not just a daddy whom you go to for things. He's strong enough to carry you through, or else you have nothing. And each of my four children said that. The first Christmas after my divorce, they were all home, and we decided to each write down a prayer that we would say for one another throughout the coming year. That was our gift to one another—we couldn't afford anything else. It was the most wonderful Christmas I ever had. We carried those prayers in our Bibles all year long.

Don: When I got out of the military service, I said that I would never want to do that again, but I wouldn't take anything for the experience, either. And I think divorce is the same way. But it's a choice. You have an opportunity to accept the changes in your emotional and spiritual life, or you can just turn away and wallow in the pity. Personally, I discovered an attribute of God that we all know of, and that is God's love. I had someone who chose to withdraw their love and leave me, but I found out that God will never withdraw His love from me.

Mike: It changes you. You're not the same. You either run toward God or you move away. When you run toward Him, He becomes an active God who makes changes that even you may not want, but He changes you, and it's for the better. He makes you grow. So many times and in so many ways I have put it on the line—with my kids, with my house, with my job and finances—and said, "Lord, it's all yours. I release it to you." The concept is that you give *everything* up to Him. He has never failed me.

Marie: By far, I have to say amen. During that first year, I was driving one day and crying, and a Christian song called "Through It All" came on the radio. It was the brokenness and shame and my weakness that caused me to realize that "through it all" I could depend on the Lord and His Word. He has become the Lord of my *daily* life. I have turned my son over to Him. Actually, he just accepted the Lord at age eight through a Christian teacher at his school—he is growing by leaps and bounds. And for me, I learned that the Lord broadens the path so our ankles don't turn. I have never been denied in prayer Him giving me wisdom and guidance. It's not that the answer has always been the one I wanted, but in retrospect, I can honestly say that He has indeed guided me through the desert . . . He got me to Canaan.

🥭 INSIGHT 🥭

Ten Ways to Support Single Parents:

- **Pray** for wisdom about what to say. Listen and be available.
- **Reach out** to the children. Invite them on outings or to church.
- **Offer practical help** such as free babysitting, yard work, car or plumbing repairs, etc. Cook a meal—set a date and follow through.
- **Invite** single friends to dinner and don't forget holidays and birthdays.
- **Reaffirm** their self-worth—accept and uplift.
- **Empathize.** Put yourself in their place.
- **Encourage** them to visit their pastor for counsel.
- **Contact**—cards, notes, poems, Bible verses, phone calls.
- **Take them somewhere normal and fun**—a picnic, a ball game, a church program, or the gym.
- **Fellowship.** Invite them to join your Bible study or Christian support group; introduce them to a single parents fellowship group.

53

"AND ONE IN HEAVEN"

Christine Willett Greenwald

How many children do you have?" As a seminar leader and the wife of an ordained minister who is a Christian camp administrator, that's a question I answer often.

"Three," is my usual happy answer. "Two boys and a girl." But inwardly—and sometimes outwardly—I add, "And one in heaven."

My husband and I experienced a miscarriage in 1981, early in my third pregnancy. We've since been blessed with a healthy baby, but grief has left its mark on our hearts. We are now well-tuned to the pain of other couples who are bereaved as we once were.

I was numb with disbelief, and full of guilt over my lack of tears after I returned home from that sad trip to the hospital. I should have been grateful for the numbness—the merciful buffer of shock. I didn't know that month after month of anguish lay ahead—anguish complicated by the fact that many people are uncomfortable in dealing with the profound sense of emptiness that may follow even the very early death of an unborn child.

And no wonder. Offering consolation to any bereaved friend is difficult. The special circumstances surrounding a loss in pregnancy often leave well-intentioned comforters feeling especially awkward.

369

Current figures from the Pregnancy and Infant Loss Center in Wayzata, Minnesota, indicate that nearly one million families each year experience a loss in pregnancy. Consequently, almost everyone knows someone who has had this experience.

But statistics don't lessen the lonely ordeal of losing a much-wanted child. That loss may be intensified in the increasingly common scenario of first-time parents over 30 who fear that the lost pregnancy might have been their "only shot" at having a family.

As my husband and I worked through our own maze of grief and frustration, and as I listened to other couples share similar experiences, I sensed a common plea for compassionate understanding. Now when I hear that friends have lost an unborn child, I try to apply the following tips:

Allow Parents the Right to Grieve

While it is normal for some couples to sustain a loss in pregnancy—especially a very early loss—with minimal emotional distress, other couples will go through a period of mourning. In most cases involving a miscarriage, no funeral or memorial service is observed, usually because there is no body.

Without the formal rituals of bereavement to "legitimize" their sorrow, these couples may experience guilt in addition to the normal stages of grief—denial, anger, bargaining, depression and acceptance. "Do I have a right to grieve for a nameless child I've never even held?" they ask.

Well-meaning comforters may unwittingly contribute to this guilt by making cheerful statements like, "You're young, you can try again," or "It's probably for the best." Such comments, in effect, deny that a life has been snuffed out, or imply that the baby who died is a "non-person." The death of an unborn child is an irreplaceable loss, and we need to respect the fact that victims of miscarriage have the right and the need to grieve in their own way.

Allow Parents the Time to Grieve

Experts on death and grief agree that it may take a year, more or less, for most bereaved persons to come to terms with the death of a loved one. Even then, the grieving continues, but on a less intense basis.

Recovering from the physical effects of a miscarriage usually takes the mother from one to six weeks. While a couple may quickly resume an outwardly normal routine, friends and relatives can best help by remaining alert to their feelings and sensitive to their readiness for outside help, if it seems warranted.

Some couples may benefit from participation in a hospital or church-sponsored support group for those suffering from a miscarriage. These have been organized all over the nation, and a listing of support groups in your area can be obtained by writing and sending a self-addressed, stamped envelope to:

> The Pregnancy and Infant Loss Center
> Suite 22
> 1415 E. Wayzata Blvd.
> Wayzata, MN 55391.

Judy Prawdzik, a delivery-room nurse and advisor to a bereaved parents' support group in Pennsylvania, volunteers another suggestion that comforters can make when the time is right. She says that all couples who have miscarried should be encouraged to schedule a post-miscarriage visit with their physician. This will provide a setting that will allow the couple to ask the many questions gnawing at their peace of mind.

It is vital to answer such anxious queries as "Would the baby have lived if I had gone right to bed?" or "Did I cause the miscarriage by lifting the box that day?" and "What happens next?"

Above all, remember to offer listening ears, thinking-of-you cards, occasional casseroles, babysitting and cleaning help in the weeks and months following a loss. These loving gestures will acknowledge your friends' need for time to grieve.

Don't Forget the Grieving Father

Understandably, more attention is focused on the physical and emotional state of the mother. But a father has his own feelings. Concern for his wife and lingering cultural expectations of "the strong, silent male" may cause a husband to bury his grief, only to have it surface later under the guises of job stress or marital tensions. My husband, Gary, will never forget the loving pastor who approached him after our miscarriage and said, "Everybody's worried about Christine, but how's Gary doing?"

Listen for God's Leading in Offering Scriptural Comfort

Early in the grief process, glib use of Biblical quotations can come across as "canned comfort," lacking understanding of the parents' need to express their feelings. At this stage, even the most devout couple may be blaming God—consciously or unconsciously—as the cause of their sorrow.

Gentle reminders of His love for little children (Matthew 18:4–6; Matt. 19:13, 14), His watchful care over each of His creatures (Matthew 10:29–31), and His empathy with Mary and Martha when Lazarus died (John 11:1–36), will help them to focus on God's loving kindness and sustaining presence.

Later, when the parents have reached the stage of accepting their loss, the truth of Romans 8:28 will offer its ageless hope: "For we know that all things work together for good to those who love God, and who are called according to His purpose." That's reassurance to live on!

54

OUR NIGHTMARE WITH MELANIE: A BATTLE AGAINST ANOREXIA

B. J. Bassett

My daughter and I laughed hysterically while sitting on her bedroom floor trying unsuccessfully to store her wedding dress. After folding yards of rebellious satin and lace, we placed it in the dress box. But the lid kept popping up.

On my knees, I positioned myself on top of the box with my derriere in the air. (I never do things the easy way.) "I know you wanted candid photos of the wedding, but I hope you don't plan to take a picture of this!" I joked. Giggling, Melanie struggled to tie string around the huge box.

Melanie and I have always shared a close relationship, and this was a happy time for us; but six years ago, I didn't know if she would have a wedding day—or even a future. At that time, she was the victim of anorexia nervosa.

As a child, Melanie had a sweet, agreeable disposition that my friends with children envied. One friend once remarked, "Not everyone is lucky enough to have a Melanie." My buttons popped with pride. Yes, I did feel lucky.

During Melanie's freshman year of high school, she would bounce through the front door each day after school, bubbling with excitement over the day's events. Her enthusiasm filled our home and overflowed to our other three children.

One day, when the door flew open she shouted, "I won! I'm a cheerleader!" That, along with being the class secretary and an honor student, kept her surrounded by oodles of friends. We supported her activities and her life seemed as "perfect" as she was. Physically, her 5'4", 105 pounds of soft curves fit nicely into size 7's. Yet emotionally, she was starving.

Melanie's route to anorexia began innocently. At the end of her freshman year, Melanie had a bout with the flu and lost about five pounds. When she returned to school after being sick, her friends commented that she looked terrific.

Delighted, Melanie decided she'd look even better if she lost more weight. So she put herself on a strict diet of apples and vegetables, coupled with an excessive exercise program—100 sit-ups, jogging, and floor exercises. By consuming only 300 calories a day and working out compulsively, Melanie lost a great deal of weight in only a few weeks.

At first, I wasn't overly concerned; I'd been skinny myself as a teen. When you see a person daily, you tend not to notice changes. I was aware, however, that Melanie was preoccupied with food.

She would make elaborate meals for the rest of the family, but her plate was sparse with tiny pieces of food that she cut into even tinier pieces and pushed around with a fork. She loved to smell and touch food—she seemed to worship it—but she would not eat it. Our nightmare had begun.

Shocking Changes

That summer we went on a vacation with friends we hadn't seen in a while. In a swimsuit, Melanie's once shapely figure had become flat-chested and boyish. Our friends were shocked by her appearance. "What's wrong with her?" they asked.

I helplessly shrugged my shoulders. I didn't know. Then my friend told me about anorexia nervosa. At that time I was not familiar with the disease. The more we talked about it, the more frightened I became.

When I approached Melanie with the possibility of being anorexic, she snapped, "I just like being thin." Her sweet disposition now turned to moodiness and anger, especially when food was mentioned. "At least include some grains, meats and milk in your diet," I suggested. But she resisted. "Vegetables and fruits are good for me," she replied. Somehow, she believed her skeletal frame was attractive.

No one in the family wanted to sit across from Melanie in a restaurant. When it was time to order, she would screw up her bony face into a painful look and say, "A green salad, please, no dressing." I wanted to scream, "Eat the dressing!"

I wondered what the waitress and the people in the restaurant thought. I felt like a failure as a mother, and I had tried so hard to be a good one. I became more and more worried, and so did my husband who pleaded with me to take her to a doctor.

But Melanie remained firm. "I don't need help. I like being thin," she told me. I knew that she could not be helped until she agreed that she had a problem.

By the end of summer, the problem turned into a life-or-death situation. Shopping for clothes was grueling. I watched Melanie try on size 1's; all her bones were visible. I was sick inside and afraid she would eventually die. She was 75 pounds and starving herself to death.

In desperation, my husband and I cried out to God for a miracle. After trying to solve the problem ourselves, we poured out our hearts to our Heavenly Father. "Please save her," we prayed.

The Road to Recovery

A lot is said about negative peer pressure, but God chose peer pressure as the means to answer our prayer.

Melanie had left school the previous June as a pert 100-pound freshman. When she returned for her sophomore year, emaciated at 75 pounds, her friends were shocked.

One day while strolling down the school corridor, Melanie over-heard some boys talking behind her. "What happened to Melanie? She looks ugly," one of the boys said.

That was the turning point. It was the first time she had realisti-cally looked at herself in months. The word "thin" had been a com-pliment to her, but "ugly" was what she needed to hear. It would take more than honest words to put weight back on Melanie, but God's miracle had begun.

Melanie's girlfriends showed love in action. They persisted in their attempts to get food into her. "Why won't you eat this candy bar? What are you afraid of?" After their badgering, Melanie would eat it and then hurry home and exercise for hours to work off the calories.

When her friends forced food on her, Melanie became angry. But they were more concerned about her life than about losing her friendship. They bought food and watched carefully to make sure she ate it.

Melanie regained her weight almost as quickly as she had lost it. At that time, I didn't know there was any danger in regaining weight quickly. Later, I learned that singer Karen Carpenter died of heart failure after an eight-year battle with anorexia nervosa. (While undergoing treatment, she had brought her weight up from 80 pounds to 110 pounds in a short time.)

Melanie seemed to be getting better. But difficult times contin-ued because she still had the characteristics of an anorexic, and she desperately wanted to be thin. Sometimes, she'd binge on food and want to vomit, but she was afraid to start in case she couldn't stop.

Questions to Ask

I have often wondered why Melanie became anorexic. Could it have been because she had a sister who received a great deal of at-tention for rebellious behavior? Did Melanie try to compensate with perfect behavior? Was it because she felt comfortable being a little girl and didn't want to grow up ? Did she feel she had to achieve success to fulfill her parents' high expectations? Was she passively rebelling by having a say in *something*—her body?

The "why" isn't important. What is important is that God can—and does—turn bad situations into good.

Today, as a radiant bride and university student, Melanie pursues her dream of becoming an elementary school teacher. Her gaunt look is gone, and her smile comes from within. Because of her suffering, she is a compassionate, strong adult who can help others.

Melanie has given me permission to tell her story with the hope that it will help someone else.

"Just thinking about what I looked like that summer makes me feel sick to my stomach," she told me recently. "I can't even look at the pictures for more than a glance before the self-inflicted nightmare is recalled. I now look back, and I see all the hurt that I caused."

If you know an anorexic, don't hesitate to help. The person may be stubborn and unreasonable, but don't give up. Pray and seek professional help for the sake of your loved one. She will be endlessly thankful, like Melanie and I are today.

❦ INSIGHT ❦

Facts about Anorexia Nervosa

- One out of 250 female adolescents may develop anorexia.
- Only about five–10 percent of all patients are males.
- If not treated, 15 out of 100 anorexics will die.
- Early detection is vital.

What to Look For

With many teenage girls on diets these days, how can you identify one with anorexia nervosa?

Here are some common characteristics. (Please be mindful that not every anorexic exhibits all of these.)

- Starts out slightly overweight, if at all.
- Sensitive about remarks concerning weight.
- A perfectionist.
- Sometimes refuses to eat.
- Exercises and moves constantly.
- Loves dieting.
- Preoccupied with weight; enjoys being thin.
- May cut food into little pieces; moves food around the plate.

- Most times will want to go far below desired weight, and succeeds.
- Sometimes will vomit and take laxative to feel thin.
- Periods will stop.
- The thinner she is, the better she likes herself.
- Extremely well-behaved.
- A distorted self-image (when thin, she will think she is fat).
- A child-like body (fear of growing up).
- Will deny having the illness.
- Sensitive to cold.

RECOMMENDED READING LIST

Adler, Mortimer J. *Great Books*.

Arterburn, Steve and Jim Burns. *Drug-Proof Your Kids*. Focus on the Family, 1989.

Baehr, Ted and Bruce Grimes. *The Christian Family Guide to Movies and Video*. Brentwood, TN: Wolgemuth and Hyatt, Publishers, Inc., 1989.

Barnes, Emilie. *Survival for Busy Women*. Harvest House Publishers, 1986.

Blue, Ronald. *The Debt Squeeze*. Focus on the Family, 1989.

Bly, Stephen and Janet. *How to Be a Good Mom*. Moody Press, 1988.

Bovde, Jeanne. *A Horse Named Cinnamon*.

Buck, Pearl S. *The Good Earth*. Buccaneer Books, 1981.

Buckingham, Jamie. *Let's Talk About Life*. Strang Comms Co., 1987.

Burkett, Larry. *Answers to Your Family's Financial Questions*. Focus on the Family, 1987.

Cuber, John. *The Significant Americans*.

Dobson, James C. *What Wives Wish Their Husbands Knew About Women*. Tyndale, 1977.

_____. *Love For A Lifetime*. Multnomah Press, 1987.

_____. *Parenting Isn't for Cowards*. Word Books, 1987.

_____. *Dare to Discipline*. Tyndale.

_____. *Love Must Be Tough*. Word Books, 1983.

Evans, John. *Recommended Movies on Video.*

————. *Preview Movie Morality Guide.*

Fadiman, Clifton. *Lifetime Reading Plan.* Harper & Row, 1988.

Forrester, C. S. *The African Queen.*

Fuller, Cheri. *Home Life: Preparing Your Child for Success in School.* Honor Books, 1988.

Golding, William. *Lord of the Flies.* Perigee Books.

Groothuis, Douglas. *Unmasking the New Age.* InterVarsity Press, 1986.

Hawthorne, Nathaniel. *The Scarlet Letter.*

Hearne, Betsy. *Choosing Books for Children: A Common Sense Guide.* Delacorte, 1981.

Hocking, David and Carole. *Romantic Lovers.* Harvest House Publishers, 1986.

Holt, Pat and Grace Ketterman, M.D. *When You Feel Like Screaming: Help for Frustrated Mothers.* Harold Shaw Publishers, 1988.

Kesler, Jay. *Ten Mistakes Parents Make with Teenagers (and How to Avoid Them).* Brentwood, TN: Wolgemuth and Hyatt, Publishers, Inc., 1988.

Kimmel, Tim. *Little House on the Freeway.* Multnomah Press, 1987.

Lewis, C. S. *Chronicles of Narnia.*

Little, Paul. *Affirming the Will of God.* InterVarsity.

Lush, Jean and Patricia H. Rushford. *Emotional Phases of A Woman's Life.* Fleming H. Revell Company, 1987.

Mains, Karen Burton. *Making Sunday Special.* Word Books, 1987.

Merrill, Dean and Grace. *Together at Home.* Focus on the Family, 1989.

McCloskey, Robert. *Make Way for Ducklings.* Penguin, USA, 1941.

Melville, Herman. *Moby Dick.*

Peel, Kathy and Joy Mahaffey. *A Mother's Manual for Summer Survival.* Focus on the Family, 1989.

Potter, Beatrix. *The Tale of Peter Rabbit.*

Publications, SP. *Parents' Most-Asked Questions About Kids and Schools.* Victor Books, 1989.

Rainey, Dennis. *Lonely Husbands, Lonely Wives.* Word Books, 1989.

Reed, Bobbie. *Single Mothers Raising Sons.* Oliver-Nelson Books, 1988.

Remarque, Erich M. *All Quiet on the Western Front.*

Rickerson, Wayne. *Getting Your Family Together.*

Seamonds, David. *Putting Away Childish Things.*

Siegel, Robert. *Alpha Centauri.*

Smalley, Gary. *The Key to Your Child's Heart.* Word Books, 1987.

_____. and John Trent. *The Language of Love*, 1988.

Sneed, Sharon. *PMS: What It Is and What You Can Do About It.* Baker Book House Company, 1988.

St. John, Patricia M. *The Tanglewoods' Secret.*

Strauss, Richard and Mary. *When Two Walk Together.* Here's Life Publishers, Inc., 1988.

Tournier, Paul. *To Understand Each Other.*

Trelease, Jim. *The Read-Aloud Handbook.* Penguin, 1989.

Twain, Mark. *Huckleberry Finn.*

U.S. Department of Education. *What Works: Research About Teaching and Learning.*

Wallerstain, Judith. *Second Chances: Men, Women, and Children a Decade After Divorce.* Basic, 1982.

Wilkinson, Bruce. "Family Walk."

Wilson, Elizabeth. *Books Children Love.* Crossway, 1987.

Wyss, J. D. *The Swiss Family Robinson.*